Friendly Foods

Mr —

We hope you try out
some of these recipes
on the Wednesday night
group!

Love,
Rosie + Caroline
Christmas 1993

Gourmet Vegetarian Cuisine

FRIENDLY FOODS

Brother Ron Pickarski, O.F.M.

 TEN SPEED PRESS
Berkeley, California

1⊜

TEN SPEED PRESS
P.O. Box 7123
Berkeley, California 94707

Cover design by Nancy Austin
Book design by Sarah Levin
Illustrations © 1991 by Ellen Sasaki

Library of Congress Cataloging-in-Publication Data

Pickarski, Ron.
    Friendly foods / Brother Ron Pickarski.
        p.   cm.
    Includes index.
    ISBN 0-89815-377-8
    1. Vegetarian cookery.   2. Cookery (Gluten)   I. Title.
TX837.P528   1991   90-43279
641.5'636—dc20   CIP

            5 — 95   94   93   92

Printed in the United States of America

SPECIAL THANKS

To my mother, who died on August 23, 1989. I wish to thank her for her dedication as a mother in raising and supporting me in my sojourn, as only a mother can do.

To the Sacred Heart Province of the Friars Minor, who have let me pursue my dream. They were always open and supportive of my quest to serve the cause of humanity, which entailed allowing me the time to create this book.

To Sandra Roscoe, for her loving support of my artistic endeavors and for her helpful counsel. We spent many precious hours together in the kitchen baking while at Valentina's Corner. She is truly a shining star.

To Chris Metzger, an endearing friend and professional chef trained in French technique. Chris fine-tuned several of my techniques and added his creative genius in several of the recipes.

To Jean-Marie Martz, a French-born ballet dancer who loves to cook and who spent three months studying with me and helping me start the final version of the recipes for the book.

To Susan Carskadon, for helping organize my outline and for helping me become more focused on the book.

To Stewart Kerrigan, for helping me organize my original recipes and for assisting in their development.

To my Brother Friars at St. Anthony's Shrine, for the use of their kitchen in the final stages of recipe development and retesting of the recipes.

To Paul Van Hoesen, an endearing friend and the man of the hour when my computer acts up.

To Amie Hamlin, for her support in coordinating further testing of recipes.

To the staff at Ten Speed Press, who put a great deal of energy into making this book possible. They were very sensitive to my artistic endeavors and to me.

When I look back at writing this book, all I can say is that the task is far more than I could have done myself. My prayer and hope is that those who read this book are touched by its endeavor. I'd like to dedicate this book to the quest for an inner life, because it is only there that any true resolve and transformation can be born and nurtured to maturity. Dietary transformation, I believe, is but one manifestation of that quest on the cosmic level.

CONTENTS

INTRODUCTION

*F*rom the age of 12, I was raised in the restaurant business. When I was in high school, my father asked me if I would consider taking over our family restaurant. I told him that it would be a rainy day in hell before I would go into the restaurant business. Well, it must be pouring down there now. But, as you will see, my culinary experience is unique.

Although I am a chef, I am also a Franciscan Brother. The Franciscans are a religious order under the auspices of the Roman Catholic Church. I joined the Order in 1968 and completed my training in 1976. During this time, I also attended Washburne's Culinary School in Chicago, the oldest school of its kind in the United States. I graduated from Washburne's in 1973 and have worked as a professional chef since then.

Ironically, it was my deteriorating health that led me to the kitchen. As a youngster, my diet consisted of hamburgers, french fries, and milkshakes, which was standard fare at my parents' restaurant. I suffered from lethargy, hypoglycemia, and other conditions of poor diet. Upon entering the seminary, I weighed in at 198 pounds—an astonishing weight for me. I finally realized that I needed to take an active interest in my health. What was so unique about this was that, as I was entering one spiritual path, my ministry was beginning to surface, although I didn't realize it at the time. Meanwhile, during my first year in the seminary, I studied nutrition, diet theory, and the basics of cooking; in the process, I lost 60 pounds.

With experience and growing knowledge, I began to view food as preventive medicine. In 1976, I became a vegetarian. As a result of this new change, I developed an intense interest in nutrition. Gradually, I became a vegan. By now, my diet has become my way of life. I no longer have to think about eating according to a particular diet, and I no longer think of my food choices as a "special diet." However, it took many years for this change to take place. My view toward eating evolved slowly with my understanding of what constitutes the ideal diet. For me, learning how to live has meant learning how to eat.

Commitment to a healthy diet is important. But it is also important to remember that we are human. There is no such thing as eating "perfect." Let me relate a few stories. Shortly after I gave up cheese, I had a craving for a piece of my favorite cheese. I promptly went to the refrigerator, sliced a piece from the block, put it between two slices of whole wheat bread, and enjoyed it to the last bite. But I have never eaten another cheese sandwich since. A few months after giving up fish, I was invited to a restaurant by a friend, a Greek Orthodox priest, who insisted that I try the fish, not knowing that I don't eat fish. Had I told my friend that I couldn't eat the fish, it would have hurt his feelings. So I ate it and enjoyed it. But that was the last time I ate fish. Another time, I was inadvertently served a hamburger in place of a vegy burger at a restaurant. Upon biting into the burger, I realized the mistake. Still, I swallowed that one bite, called for the waiter, and politely returned the remainder. The point of these stories is that we can become so wrapped up in our diets that we lose touch with reality. Being sensitive to our biological needs also means being sensitive to who we are. Be realistic and enjoy a "slip-up" once in a while. Sometimes those "slip-ups" actually can test us.

My Professional Background

My culinary education and experience as a chef have given me a comprehensive knowledge of food preparation—with traditional foods, gourmet foods, and natural foods. In addition to training at Washburne's, I completed a course in specialized meat cutting (although I have since retired my meat-cutting and meat-cooking skills) and have worked as a professional pastry chef. My background is unusual, I suppose, for someone devoted to a vegan eating style.

By the late 1970s, I became more and more interested in working with whole foods. I traveled to Boston to work with some friends experienced in the use of natural foods. Then I hosted the first vegetarian Escoffier dinner at a country club near Chicago. This was the birth of my style of elegant vegetarian cooking, a style that led me to the 1980 International Culinary Olympics, where I won my first bronze medal. (I competed again in 1984 and 1988 and won bronze and silver medals for vegan foods in those years.)

In 1980, I opened a natural foods restaurant in Milwaukee. In 1982, I moved to Miami, where I became executive chef at a natural foods restaurant and, subsequently, executive pastry chef at a Miami yacht club. Later, I taught pastry making and basic cooking through the Dade County school system in Miami.

During this time, I also received certification as executive chef with the American Culinary Federation, becoming the first professional vegetarian chef to receive such certification. Currently, I work as an educator, consultant, and food technologist in the natural foods industry. I help create menus for restaurants and develop product lines for nationwide packagers of high-quality natural foods.

Vegetarianism is on the rise in America. And for each vegetarian in America today, there are many others who are tending toward this diet. I believe that the food service industry and retail food sales will become more sensitive to the market demands for more nutritious foods as the demands arise. Vegetarianism will progress rapidly when it is integrated into mainstream commercial food service.

What Are Friendly Foods?

This book is all about preparing friendly foods. So, what are friendly foods? They are foods that are friendly to our bodies, our pocket books, our busy schedules, and our environment. Friendly foods are transitional, natural, healthful foods designed to help people make the gradual change from the typical American diet to a natural-foods American diet. Friendly foods require no dietary semantics or paraphernalia. They are just beautiful, delicious foods that are fairly easy to prepare, and that accommodate the busy schedule of a typical modern household.

I have tried to adapt many popular American foods, improving on their nutrition, taste, and appearance. Friendly foods are familiar foods such as lasagna, burgers, pizza, fruit pies, vegetable soups, stir-fried vegetables, quiches, cakes, and desserts.

The basic premise of this book is whole foods vegetarianism, which I consider the ideal diet. Most recipes, however, can be adapted quite easily to include dairy products such as milk, cheese, or sour cream, or to include eggs or meat. This makes them especially useful for "transitional" diets—for those people attempting to go from a traditional meat-based diet to a purely vegetarian diet.

In fact, the recipes in this book should build on to your diet—your way of eating. This book is designed to nurture your dietary space. If you so desire, it may help transform your diet gradually, in an easy, friendly manner. The foods presented are innovations of many common foods.

Friendly foods are based on sound principles of nutrition, affirmed by medical research. Most of my recipes produce dishes that are about 95 percent cholesterol-free, use fresh or frozen vegetables, and are loaded with dietary fiber. I don't just try to make these dishes taste as good as traditional foods; I make them taste better!

A Note about Ingredients

A number of ingredients called for in the recipes are unusual and possibly unfamiliar. The glossary (page 261) describes these ingredients and provides background information about any ingredient that might be considered to fall outside the confines of an American meat-and-potatoes diet. With the growing cosmopolitanism of our society, many of these ingredients are becoming almost staples; others may still be novel.

I would suggest that, before using a recipe, you read through the list of ingredients first and check the glossary for anything unfamiliar. That way, you will understand how to use the item before you plunge into cooking it. The received wisdom that one should always read a recipe all the way through before doing anything else still holds true.

THE IDEAL DIET

*T*he ideal diet is high in complex carbohydrates and low in protein and fat. This is relative to one's individual condition, though. For example, if someone has just experienced a physical injury, he or she will need more protein, since the function of protein is to heal the body. If someone has diabetes, her or his use of even naturally sweet foods must be carefully controlled and monitored. Some other factors that dictate dietary needs include age, gender, season, and geographic region.

Here are the recommended U.S. dietary guidelines as endorsed by C. Evert Koope:

1. Eat a variety of foods.
2. Eat enough to maintain a desirable weight.
3. Avoid excessive amounts of saturated fat and cholesterol.
4. Eat foods that contain adequate starch and fiber.
5. Avoid too much sugar.
6. Avoid too much sodium.
7. If you drink alcoholic beverages, do so in moderation.

These are practical, no-nonsense guidelines that probably seem quite familiar. In fact, they are the core of nearly every sound diet.

The key to eating well is to focus on the foods that comprise that particular way of eating. This is more beneficial than focusing on what foods to avoid. Most people should eat about 70 percent complex carbohydrates, 20 percent protein, and 10 percent fat or oil. Complex carbohydrates include whole grains, vegetables, and fruit. Beans, tofu, and tempeh are the main sources of vegetable-based protein.

Raw Foods

Eating raw foods helps one meet many of the guidelines of the ideal diet. It's a good idea to consume about 25 to 50 percent of your food by volume, not calories, in the raw state. Salads, of course, are the best way to do this. Raw foods provide fiber and they are filling, so they may help maintain desirable weight. Raw foods are fairly low in sodium, depending on the food, of course. But, in general, we receive higher sodium intakes from prepared foods. Perhaps most important, because heat destroys or diminishes most nutrients, raw foods offer the best nutritional value.

The Protein Myth

Many people mistakenly believe that protein is intended for a body fuel. For example, after donating blood it is generally recommended to eat a steak. This recommendation is in error. With a balanced diet and a healthy body, protein is not intended for use as an energy source, although it can be if the remainder of one's diet doesn't provide enough energy. Times of starvation and famine are an example of when the body will use any incoming protein as an energy source. Unfortunately, however, the body goes through a convoluted process to convert protein into an energy source. Using protein as a fuel is something akin to using ''gasahol'' in your car instead of gasoline. Therefore, consuming proteins to provide energy puts more stress on the body than consuming either carbohydrates or fats as an energy source.

Fats

Oils and fats are refined foods, whether they are from an animal or vegetable source. There are three categories of fats: saturated, monounsaturated, and polyunsaturated. The polyunsaturated fatty acids are the essential ones since our bodies cannot produce them. Saturated fats of the hydrogenated nature should be limited in consumption since they tend to raise cholesterol. Cholesterol is not a lipid but a fat-soluable alcohol called sterol. Because a fat is saturated doesn't mean that it is high in cholesterol, or that it will raise cholesterol.

Vegetable-based proteins such as tofu and seitan have no or very little saturated fat in them whereas animal-based proteins tend to be higher in saturated fats and cholesterol. The ADA (American Dietary Association) recommends that about 30 percent of our calories come from fat with no more than 10 percent of those coming from saturated fats. I am comfortable with about 15 percent of my calories coming from fats. Some of your fat consumption can be monitored by using low-fat cooking methods.

Prince Charles plans to go totally organic with his 770-acre farm in western England. The expense of converting to organic farming, he says, is worth it if it can help save the environment. The prince also has urged 1,500 tenants on his Devon and Cornwall farmland to cut back on pesticides.

Diet as a Way of Life

Our word *diet* comes from the Greek word *diaita*, meaning "a way of life." The ideal diet is more than just eating or avoiding certain foods. It is tied to such things as environmental factors. For example, fresh air and water are actually nutrients. The quality of each relates directly to proper nutrition, because these factors affect our ability to digest foods properly. Oxygen "fires" our biological pistons; water is needed to cool the system and regulate metabolism and digestion.

The ideal diet is also related to stress in our daily lives, our attitudes about life and ourselves, and our inner life, or spiritual outlook. Diet, especially vegetarianism, relates to ethics and morals as well. It is therefore not possible to say that the ideal diet always includes a given set of foods or always excludes certain foods. And there is no prescriptive "ideal diet" that is right for everyone, although there are basic principles that apply to the ideal.

FOOD QUALITY

*C*hoosing high-quality, nutritionally dense foods is the first step toward improving one's diet. I apply several criteria in defining food quality. First, I look for organically grown foods. Second, I choose foods that are not refined. Third, I consider whether the food has been irradiated or contains additives. Finally, I consider the way in which the food is packaged. All of these features affect the quality of food.

Nutritional Density

I often hear people comment that a food is too high in calories for them to partake of it. What these people may not be considering is the nutritional density of the food. Basically, nutritional density is stacking up calories against the amount of nutrients the food contains: a particular food may have a lot of calories, but it also may have many essential nutrients. For example, suppose you consume 100 calories worth of sesame butter; in this amount, you obtain some of your daily calcium requirement. The ratio of calories to nutrient is favorable, so the food is nutritionally dense, compared to sesame oil which has no calcium in it. Considering the nutritional density of foods is a step ahead toward eating high-quality foods.

Health Food Stores versus Supermarkets

Shopping in health food stores rather than supermarkets is not enough to guarantee food quality: you will find so-called "healthful" junk foods in natural foods stores, and you will find high-quality natural foods in supermarkets. It goes back to that old adage: Buyer beware. This section is designed to help you make intelligent decisions in the supermarket and the natural foods store alike. It includes some helpful hints on nutrition, organic foods, irradiation, and labeling on packaged foods.

Cost is a major factor for people in selecting food products. Luckily, paying more for a product doesn't mean that it is of better quality. Costs generally are higher at natural foods stores. Although such stores usually stock high-quality foods, the higher costs are not necessarily due to higher quality. I believe that these higher costs are due in part to the system of distribution and to smaller product volumes. Perhaps with time, the natural foods industry will become more efficient in marketing and distribution and their stores can compete better with mainstream supermarkets.

On the flip side, supermarkets have their own strategy with natural foods. Because a product is labeled natural, supermarkets sometimes charge more for it. The word natural helps to sell products. You should be aware, however, that Food and Drug Administration (FDA) standards complicate the issue of what is natural. In the first place, a product does not have to be 100 percent natural in order to be called natural. For example, vitamins can be labeled natural as long as 10 percent of the product is derived from a natural source. Furthermore, many high-quality whole-food products do not qualify as "natural" foods with the FDA. Two examples are catsup sweetened with honey and imitation mayonnaise that is low in fat and cholesterol. The FDA requires that catsup include sugar and that mayonnaise contain a certain level of oil in order to be called natural. So, just because a product is labeled natural does not mean it is good for you; conversely, just because a product is not labeled natural does not mean it is not good for you.

Organic Foods

Organic produce is food grown without chemical fertilizers or pesticides. The semantics of the matter can become very technical. But the essence of the issue is producing high-quality food while nurturing the environment that produces it.

Trace elements in organically grown produce play subtle roles in the electrochemical balance of the body. Although these trace elements are not well understood, they clearly are vital to good health and are not mere impurities. When they are missing, vitality and resistance to disease is diminished.

The availability of organic foods has increased 20 percent since 1980. It is now a highly successful segment of the agriculture business. So, how does one know when food is really organic? Some states have standards for organic farming. Some states do not have standards, which means the term *organic* can be used freely. The best advice is to look for organic products that have been certified by the state (when appropriate) or by private farm associations.

Besides causing confusion for consumers, the lack of national standards regarding the label organic has generated barriers to interstate trade. Produce that meets one state's organic labeling standards may not qualify as organic in states that have tougher regulations. There is currently a move to create national standards for organic produce. For more information on organic farming, check with your local natural foods store or contact the California Certified Organic Farmers, P.O. Box 8136, Santa Cruz, CA 95061.

Chemicals in Our Food

There are two main types of pesticides used in chemical farming—systemic and nonsystemic pesticides. Systemic pesticides end up inside the plants, not on them, and therefore cannot be washed off. Hence, we consume the chemical along with the food, and there is no label to warn us of this fact. Nonsystemic chemicals can be washed off, however. The Environmental Protection Agency (EPA) allows about 400 different pesticides into our food supply.

The government's efforts to control pesticides in our food are in a shambles. For example, from September 1983 through July 1985, the FDA discovered 179 shipments of food containing illegal pesticide residues. For 107 of these cases, the agency took no action to prevent the food from reaching the public. Furthermore, the EPA's tolerance levels for such chemicals may be grossly inaccurate. As consumers, all we can do is learn as much as we can about the use of chemicals in farming and try to buy organic produce.

One percent of Europe's farmland is organic.

Since 1950, the amount of chemical fertilizers used in farming has doubled every 10 years. In the 1980s, the United States used approximately 17 million pounds of chemical fertilizers. Chemically fertilized foods may lose a lot of their minerals, which add flavor as well as nutritional value to the food. This may be one reason why Americans use so much salt and sugar and so many spices and flavor enhancers in their food. It is easy to see how a destructive cycle could develop when one natural step in the process is alleviated.

Government practices regarding the use of chemicals on foods is puzzling. For example, the FDA has allowed farmers in the United States to spray six times the determined-safe level of a carcinogenic chemical on grapes; yet this same agency once stopped the import of grapes from Argentina because it found arsenic on a single grape! The Delaney Amendment, passed in the 1980s, prohibits the addition of carcinogenic chemicals to any food; yet such chemicals are often found in our food.

Currently, about 2,800 chemicals may be added to foods, and about 10,000 chemical compounds may be used directly in the food or in the processing of food. This does not include herbicides, fungicides, insecticides, and detergents, which also affect our produce. The Pesticide Chemicals Amendment of 1954 regulated the use of chemicals in foods. However, because scientists lacked the technology to measure low levels of chemicals in foods, and perhaps because there was little concern for the effects of such chemicals, fighting the widespread use of chemicals in agriculture and the food industry was impractical.

As many as 1,500 chemicals are used as additives in ice creams; none of these chemical additives will be listed on the label.

The Delaney Amendment was meant to improve things. But business has been successful in dodging the law. One way has been creating the GRAS list, which identifies substances "generally recognized as safe." For regulatory purposes the GRAS substances are not considered food additives. For each substance on the GRAS list, qualified experts stated that, in their opinion, the substance was safe; no tests were necessary to substantiate their claims. About six percent of the GRAS substances are being investigated further. These include caffeine, monosodium glutamate (MSG), protein hydrolysates, licorice and licorice extracts, ammoniated glycerine, sucrose, nutmeg and mace (and their essential oils), sulfites, saccharin, nitrates, and nitrites.

Fresh versus Preserved Foods

Using fresh fruits and vegetables is one of the most obvious ways to maintain quality. As a general rule, fresh is best. Fresh fruits and vegetables lose nutrients if they sit around in the refrigerator for more than a few days, though. In some cases, then, it may be better to rely on frozen foods.

In general, frozen fruits and vegetables are superior to canned fruits and vegetables—both in nutrition and in taste. In the canning process the cans are sterilized and filled, and the food is cooked in the can and sealed while hot. This process radically overcooks food, since the cooking process goes on for several minutes after the can has been sealed. Nutrients generally are lost in the liquid, which often is discarded. Frozen foods, on the other hand, are first washed, cut, cleaned, and often blanched. Then they are flash-frozen to retain flavor, color, and nutrients.

The quality of food has changed drastically since the turn of the century, largely due to food preservation techniques. However, other advances in food technology are less beneficial. Overrefining of foods has reduced their nutritional density; furthermore, soil deterioration and contamination due to farming methods have compounded the problem.

Refined Foods and Processed Foods

Refined foods and processed foods are not the same. I generally avoid refined foods. Some examples are juices, white flour, and oils. Processed foods, on the other hand, include foods that have been preserved without breaking down or significantly changing the whole food. Tempeh, canned beans, and frozen vegetables are examples of processed foods.

I have a tremendous respect for technology, but sometimes I wonder about the objectives. I believe that food technology sometimes applies the wrong solutions to a problem. Take for example the development of a fiber supplement. Wouldn't it be better to stop refining sugars and flours and forget about the fiber supplement? Another example is brown sugar, which is a refined product made in some cases by adding a caramel color to white sugar. Wouldn't it be better to produce a sugar in which the molasses, with all its nutrients, is left intact?

The food refining process often changes the levels of nutrients in foods and destroys the balance of those nutrients, which helps in their absorption into the body. I doubt that technology can fully compensate for this imbalance. For example, if we use lecithin as a supplement, we need a calcium supplement to counter the calcium lost, because lecithin draws on our calcium stores. But magnesium is needed to assimilate calcium, which is why most lecithin supplements are calcium-magnesium balanced. This is one reason I try to avoid refined foods. Most diets that consist of a balance of high-quality whole, natural foods will not need supplements.

While we're on the subject of supplements, I'd like to point out that I distinguish between whole food supplements (such as blue-green algae or bee pollen) and vitamin supplements. I advocate whole food supplements and would take vitamin supplements only under the care of a qualified nutritionist. Before taking such vitamin supplements, I would expect a nutritionist to first determine (through medical tests) if I have any vitamin deficiencies. Then I would address the source of the deficiency, attempting to determine if it is related to my diet or to a biochemical imbalance.

Nutrient Stability

Some nutrients remain stable in light. That is, they don't deteriorate when exposed to light. Nutrients that are not light sensitive do not break down when exposed to light. Some nutrients break down when exposed to oxygen, whereas others do not. The chart that follows shows the stability of various nutrients.

Riboflavin is one example of a light-sensitive nutrient. A study conducted at the University of Minnesota analyzed packaged dried pastas and discovered that the riboflavin in these pastas deteriorated most rapidly when the pasta was packaged in a clear plastic container. Cardboard packages enabled the riboflavin to remain more stable.

NUTRIENT	LIGHT STABLE	LIGHT SENSITIVE	OXYGEN STABLE	OXYGEN SENSITIVE
Biotin			x	
Carotene (pro-A)		x		x
Choline	x			
Essential fatty acids (oils)		x		x
Folic acid		x		x
Inositol	x		x	

NUTRIENT	LIGHT STABLE	LIGHT SENSITIVE	OXYGEN STABLE	OXYGEN SENSITIVE
Niacin	x		x	
Riboflavin		x	x	
Thiamine	x			x
Pantothenic acid	x		x	
Vitamin A		x		x
Vitamin B_6		x	x	
Vitamin B_{12}		x		x
Vitamin C		x		x
Vitamin D		x		x
Vitamin E		x		x
Vitamin K		x	x	

Food Contamination Due to Bacteria

Chemical additives and pesticides are not the only causes of food contamination. Bacteria may pose a far greater risk than chemical additives and preservatives. Salmonella poisoning, for example, results in direct deaths and may cost as much as two million dollars a year in medical bills; other illnesses related to food contamination may cost 600 million to 1 billion dollars annually.

Irradiation of Foods

Food irradiation is a treatment that involves very large doses of ionizing radiation. Currently, irradiation is used:

- To eliminate trichinosis in fresh pork
- To stop potatoes from sprouting
- To kill insects and vermin in grains and herbs
- To increase the shelf life of perishable produce
- To kill bacteria

In addition, food technology scientists are exploring a process that uses even larger doses of radiation and will allow meat, milk, and other products to be packaged in such a way that they can remain at room temperature indefinitely.

Let's take a look at how irradiation works. When radiation strikes something, an energy transfer takes place. At a certain level, radiation has sufficient energy to knock electrons from the atoms of the material bombarded. This can break down the molecular structure of the material, leaving positively and negatively charged particles (ions). At or above a given level the radiation is called ionizing radiation. The ions are chemically active and easily recombine or initiate chemical reactions with surrounding material. Thus, ionizing radiation alters the chemical structure of material, which in turn may affect the organisms that feed on that material.

> *A food product label need not indicate irradiation, since this is a process, not an ingredient.*

High-energy ionizing radiation can cause radioactivity in the material bombarded. Even with low-energy radiation, it is possible for some compounds in the food to be made radioactive. However, this induced radioactivity decays rapidly; so, if the food is stored before use, the level of radiation is likely to be insignificant and well within the range of the natural radioactivity already found in food. Therefore, if irradiation is properly controlled, food should not become measurably radioactive. There are, however, several other health concerns regarding irradiation.

One problem is that irradiated foods have unique radiolytic products (URPs), of which very little is known. URPs are not found in conventional food processing, and the FDA has expressed concern that irradiated foods may contain enough URPs to warrant toxicologic evaluation. Another problem is the increased incidence of aflatoxins on irradiated foods. Aflatoxins are potent cancer-causing chemicals created by fungi. They occur naturally in some foods, such as peanuts. Several studies have shown that aflatoxins occur more abundantly on irradiated foods. This may constitute a serious health concern, since aflatoxins are 1,000 times more potent than the banned pesticide EDB, for which irradiation is a substitute.

Finally, even if irradiation is proved to be safe, it may have other adverse effects that would negate any benefits. Beatrice Trum Hunter, author of *Consumer Beware!*, documented the levels of nutrients that remain in irradiated foods and found that most vitamins are radiosensitive (that is, they are likely to be adversely affected by irradiation). Vitamin A and carotene, vitamin C, thiamine, B complex, and vitamin E especially are affected. Hunter found that irradiated oranges, for example, lost 28 percent of their ascorbic acid. Corn lost up to 29 percent of its ascorbic acid and 44 percent of its carotene. And whole milk lost 61 percent of its vitamin E.

I believe that, before the practice of irradiation is allowed to continue, there should be some conclusive, scientific evidence—verifiable by independent researchers—that proves that food irradiation is safe. Researchers should agree on exactly what is a "safe" dose of radiation. They also should know more about the health hazards that may result from irradiation and about what nutrients are lost through this process. In addition, there are many other issues that should be resolved. For example, we should know if workers in irradiation facilities may be exposed to dangerous levels of radioactive materials. We should know if it is possible for radioactive materials to be dispersed accidentally through the environment. And we should have some way of preventing the misuse of irradiation to "clean up" substandard, decaying foods, which may then be sold as fresh, high-quality products.

Protecting consumers from irradiated foods is difficult. In the first place, it is impossible to detect that a food product has been irradiated. Most food package labels do not reveal that such a process has been applied to the food. Even if labeling does occur, products will be labeled only if the entire product has been irradiated—not if an ingredient in the product has been irradiated.

Another problem is that government inspectors cannot verify levels of radiation used in the commercial process of irradiation. Although specified doses are supposed to be harmless, there is no simple way to ensure that foods have not been exposed accidentally to greater, unsafe levels of radiation. Then, too, if the industry begins to use larger doses of radiation for some purposes, food package labels probably should indicate doses of radiation used on all irradiated foods.

One group that is trying to ban irradiated foods from supermarkets is Project Cure. Its headquarters are 2020 K Street, N.W., Suite 350, Washington, D.C. 20069.

Labeling Food Products

Labels are the primary indicator of the quality of a product, but they do not always tell the whole story. Furthermore, labels sometimes are designed to mislead the consumer. For example, a label that reads "no sugar added" does not mean that the product does not contain sugar. A label that announces a product has been "fortified" or "enriched", which is good, does not necessarily claim that the refined product has more nutrients than the source foods. In most cases, enriched products may have far fewer nutrients than the source foods. A wise consumer will read between the lines when it comes to reading labels.

Some companies put chemical preservatives on the inside of packages to preserve food and prevent having to declare the use of chemical additives on the package label.

Nutrient labeling by supermarkets is on the rise. Labels usually emphasize low-sodium, low-fat, and low-calorie food items. According to the FDA, before supermarkets instituted such labeling, consumers generally did not realize that some common products, such as pasta, are low in sodium. As a result, these products have experienced increased sales. This is good, but it actually would be more helpful to consumers if there were danger signs beside high-sodium, high-fat, and high-calorie foods. When that happens, we'll know that a profound change has taken place in the food industry. But then, Rome wasn't built in a day.

LABELING FOR ADDITIVES

Unfortunately, ingredient labels need not list all additives. Of course, not all additives are harmful; some, such as guar gum, are actually beneficial. But it would be helpful if packagers were required to list all ingredients contained in packaged food. Naturally, this would be cumbersome.

Two common types of food additives are preservatives, which prevent foods from spoilage due to microorganisms, and antioxidants, which prevent or retard changes in color, flavor, and texture of processed foods. Some common preservatives are sodium benzoate, sorbic acid, sulfur dioxide, nitrites, and nitrates. Some common antioxidants are ascorbic acid, citric acid, BHA (butylated hydroxyanisole), and BHT (butylated hydroxytoluene). Recently, scientists discovered that the mustard seed contains a unique ingredient that may act as an antioxidant. They hope to be able to use it in place of the more suspect additives BHA and BHT.

MISLEADING LABELS

My personal interpretation of the label *natural* is that nothing artificial has been added to the product. It does not mean that the product is good for you. Many "natural" food products are high in sodium, fat, and/or sugar. Don't rely on such labels to tell you that a product is good; instead, read the ingredients and the nutritional information listed on the package label.

The labels *no cholesterol*, *light* or *lite*, and *low in calories* may leave the consumer thinking the food is healthier. The product actually may offer little if any health benefits. In fact, the term *lite* may refer to color, texture, or sodium content as well as to calories or fat content. In one nutrition study, a researcher found that the "light" version of a leading brand of pancake mix was actually higher in calories than the standard pancake mix, although it was lighter in texture. It's always a good idea to read the "fine-print" nutritional information and list of ingredients on a product. That way, you can find out for yourself what is the basis for any claims on a product.

Only ingredients that comprise one tenth of one percent of the food product must be listed on the label.

The label *no salt added* is another confusing claim. Most consumers think "low sodium" when they see a label claiming no salt added. Salt and sodium are not the same thing; rather, salt is composed of sodium and chloride. Just because a product claims that no salt was added does not mean that no sodium was added. The manufacturer or packager may have added sodium in the form of sodium caseinate, sodium saccharin, or monosodium glutamate (MSG). In addition, some foods (such as pickles) are naturally high in sodium; so a manufacturer may legally claim that no salt has been added to the pickles, even though the product is high in sodium.

Sugar is another sticky issue. The labels *no sugar added* or *sugar free* can be misleading, because the products still may contain other added sweeteners, such as glucose, fructose, maltose, honey, or molasses. Just because a label claims that no sugar has been added does not mean that the food is low in calories. Even more aggravating, the claim of "no white sugar added" does not mean that there is no white sugar in the product; white sugar may have been added to another sweetener, such as honey, which was then added to the product.

The labels *no cholesterol* and *made with pure vegetable oil* often mislead the consumer. A product labeled *no cholesterol* most likely contains margarine or vegetable oil—foods that do not contain cholesterol but that promote the natural production of cholesterol in the body. The manufacturer's claim leads the consumer to suppose the product is fat-free, which isn't true. The claim "made with pure vegetable oil" fails to reveal the type of vegetable oil used. Tropical vegetable oils such as palm oil or coconut oil may rival animal fats in their effect on blood cholesterol. Therefore, the claim of "pure vegetable oil" is not synonymous with "healthful."

The American Heart Association recommends that we limit fat intake to no more than about 30 percent of our total caloric intake. Generally, we should choose foods that contain less than 30 percent of their calories from fat. But how are the percentages determined? The label on a food product should list the grams of fat per serving. You would multiply this figure by nine, since there are nine calories in each gram of fat. Next, divide this figure by the total number of calories per serving (which also should be listed on the package label), and then multiply by 100.

THE IDEAL PRODUCT LABEL

Product labeling is an issue of great concern. Labels may be ambiguous and difficult to read; they often provide useless information and lack uniformity. The Center for Science in the Public's Interests (CSPI) has designed what may be called the ideal label. Their product label includes a pie chart that breaks down calories into protein, carbohydrates, and fats. It gives the percentages of unsaturated, saturated, and cholesterol fats in the product and identifies each source of oil or fat. The label lists all major ingredients—those that make up five percent or more of the product by weight. It also identifies other ingredients—those that comprise less than five percent of the product by weight. The label lists vital statistics such as information on fiber, cholesterol, cholesterol-raising fats, sodium, carbohydrates, proteins, calcium, iron, and vitamins A and C. Finally, a label would appear on the front of the package and would include four spotlights, telling the consumer if the product is high or low in a particular nutrient. Red labels would denote undesirable features, such as a high cholesterol content; yellow labels would denote desirable ones, such as being low in calories.

Maintaining Quality with Special Foods

The recipes in this book are vegan. Personally, I do not eat any animal proteins. However, for transitional diets you may wish to introduce or substitute dairy products or eggs. For this reason, I think it's important to discuss the quality of these foods as well as other, more recommendable foods.

One cup of cooked collards has more calcium than a cup of milk. Kale, broccoli, and tofu are other good sources of calcium and are more healthful than milk.

DAIRY PRODUCTS   Regular milk is high in fat and low in complex carbohydrates and fiber. It is generally not a balanced food; as recent studies have indicated, milk actually may help deplete calcium stores in the body. The process of homogenizing milk has become a major issue in terms of health. In this process, fats are broken down and integrated into the milk. The fats are then assimilated into the bloodstream, creating buildups of cholesterol or plaque in the artery walls. In contrast, the fats in unhomogenized milk cannot pass through the cell membrane.

The addition of vitamin D is another issue with milk. Vitamin D does not occur naturally in milk; most cow's milk is enriched with vitamin D, which is critical to the metabolism of calcium. But dairy processors use a synthetic vitamin D that may even be carcinogenic. There are many sources of vitamin D available to us, and I cannot recommend a product that is enriched with synthetic vitamins. The main reason I do not recommend milk, however, is that it promotes the production of mucus in the body, which I believe is not healthy.

The fact that most cheese is relatively high in sodium has come as bad news for cheese lovers. Researchers at the University of Wisconsin are working on an ultrafiltration process, which removes the salt from the milk but preserves high levels of phosphorus and calcium, giving the cheese a salty taste. The process can cut sodium levels from 30 to 60 percent in most kinds of cheeses. The unique element of this process is that it doesn't leave the bitter aftertaste that regular low-sodium cheeses have.

EGGS Nutritionally speaking, the egg has a net protein utilization (NPU) of 98 percent. That means that 98 percent of the protein in the egg is absorbed into the body. This is far higher than that of meats, which is roughly 60 percent. (The NPU may not be the same when the egg is baked into a product such as a cake.)

It's best to avoid powdered whole milk or powdered eggs, because oxidized cholesterol may be harder on the system than regular cholesterol.

Eggs are high in cholesterol, though, and should be used in moderation. One large egg has about 275 mg of cholesterol. Because most health experts recommend limiting daily cholesterol intake to 300 mg, many people consider eggs off-limits. Now, however, low-cholesterol eggs are available: in the 1980s, a firm in Pennsylvania was trying to develop eggs that have thicker shells; inadvertently, they produced eggs that have less cholesterol—about 180 mg per egg. Personally, I do not eat eggs. If I did, I probably would eat these lower cholesterol eggs. Keep in mind, though, that even these low-cholesterol eggs are quite high in cholesterol.

MAYONNAISE Imitation mayonnaise is readily available at natural foods stores and some supermarkets. There are several brands, and ingredients vary. Some contain whole eggs, egg yolks, and soy oil or canola oil. Some are entirely eggless and may contain tofu. In any case, most imitation mayonnaise produced by whole foods companies contain less cholesterol and fewer calories than regular mayonnaise. In general, therefore, they are of higher quality. These new mayonnaises are called imitation because they don't meet the FDA's standards for a high oil content.

DAIRY-LIKE PRODUCTS   There are four dairy-like products of concern here. They are nondairy creamers, soy milk, soy cheese, and tofu "ice cream." In general, nondairy products are more healthful than the more familiar dairy products they imitate. Nondairy creamers are one exception to this general rule.

Nondairy creamers sometimes are popular with folks who are trying to cut down on cholesterol. Usually, though, nondairy creamers are very high in saturated fats, contributing to cholesterol. Typically, nondairy creamers contain corn syrup solids, partially hydrogenated vegetable oil (including coconut oil, cottonseed oil, palm oil, or palm kernel oil), sodium caseinate, sodium phosphates, mono- and diglycerides, sodium silico aluminate, and artificial color. I do not consider this type of product to be an example of a high-quality food.

Soy milk is an example of a high-quality food, but this product varies among producers. Read the package labels and check for added oils, flavoring, and sweeteners. Plain soy milk that does not have added ingredients will be low in calories, fat, simple sugars, and sodium. Several companies produce flavored soy milk drinks. They are nutritious, but they are fairly high in calories, due to added sweeteners and oils.

Soy cheeses are another alternative to dairy products. Their nutritional densities vary, but they are generally high in fats or oils, with the softer cheeses being especially high. For this reason, I recommend using soy cheeses sparingly; I like to reserve them for special menus.

In general, soy-cultured cheeses are high in oil and therefore are more nutritionally dense. Most soy-cultured cheeses are not vegan, though, because they contain enzymes (casein) from the cow. As a side note, some soy cheeses will not melt under the broiler in the same way that dairy cheese does.

One last nondairy product of concern here is tofu "ice cream." There are a few different brands of this dessert available, and most are fairly high quality—particularly those that contain brown rice syrup or similar sweeteners. Again, check the carton labels; make sure you purchase brands that contain a substantial percentage of tofu and are free of lactose and cholesterol; these will be high-quality, tasty substitutes for dairy ice cream. You should also be aware that plainer flavors contain far fewer calories than fancier flavors, such as chocolate chip or nut flavors.

OILS   All fats and oils are composed of fatty acids. Plants and animals convert energy into fatty acids as a means of storing energy for future use. There are three types of fatty acids—polyunsaturated, monounsaturated, and saturated. Polyunsaturated fatty acids, called essential fatty acids, are needed for good health but cannot be produced by the body. The chart below shows the make-up of several different types of oils.

OIL	POLY-UNSATURATED	MONO-UNSATURATED	SATURATED
Canola	32%	62%	6%
Safflower	75%	12%	9%
Sunflower	66%	20%	10%
Corn	59%	24%	13%
Soybean	59%	23%	14%
Olive	9%	72%	14%
Peanut	32%	46%	17%
Sesame seed	40%	40%	18%
Cottonseed	52%	18%	26%
Palm kernel	2%	10%	80%
Coconut	2%	6%	87%

Most nutritionists agree that consuming fats, especially saturated fats, tends to contribute to cardiovascular disease. The consumption of oils, on the other hand, may contribute to colon cancer. When heated to the breaking point, oxidized oils cause particles to form in the body which can lead to precancerous conditions. This does not mean that oils should be avoided; they are an important carrier for the fat-soluble vitamins A, D, and E, as well as providing essential fatty acids. Oils are also important for the efficient use of the B vitamins. Otherwise, though, oils are nutritionally deficient.

The labeling of oils can be misleading. For example, the label *cold-pressed* leads one to believe that the oil was extracted from the source without involving heat; this assumption is incorrect, because all oil extracting involves heat. For the highest quality oil, look for the label *unrefined*. This term means that very little heat and no chemicals were used in extracting the oil from the source product. Even this term is misleading, though, because all oils—even "unrefined" ones—are refined by-products of a natural food.

In the processing of olive oil, the olive is crushed in a mill that breaks up the pulp but not the kernel. The first pressing is gentle and does not heat the oil much above room temperature. This pressing is labeled *virgin olive oil*. There are different grades of olive oil that carry this label. Extra virgin olive oil has superior aroma; fine virgin olive oil usually has a high acidity; and virgin olive oil is less flavorful and has an even higher acidity. This varies, however, according to the brand. For example, a fine virgin olive oil of one brand may actually be comparable to an extra virgin oil of another brand.

Unrefined corn oil (which actually is refined somewhat) is an excellent substitute for butter, because it has a rich buttery flavor. It is my favorite oil to use in making pastries. It is less desirable for sautéing, though, because it tends to foam easily. Unrefined corn oil is high in linoleic acid, one of the essential fatty acids, as well as vitamin E. This oil stores for a fairly long time without becoming rancid.

Sesame oil is one of the oldest oils. Produced in China about 5,000 years ago, it was also important for cosmetics and ink. It comes in two forms— roasted, which is dark and has a strong flavor, and unroasted, which is light and has a mild nutty flavor. Sesame oil is shelf stable and is good for frying and sautéing. (My recipes that call for sesame oil generally mean unroasted sesame oil; if the strong flavor of roasted sesame oil is appropriate in the dish, the recipe will call for roasted sesame oil.)

Canola oil, or rapeseed oil, is the lowest in saturated fats and is 100 percent expeller pressed. Like olive oil and sesame oil, canola oil has a long history. It was one of the world's most popular oils, favored in China, Japan, and India. The rapeseed resembles a mustard seed; canola ("Canadian oil") is a result of selective plant breeding designed to product the ideal oil seed. This oil has 25 percent less saturated fat than safflower oil and is one of the few vegetarian sources of omega-3 fatty acids, commonly found in fish oils. Canola oil has a bland flavor but a delicate aroma. Because it has a high smoke point, it is excellent for cooking and baking. It blends well, making it excellent for mayonnaise and salad dressings, and resists becoming rancid.

> *Because oils will oxidize and become rancid when exposed to light and oxygen, they should be stored in dark-colored glass bottles rather than clear plastic.*

MARGARINE   By FDA standards, margarines must be at least 80 percent fat or oil. Refined oils are best suited for margarines, because they are neutral in flavor and color. Most margarines are high in saturated fats.

Margarine is not a high-quality food, and I do not use it very often. When I do use this product, I use margarine made from soybean oil rather than corn oil. Both are all-vegetable products that contain no animal by-products, and both contain partially hydrogenated oils. But corn-oil margarines often contain preservatives and other additives. Most soybean margarines, on the other hand, contain no preservatives or artificial flavoring. In addition, the nutritional value of the soybean, in my opinion, makes soybean margarine a superior, more desirable product.

LECITHIN   Lecithin is a food that has several uses in the diet. Lecithin choline is transformed into acetylcholine, a vital compound for the transmission of messages from one nerve to another. Lecithin helps prevent cholesterol and other fats from accumulating on artery walls. (It works on cholesterol like rock salt on ice.) It also helps prevent or retard liver degeneration. In the digestive tract, lecithin helps the body to absorb vitamins A and D and to utilize fat-soluble nutrients like vitamins E and K. Finally, lecithin may help protect the myelin sheath around nerve fibers. Because lecithin draws calcium from the system, it may cause calcium depletion. The key is to buy a lecithin that is calcium-magnesium balanced. (Calcium needs magnesium to become assimilated into bodily tissues.) I generally use liquid lecithin in baking and lecithin granules (especially fruit-flavored granules) in beverage drinks.

NUTS AND SEEDS   Nuts and seeds are high in oil—nuts more so than seeds. Therefore, these foods should be eaten in moderation. Still, they are nutritionally dense. The following table shows the amount of saturated fat as a percentage of total fat in various nuts.

NUT	SATURATED FAT AS PERCENT OF TOTAL FAT
Hazelnuts	6.2%
Pecans	6.2%
Almonds	8.2%
Walnuts	8.2%
Pistachio nuts	12.1%
Peanuts	12.2%
Cashew nuts	13.7%
Brazil nuts	15.9%
Chestnuts	18.1%

When buying packaged nuts and seeds, check to see if they are nitrogen packed. If so, they probably will be safe to consume if used before the expiration date. Whole nuts usually stay fresh longer than chopped nuts, which oxidize more quickly.

Like nuts and seeds, nut butters are a high-fat food that are nevertheless a high-quality food. You should be aware that some nut butters have additives; pistachio butter usually has added salt; cashew butter usually has added oil. Choose fresh nut butters, especially when it comes to peanut butter. Avoid products that contain added sugars or flavorings; avoid peanut butter that contains added salt or hydrogenated oils, too.

There is some controversy over the value of raw sesame tahini as opposed to cooked tahini. In the case of tahini, quality depends mainly on the process of manufacturing. Most tahinis on the market today are rancid (unless they are heat treated). Raw tahini turns rancid quickly because of the moisture content of the seeds. As a result, it leaves a bitter taste in the back of the mouth. Look for tahini that uses a light roasting process. This process causes any moisture on the seeds to evaporate. Tahini processed in this way tends to stay good for a long time.

One other factor in the process of making tahini affects quality. The hull of a sesame seed contains calcium oxilate, which is indigestable. Most manufacturers spray the sesame seeds with lye to remove the hulls. Some manufacturers hull the sesame seeds mechanically, without chemicals. Obviously, I recommend the mechanical process. In purchasing tahini, try to find those produced using this process.

Quality in Seasonings

Salt is probably the most common form of seasoning. Table salt is a highly refined product. Typically, it contains salt, sodium silico aluminate, dextrose (a sugar), and potassium iodine. It is heated at high temperatures, and anticoagulants are added to prevent clumping. Some studies have suggested that sodium chloride may be more detrimental than any other form of salt. I often use sea salt in my own cooking, because it contains more minerals than a more refined table salt.

Herbs and spices are an integral part of cooking. They must be used to complement and bring out the pristine flavors of the foods, not overwhelm them. Use fresh herbs and spices as often as possible. When buying dried herbs and spices, check the label to make sure there are no additives such as sugar, salt, or MSG. Check the expiration date on the containers; older spices and herbs will lose their aroma. Many spices are irradiated, which is not indicated on the label and cannot be detected. Consult your local health food store for information on spice companies that do not irradiate their products.

In purchasing miso, find out how it was made. Try to buy miso that has been made by the traditional fermentation process. There are many different types of miso. (See the glossary for descriptions.) Avoid miso that has chemical additives.

One of the most important seasonings in my kitchen is prepared vegetarian soup stock, or base. You can buy powdered soup base in packages or in bulk. In purchasing this seasoning, make sure you are getting one that is truly vegetarian. Some powdered vegetable soup bases contain animal proteins. Also look for ones that are low in sodium and free of additives.

FOOD PREPARATION TECHNIQUES

*T*he way in which we prepare foods has a direct effect on the nutritional density of the end product. Food preparation techniques also affect the way the food looks, tastes, and feels in the mouth. One of the most effective ways to develop flavor is to cook the food. Ironically, heat can also be the most destructive element to the quality of food.

Some nutrients, such as choline, vitamins B_{12} and K, niacin, and essential fatty acids are heat-stable nutrients. This means that heat will not destroy the nutrient significantly when the food is cooked properly. Most other nutrients are not heat-stable. The following chart shows the value loss of various nutrients. Note that although niacin is a heat-stable nutrient a substantial percentage of its value can be lost through excessive heat.

NUTRIENT	PERCENT OF NUTRIENT LOST IN COOKING
Heat-Stable Nutrients	
Vitamin B_{12}	up to 10%
Vitamin K	up to 5%
Choline	up to 5%
Essential fatty acids	up to 10%
Niacin	up to 75%
Heat-Unstable Nutrients	
Vitamin A	up to 40%
Vitamin B_6	up to 40%
Vitamin C	up to 100%
Vitamin D	up to 40%

NUTRIENT	PERCENT OF NUTRIENT LOST IN COOKING
Vitamin E	up to 55%
Biotin	up to 60%
Carotene	up to 30%
Folic acid	up to 100%
Inositol	up to 95%
Pantothenic acid	up to 50%
Riboflavin	up to 75%
Thiamine	up to 80%

Cooking Methods

When foods are cooked quickly, there is generally a better chance to lessen nutrient loss. For example, when broccoli is cooked quickly in a small amount of water, it loses only half the vitamin C. Potatoes cooked for half an hour retain 66 percent of their vitamin C. When cooked for an hour they retain 50 percent; after 90 minutes, only 17 percent of the vitamin C remains. One way to curb the loss of water-soluable vitamins is to bring the water to a simmer before adding the vegetables; then cook for a minimum amount of time. Cooking vegetables in covered saucepans also minimizes exposure to air, which causes the cooking time—and the loss of vitamins—to decrease. There is also an advantage to slow cooking, though. I find that slow cooking allows the flavors of foods to develop. Because there are advantages and disadvantages to each type of cooking, it is important to know when to choose each type.

There are several basic methods of cooking, including baking, boiling, braising, broiling, deep-frying, sautéing, steaming, and poaching. Cooking vegetables in water seals in the flavor; in contrast, sautéing extracts the flavor from vegetables. Slower sautéing (low heat) is recommended for starchy vegetables, because it develops the starches into a sweet flavor. A quick-sauté method is acceptable for nonstarchy vegetables, such as in a stir-fry.

To sauté means to fry lightly and quickly in a small amount of oil. Only tender proteins can be used for this method of cooking, since the cooking time generally is very short. To sauté, preheat the skillet over medium-high heat. Use about one to two tablespoons of oil, depending on the quantity of food. (Butter is not recommended for sautéing because it burns quickly.) Add the vegetables or other food when the oil is hot but not smoking. If the oil is not hot enough, the food will stick to the skillet. Lower the heat and continue to cook the food, stirring occasionally.

Pseudo-sautéing is the state of the art in cooking. This slower cooking method uses less oil and relies on the natural moisture from the vegetables to fully cook the food. When pseudo-sautéing, use a medium-low heat and stir the vegetables constantly to evenly coat them with or oil and prevent burning. High-moisture vegetables such as onions, carrots, and mushrooms need very little oil. Adding a little salt will extract the moisture from the vegetables, so you may not need to add any water at all. When cooking low-moisture vegetables, you can add small amounts of water, about two tablespoons at a time, toward the end of cooking to prevent burning.

Toasting can significantly lower the nutritional density of food.

Boiling is one of the cleanest ways to cook, because it uses no oils. But it results in the loss of nutrients, unless the boiling water is used to make soup or sauces. In any case, you will boil away some of the nutrients from the vegetables. When I do boil vegetables, I use just enough water to cover the vegetables—not the copious amount of water used in traditional cooking.

Steaming vegetables is preferable to boiling them; because the vegetables are not in direct contact with water, the water-soluble vitamins are less likely to be drawn out. When I have liquid left over from cooking vegetables, I like to make a light glaze from it. I generally reduce the excess water to about one-half cup, season and thicken it to a light glaze (using kuzu or arrowroot), and pour it over the vegetables. I often use sauces or glazes with vegetables that are cooked by steaming. That's because the cooking process does not impart any additional flavor to the food, and steamed vegetables sometimes can seem dull.

Boiling pastas and grains is another matter. With pasta, you need a much greater amount of water than with vegetables, but you don't need an exact amount of water. In fact, I usually use one third more water than the package label indicates, just so the pieces of pasta have plenty of room to cook without sticking to themselves. With grains, on the other hand, the amount of water should be exact. The quantity of water should be calculated so that the grain becomes tender at just the same time that it absorbs all of the water.

Poaching is another method of cooking with liquid. It is generally associated with the preparation of eggs and fish, but it can be quite successful with vegetables also. To poach vegetables, you first preheat a small amount of water, broth, or wine. Then you either pour the liquid onto the vegetables or stir the vegetables into the simmering liquid. There should be enough liquid to cover the vegetables by about half an inch. Cook until *al dente* and immediately remove from the broth. To make a complementary sauce, thicken the broth to a sauce consistency, adjust the seasoning, and serve with the food immediately.

Broiling and grilling are quick-cooking methods that generally use an open flame or otherwise exposed heat. The high heat browns the surface of the food, producing the characteristic effect. Tofu, seitan, tempeh, and fresh vegetables can all be broiled successfully. When broiling vegetable proteins, it is imperative to lightly coat the food with oil to keep it moist. With precooked foods such as tofu, the only concern beyond browning them is to thoroughly heat it for flavor and to kill any bacteria.

Braising is a method that combines dry heat and moist heat. Usually, the foods are browned first in oil over high heat. Then a liquid such as a rich stock is added. The pan is covered and the food is allowed to simmer gently until tender. A roux or "demiglace" may be added along with the cooking liquid. Braising, like sautéing, develops the flavor of the food. In traditional cooking, this method is used most often with large cuts of meat; vegetables are then added along with the cooking liquid. Likewise, braising is appropriate with a whole piece of seitan.

Roasting is a dry-cooking method that takes place in an area of enclosed heat, such as an oven. To make a seitan or tofu roast, first preheat the oven to 350 degrees F. Place a layer of vegetables in a pan, along with some herbs and spices. Then place the piece of seitan or tofu in the pan and put it in the oven. Reduce the heat to 300 degrees F and cook the food slowly for about one and a half hours. With precooked vegetable proteins, the purpose of cooking is to instill flavor and to cook the accompanying raw vegetables. Tempeh must be cooked thoroughly, though, to kill the bacteria. Also, if you are using raw seitan, it will need to be cooked longer and will need additional water; raw seitan will absorb up to 25 percent of its raw weight in water. When the food is cooked, it is best to allow the roasted protein to stand for ten minutes before cutting. Always roast seitan and tofu in a covered pan, since these foods have no oils in them and will dry out.

It is easier to deep-fry tofu, seitan, and other vegetable proteins because these foods usually are precooked. Deep-frying meat is comparatively more difficult because the hot oil has to cook the food all the way through. With tofu, seitan, or tempeh, you are basically heating the food throughout and cooking only the surface of the food. The frying oil must be hot enough to brown the food and make it crisp without burning it. If the temperature is too low, the oil will permeate and saturate the food.

When deep-frying foods, avoid overloading the frying pan. The more food you add to the fryer at one time, the more quickly the oil temperature will drop, especially if you are frying cold or frozen foods. To give your oil a longer life, it is best to strain it after each use. Food particles left in the oil will cause the oil to break down, which will affect the way in which the oil fries foods.

Storing Cooked Foods

Allow hot cooked foods to cool down before sealing and refrigerating them. If you seal hot foods, the heat that is trapped inside the container will incubate bacteria. There are two ways in which you can cool foods quickly. One way is to put the food in an open container and spread it out to allow the heat to escape more rapidly. Stir the food about every five minutes to release heat. When the food becomes lukewarm, you can transfer it to a clean container and refrigerate it. Another way is to put the food container in an ice bath.

Marinating Foods

The main purpose for using marinades in food preparation is to fuse a flavor into the food. To intensify the marinade, you can use the hot-infusion method, in which herbs are cooked with liquids to release the flavor of the herbs immediately. The marinade can then be cooled or used hot. If you are marinating tofu, for example, you may want to add it to the hot marinade to kill any surface bacteria. (Sometimes, I let foods half-cook in hot marinade.) High-acid marinades will cause protein cells to break down slowly. This "tenderizing" effect (in reality, a denaturing of the protein cells) is not an important goal in marinating vegetable-based proteins.

Plan to marinate foods for several hours (or overnight) in order for the marinade to significantly affect the food. Marinating foods for less than half an hour will not affect the flavor much more than basting it during the cooking process. Use strong marinades in foods that will be cooked slowly over a long period of time; the flavors will mellow out in the cooking process.

Seasonings

The fundamental purpose of seasoning food is to enhance the existing flavor or, in some cases, to provide a dominating flavor. Herbs and spices also are used to lighten the taste of food and sometimes to make it easier to digest. In warm climates, spices are used to preserve foods. Proper cooking techniques are essential to the effective use of spices and herbs. For instance, if the cooking oil is too hot when you sauté garlic, the garlic will burn and take on a bitter taste.

In general, a little salt should be added to foods during the cooking process to help bring out the flavor. If you want to add more salt to adjust the flavor, it is best to do so while the food is still hot. Salt is used in macrobiotic cooking to help retain minerals in vegetables. Water is yin and will release minerals; salt is yang and is therefore believed to prevent minerals from being leached out of the vegetable.

I prefer working with fresh herbs whenever possible. I realize, however, that fresh herbs are not always readily available in some parts of the country or at some times of the year. When a recipe calls for fresh herbs and you must substitute dried herbs, the rule of thumb is to use one-half to one-third the amount indicated, depending on the herb. For example, if a recipe calls for one tablespoon of chopped basil, use one teaspoon of dried. With fresh herbs, the more finely you chop them, the more intense the flavor becomes.

Dried herbs generally are more concentrated in flavor than fresh herbs, unless the dried herbs have been stored for a long time. However, fresh herbs have a superior bouquet. In general, I do not recommend using powdered dried herbs in cooked foods, because the powder is too concentrated and can affect the color of the food adversely. I sometimes use powdered herbs in small quantities to boost flavor at the end of the cooking process, if the whole herbs I used at the beginning of cooking were not sufficient.

You can get a quick release of flavor from whole herbs by making a hot infusion. This process is done by simmering the herbs in a small amount of water for several minutes. Then you can strain the mixture and add the liquid to the food.

Ginger is a great natural preservative, bacteria-killer, and tenderizer. Some studies have shown that ginger extract is effective in killing salmonella. This bulb is used in macrobiotic and Oriental cuisine. Fresh ginger can be cooked to reduce the "bite" in it. I like to simmer it in apple juice to make "ginger ale."

To give broiled, roasted, or sautéed foods the taste of ginger, add freshly grated ginger—pulp and all. If you really don't want the pulp to become part of the dish, you can wrap the ginger pulp in a piece of clean cheesecloth before using it. Some people prefer instead to squeeze the juice out of the ginger and discard the pulp. The cheesecloth method is better.

Several recipes in this book call for prepared seasoning blends. Some are available commercially, such as gomasio. However, you may wish to make your own blends. Here are two recipes for seasoning blends that may come in handy in your kitchen.

Pâté Seasoning Blend

YIELD: *1½ cups*
TIME: *10 minutes*

2 tablespoons white pepper
2 tablespoons black pepper
2 tablespoons paprika
2 tablespoons nutmeg
2 tablespoons ginger powder
2 tablespoons dried basil
2 tablespoons whole dried thyme
2 tablespoons marjoram
2 tablespoons allspice
2 tablespoons garlic powder
1 tablespoon ground cloves

Stir together the seasonings and store in an airtight container. Use about 1 teaspoon of pâté seasoning per pound of protein.

Cardamom Gomasio

YIELD: *1 cup*
TIME: *20 minutes*

¾ cup raw sesame seeds
1 tablespoon sea salt
1¼ teaspoons cardamom

Put all ingredients in a heavy skillet and cook over medium heat for about 2 minutes. Then continue to cook, stirring constantly, until the seeds cease popping. Put the mixture into a suribachi and grind by hand until the seeds are half-ground and the oils have coated the salt. As an alternative, grind the mixture in a blender for about 10 to 20 seconds. Be careful that you don't grind it into a paste.

¾ cup raw sesame seeds
1 tablespoon sea salt
½ teaspoon dried oregano
½ teaspoon celery seed
½ teaspoon dried basil
½ teaspoon garlic powder
½ teaspoon ground fennel seeds

VARIATION: *Italian Gomasio*
To prepare this gomasio, follow the directions given in the main recipe above.

Appetizers

*A*ppetizers should complement the rest of the meal. For example, if you are serving a heavy entrée, you should present a light appetizer. Generally, I serve either a soup or a salad after an appetizer; rarely do I serve both. If I serve all three—appetizer, soup, and salad—I take care that they are well balanced and not very heavy.

Appetizers cover a wide variety of foods. In general, many entrée foods can be used for appetizers, and vice versa. I consider appetizers to be the equivalent of petit fours in the pastry department in the sense that they are small, bite-sized pieces of delectable food. The primary function of an appetizer is to stimulate the appetite, not to satisfy it. That is why appetizers often are spicy.

An appetizer party is another matter entirely. At an appetizer party, the food is *not* followed by another course. In this case, the appetizers are meant to constitute a small meal by themselves. Therefore, if you are serving these appetizers at such a party, you may want to make some of them slightly larger, or at least plan to have larger quantities available. My appetizer recipes are based on traditional presentations, but many are unique in their vegetarian nature. After all, vegetarian cuisine has a rich tradition of its own.

Italian Antipasto

YIELD: *3 cups; 6 servings*
TIME: *45 minutes*

2½ teaspoons cider vinegar
¾ teaspoon lemon juice
1½ teaspoons dry wine or
 sherry
¼ cup tomato paste
¾ cup water
2 tablespoons olive oil
1 cup peeled and julienned
 rutabaga
1 cup peeled and julienned
 carrots
½ cup diced potato
1 teaspoon chopped basil
1 teaspoon fresh rosemary
2 teaspoons minced garlic
2 teaspoons paprika,
 preferably Hungarian
1 teaspoon chopped oregano
¼ teaspoon black pepper
½ teaspoon chopped thyme
½ teaspoon dry mustard
1 teaspoon salt (optional)
½ cup diced green pepper
¾ cup diced celery
½ cup quartered mushrooms
¾ cup diced onion
1 tablespoon, each, pitted
 chopped black and green
 olives or 2 tablespoons one
 kind of olive

*T*his recipe uses a heat-infusion marinade. The vegetables should be tender-crisp when cooked. The antipasto will keep, refrigerated, for about two weeks.

To make the marinade, stir together the cider vinegar, lemon juice, wine, tomato paste, and water. Set aside.

Heat the olive oil in a heavy saucepan over medium heat for a few minutes. Add the rutabaga, carrots, potato, and seasonings and sauté for about 5 minutes, stirring occasionally. Add the remaining vegetables, the olives, and the marinade. Cook for 10 minutes, covered, stirring occasionally. Cool before serving.

Serve the antipasto on a bed of lettuce accompanied by natural whole wheat crackers or other crackers of your choice.

VARIATION 1
When the mixture is cool, add ½ cup of julienned zucchini and ½ cup of cooked garbanzo beans. Instead of garbanzo beans, you may wish to add 1 cup of finely diced tofu that has been steamed for about a minute. (Because the tofu probably will be bland, you may want to add more spices or marinate the tofu for a while.)

VARIATION 2
For this pasta salad variation, begin by preparing enough small shell pasta (or other small pasta) to yield about 4 cups of cooked pasta. Allow the cooked pasta to cool. For each serving, arrange lettuce on a salad plate, place about ½ cup of pasta on the lettuce and top with ½ cup of antipasto mixture. Serve with bread or crackers.

Marinated Vegetables

YIELD: *4½ cups; 5 to 6 servings*
TIME: *20 to 30 minutes preparation; allow 1 to 7 days to marinate the vegetables*

MARINADE INGREDIENTS:
½ cup barley malt syrup (or barley-corn malt syrup)
¾ cup brown rice vinegar*
¼ cup water
¼ cup sesame oil, olive oil, or canola oil
¾ teaspoon finely chopped savory or basil
1½ teaspoons chopped tarragon
1 tablespoon minced garlic
¾ teaspoon salt

*You may use 6 tablespoons cider vinegar diluted with 6 tablespoons water.

VEGETABLES:
1 cup carrots, peeled and cut into thick matchsticks
1 cup yellow squash, cut into thick matchsticks
1 cup green zucchini, cut into thick matchsticks
1 cup Spanish onions, halved and thinly sliced
1 cup red bell pepper, cut into thick matchsticks

*O*ne afternoon, when I was the executive chef in a small restaurant in North Miami, I found the perfect marinade. This basic recipe is extremely versatile. The same marinade may be used to flavor tofu and seitan. It also may be used as a dressing for pasta salad. The savory and tarragon give it a balanced sweet and sour flavor. Marinades mellow with age. This one may be made up to a week before it is used.

In a large bowl or pan, mix together the marinade ingredients. Add the prepared vegetables and let stand for at least 1 day—preferably for 3 to 7 days. Stir every day to ensure that the vegetables marinate evenly.

To serve, arrange a bed of various greens, such as fresh spinach, Bibb lettuce, and romaine lettuce, and top with about ½ cup of the marinated vegetables per person.

1 pound tofu, cut into 16
    cubes
4 tablespoons roasted sesame
    oil
½ teaspoon minced garlic
2 tablespoons tamari
marinade ingredients (from
    main recipe on previous
    page)

VARIATION: *Marinated Tofu*

Sauté the tofu in the oil, add the garlic and tamari, and continue to sauté until the tofu is lightly brown on all sides. Prepare the marinade, add the tofu, and refrigerate for at least 12 hours—ideally for 3 days.

1½ cups cubed seitan
4 tablespoons roasted sesame
    oil
1 teaspoon tamari
water
marinade ingredients (from
    main recipe on previous
    page)

VARIATION: *Marinated Seitan*

Sauté the seitan in the oil. Add the tamari and a little water, and continue to sauté until the seitan is evenly browned. Deglaze the pan with about 2 tablespoons of water and set aside. Prepare the marinade. Add the seitan and the sauce from the sauté pan. Refrigerate for at least 12 hours—preferably for 3 days. To serve, arrange a lettuce leaf on a small plate, fan out a few slices of tomato on the lettuce, and place the marinated seitan on the tomatoes.

3 cups water
2 teaspoons oil
½ teaspoon salt
1 cup dried whole-wheat shell
    pasta
Marinated Vegetables (entire
    main recipe on previous
    page)
½ cup tomato paste (optional)

VARIATION: *Marinated Pasta Appetizer*

Bring the water, oil, and salt to a simmer. Add the pasta and stir occasionally to prevent it from sticking. Cook for 15 to 20 minutes until the pasta is tender and breaks easily. Drain the pasta and run cold water over it to prevent it from overcooking. Combine the pasta gently with the marinated vegetables and the tomato paste, if you wish.

Shish Kebabs

YIELD: *6 servings*
TIME: *40 minutes
preparation; 10 to 15 minutes
cooking; allow 1 to 7 days to
marinate the tofu and seitan*

*1 tablespoon roasted sesame
   oil
½ onion, cut into six pieces
twelve 1-inch squares red bell
   pepper
twelve 1-inch squares green
   bell pepper
6 mushroom caps
Marinated Tofu (page 41)
Marinated Seitan (page 41)
3 cups cooked brown rice*

*K*ebabs, consisting of cubes of marinated tofu and seitan interspersed with lightly sautéed peppers and onions, make light and attractive appetizers. The kebabs may be assembled without the additional vegetables, in which case a colorful vegetable garnish would be attractive.

Heat the oil in a skillet and sauté the onion and red bell pepper for about 2 minutes over medium heat. Add the green pepper, sauté for another minute, and remove immediately. (The green peppers will turn gray-green if overcooked.) Sautéing the vegetables brings out the flavor and partially cooks them so that they do not dry out on the skewer while baking. The oil coating gives them a sheen.

To assemble the shish kebabs, place the ingredients in the following order: tofu, red pepper, onion, seitan, green pepper, onion, tofu, and so forth. End with a mushroom cap.

Place the kebabs with 2½ cups of the marinade in a pan, cover, and bake in a preheated oven at 375 degrees F for 10 to 15 minutes. Pour the marinade into a 1-quart saucepan, and cook over medium heat until it thickens and use as sauce over the kabobs. Serve on a bed of brown rice.

Marinated Tofu with Scallions

YIELD: *5 to 6 servings*
TIME: *30 minutes
preparation; 12 hours to
marinate the tofu*

2¼ cups canola oil
¾ cup cider vinegar
*1 tablespoon barley malt
    syrup*
1 cup sliced scallions
*¼ cup finely diced red bell
    pepper*
1 tablespoon minced garlic
¾ teaspoon salt
¼ teaspoon black pepper
¾ teaspoon chopped basil
1 tablespoon dill weed
*¾ teaspoon paprika,
    preferably Hungarian*
1 tablespoon chopped parsley
*1 tablespoon roasted sesame
    oil*
*1 tablespoon unroasted
    sesame oil*
3 tablespoons tamari
*1¼ pounds firm tofu, rinsed
    and cut into ¾-inch cubes*

Mix together the oil, vinegar, syrup, scallions, bell pepper, garlic, salt and pepper, basil, dill weed, paprika, and parsley. Set aside this marinade.

Mix together the sesame oils and tamari and sauté the tofu over high heat for 5 to 10 minutes. Use a wooden spoon to stir the tofu to prevent it from tearing. Pour the tofu into the marinade, cover, and refrigerate until the next day.

Serve as an appetizer or a salad. You can also use this marinated tofu as a sandwich filling.

Millet Croquettes with Mustard Sauce

YIELD: *8 servings*
TIME: *75 minutes*

2 cups millet
4½ cups water
¾ teaspoon salt
6 large parsnips
*½ cup chopped toasted
   almonds*
1 tablespoon chopped parsley
1 teaspoon minced garlic
pinch white pepper
*sesame oil (or other cooking
   oil) for deep-frying*
*Mustard Sauce (see recipe
   next page)*

*T*hese croquettes are light and therefore not very filling. The sauce is what makes them superb.

Timing is important in this recipe. The croquettes must be made while the millet mixture is still warm. Then the croquettes must cool before they are fried; otherwise, they will disintegrate.

Toast the millet in a heavy skillet over medium heat, stirring to prevent it from burning. When the millet is lightly browned, remove from the pan and set aside.

Bring the water to a simmer, along with the salt, in a medium saucepan. Add the toasted millet, cover the pan, and simmer for 30 minutes, until the millet is cooked. Meanwhile, you can begin cooking the parsnips.

Peel the parsnips and cut them into small pieces. Steam them until soft (about 30 minutes) and either mash them with a potato masher, press them through a food mill, or purée them in a food processor. In a large bowl, mix thoroughly the cooked millet, parsnips, almonds, parsley, garlic, and pepper. While the mixture is still warm, shape it into small balls, using about 2 tablespoons per ball, by rolling them evenly between the palms of your hands. Deep-fry them in 1½ inches of oil until golden brown. Drain on paper towels. Serve hot with Mustard Sauce for dipping.

Mustard Sauce

1 tablespoon kuzu (or
    arrowroot or cornstarch)
2 tablespoons water
1 tablespoon mirin
2 tablespoons Dijon-style
    mustard
1 tablespoon lemon juice
1 tablespoon tamari
1 tablespoon rice vinegar
½ cup water
½ teaspoon chopped fresh
    tarragon

Mix together the kuzu and 2 tablespoons of water and set aside.

Combine the remaining ingredients in a small saucepan and bring to a simmer. Remove from heat, stir the kuzu mixture into the simmering liquid, return to heat, and simmer gently for 1 minute, stirring constantly to prevent lumps. Serve hot or warm with the Millet Croquettes.

VARIATION

Use 6 large carrots in place of the parsnips. Put a small amount of Lentil, Split Pea, or Carrot Pâté (pages 46–47) in the center of each croquette, sealing well before deep-frying.

Split Pea Pâté

YIELD: *16 small servings*
TIME: *90 minutes preparation and cooking; 1 hour to refrigerate*

2 cups dried split peas
4 cups water
one 4-inch strip kombu
1 medium carrot, halved lengthwise
6 cloves garlic
quarter of a small onion
bay leaf
2 sprigs parsley
3 tablespoons arrowroot
4 tablespoons water
2 tablespoons smoked yeast
1 teaspoon sea salt
2 pinches ground nutmeg

*T*his pâté is packed into a serving dish and may be turned out as a molded pâté if it becomes firm enough. It is very versatile and may be used for canapés or sandwiches, served as a dip with crackers and vegetables, or served with crisp greens as a salad.

Wash the split peas, sort out any tiny rocks or odd peas, and put the peas in a medium saucepan with the water. Add the kombu, carrot, garlic, onion, bay leaf, and parsley. Cover the pan tightly and simmer until the peas are very soft (about 35 to 40 minutes). The mixture should be cooked until there is very little, if any, liquid left.

Remove the bay leaf and parsley. Pour the mixture into the blender (in two batches), and blend until smooth. Return to the pan.

In a small bowl, mix the arrowroot, water, yeast, salt, and nutmeg. Add these seasonings to the pea mixture. Stir until well blended. Bring the mixture to a simmer, stirring constantly. When the pâté detaches itself from the sides of the pan, remove from the heat. If the pâté seems too liquid, just add another tablespoon of arrowroot, dissolved in a tablespoon of water, to make the mixture firmer. Turn the pâté mixture out into a lightly oiled serving dish and refrigerate. If the mixture becomes firm enough, you can unmold it onto a plate and garnish with more parsley sprigs.

VARIATION: *Lentil Pâté*
In place of the split peas, use 2 cups of lentils. Increase the amount of water to about 5 cups. Insert 4 cloves into the carrot halves. Along with the kombu, carrots, garlic, onion, bay leaf, and parsley, add the leafy tops from 4 stalks of celery. Cook these ingredients with the lentils and water for 30 to 35 minutes. Remove the cloves from the carrots. Then purée the mixture as in the recipe above.

Combine the dissolved arrowroot, salt, and smoked yeast, as in the recipe above. Omit the nutmeg and add ¼ cup barley miso and ¼ teaspoon black pepper. Add this mixture to the lentil purée and simmer until the mixture reaches the right consistency.

Carrot Pâté

YIELD: *4 servings*
TIME: *35 minutes*

2 cups sliced carrots
¼ cup diced onion
1 clove garlic, slivered
¼ teaspoon dill
2 tablespoons olive oil (or corn oil)
½ cup water
1 tablespoon arrowroot, dissolved in 1 tablespoon water
2 tablespoons white miso
¼ teaspoon sea salt
2 tablespoons tahini (optional)

*F*or this recipe you may use a food processor instead of a blender to purée the carrots. Mash the carrots roughly before puréeing them. You might need to add a little extra water; in which case, simmer the puréed, flavored carrots for a while longer. The pâté should not feel wet. The addition of two tablespoons of tahini will make the pâté taste richer and help hold the ingredients together.

In a medium saucepan, sauté the carrots, onions, garlic, and dill in the oil for 2 to 3 minutes. Add the water, cover, and simmer until the carrots are tender (about 20 minutes). Purée to a smooth paste and return to the saucepan.

Combine the dissolved arrowroot, miso, salt, and tahini, if you wish. Add this mixture to the puréed carrots. Bring to a slow simmer, stirring constantly, and cook until the pâté detaches itself from the sides of the pan. Remove from heat, turn the pâté mixture out into a lightly oiled serving dish, and let cool.

Serve the pâté with crackers or toast, or serve it as a dip with crisp raw vegetables.

Vegetable Tempura

YIELD: *10 servings*
TIME: *30 minutes*

⅔ cup unbleached white flour
*⅔ cup arrowroot (or
   cornstarch)*
2 teaspoons baking powder
1 tablespoon curry powder
1½ teaspoons salt
½ teaspoon black pepper
1 cup water
*vegetables (carrots, broccoli,
   cauliflower, potatoes, sweet
   potatoes, bell pepper,
   parsnips, and so on)*
*unbleached flour for dredging
   the vegetables*
*cooking oil for deep-frying
   the tempura vegetables*

With planning, this is a simple, last-minute appetizer. You can prepare the batter, vegetables, and sauce ahead of time; then you can assemble the dish just before serving.

Small cubes of tofu, tempeh, and seitan may also be deep-fried in this light, spicy batter and served as an appetizer. Larger pieces of these vegetable proteins may be deep-fried and served as an entrée.

Mix all of the dry ingredients together. Add the water gradually until the mixture has the consistency of a light batter. The batter can be used immediately or refrigerated until needed. Leftover batter can be saved for future use.

Cut the vegetables into manageable pieces. For example, use florets of broccoli and cauliflower; cut carrots, potatoes, and parsnips into slices of about ⅜ inch; cut bell peppers into ½-inch wide strips, and so on. Drain the vegetables. Dredge in flour and dust off the excess.

Pour about 2 inches of cooking oil into a deep frying pan and begin heating it. (The oil should be about 375 degrees F to fry the vegetables.) Dip the floured pieces of vegetable into the tempura batter to coat thoroughly. Deep-fry the vegetables until golden brown. Drain on paper towels and serve immediately, accompanied by a dipping sauce, such as Sweet and Sour Sauce, Tahini Lemon Sauce, or Miso Sauce (pages 164–165).

Gefilte Tofu with Horseradish and Charoset Sauce

YIELD: *6 to 8 servings*
TIME: *90 minutes*

2 quarts water
1½ cups chopped onion
1 cup carrots, cut in half
  lengthwise and then sliced
1 cup chopped celery
1½ teaspoons salt
¼ teaspoon white pepper
½ teaspoon thyme
1 whole clove
1½ bay leaves
5 teaspoons agar powder
Gefilte Tofu (see recipe below)

A s an appetizer, Gefilte Tofu may be served cold, on a bed of leaf lettuce, topped with sliced carrot and chopped parsley, with a wedge of lemon on the side, and accompanied by Beet Horseradish Sauce. Or it can be served hot, with Creamy Horseradish Sauce. As a lunch entrée, Gefilte Tofu may be served hot or cold, with a complementary vegetable and a starch or a salad. In addition to the sauces, you can serve the Gefilte Tofu with Charoset, a traditional condiment. A recipe for Charoset follows the sauce recipes.

Place the water in a large saucepan with the vegetables and seasonings. Bring to a simmer and reduce the liquid by half. Then stir in the agar powder to thicken the stock.

Place the gefilte tofu in a lightly oiled steam basket in a large saucepan. Gently pour the hot stock over the gefiltes and simmer for about 10 minutes. (If you are making several batches, remove the cooked gefiltes delicately and reuse the stock.) Do not overcook the gefiltes, or they will split apart. Serve with one of the sauces and Charoset.

Gefilte Tofu

2 cups chopped onions
1 cup chopped carrots
1 quart firm tofu, crushed by
  hand
6 tablespoons matzo meal
2 tablespoons Egg Replacer
6 tablespoons ground
  blanched almonds
1 teaspoon salt
½ teaspoon black pepper

In a food processor, blend the onions, carrots, and tofu until smooth. Transfer to a mixing bowl.

Mix the remaining ingredients together and add them to the tofu mixture. Make sure the mixture is thoroughly blended.

Form oval-shaped gefiltes from the mixture. (Use ¾ cup of the mixture for large gefiltes or 6 tablespoons of the mixture for small gefiltes.) Use extra matzo meal to keep the mixture from sticking to your hands. (It's a good idea to portion out all pieces before shaping them.)

Beet Horseradish Sauce

½ cup cooked beets
½ cup horseradish
¼ teaspoon salt (optional)

Mash the beets or purée them in a food processor. Mix the horseradish and salt into the beets, and refrigerate.

Creamy Horseradish Sauce

5 ounces silken tofu
½ cup soy milk
1 teaspoon arrowroot (or 1½ teaspoons cornstarch)
1 tablespoon horseradish
¼ cup water
¼ teaspoon salt
⅛ teaspoon white pepper

Put all of the ingredients into a blender and blend until smooth. Transfer to a saucepan and cook over medium heat until thickened, stirring constantly to prevent the mixture from burning.

Charoset

1 cup ground walnuts
3 cups unsweetened applesauce

Stir together the walnuts and applesauce. Serve at room temperature to complement the Gefilte Tofu.

Mushroom Duxelles

YIELD: *2 cups of filling*
TIME: *20 to 30 minutes*

*2 cups finely diced fresh
  mushrooms*
1 cup diced onions
*½ cup peeled and finely diced
  carrots*
*1 cup seitan (or 1 cup cooked
  bulgur)*
2 tablespoons tamari
2 teaspoons chopped basil
4 teaspoons minced garlic
½ cup finely chopped walnuts
*2 tablespoons soy oil or
  sesame oil*
*2 tablespoons barley malt
  syrup, dissolved in 2
  tablespoons water*
*4 tablespoons quick-cooking
  oats, finely chopped (or oat
  flour)*
*¼ teaspoon black pepper
  (optional)*
*3 tablespoons sherry
  (optional)*
*2 teaspoons Vogue Vegy Base
  (optional)*
*½ teaspoon chopped thyme
  (optional)*
*½ teaspoon chopped
  marjoram (optional)*
¼ teaspoon salt (optional)

*T*here are several ways to make *duxelles*. The classic French way is to cook the mixture down until it thickens. The American way is to cook it down partially and add bread crumbs to thicken it. My way is to add a thickening grain. In this case I use quick-cooking oats.

This basic recipe may be used as a stuffing, in vegetable loaves, salads, or Tofu Seitan Wellington (page 250).

Combine the mushrooms, onions, carrot, seitan (or bulgur), tamari, basil, garlic, and walnuts. Sauté in the oil until the onion is translucent. If you are substituting bulgur for the seitan, you may need to increase the seasonings, because the seitan is already seasoned.

Add the barley malt and water to the mushroom mixture and cook for 2 minutes. Add the oats and cook for 4 or 5 minutes longer. The sherry may be used at this stage; you may wish to add the optional seasonings for additional flavor.

VARIATION: *Mushroom Pâté*
Prepare the Mushroom *Duxelles* using 3 tablespoons soy margarine instead of 2 tablespoons oil. Purée the mixture into a paste and add ½ teaspoon of Pâté Seasoning (page 35). Spread the pâté on bread, toast, or crackers.

VARIATION: Duxelles-*Filled Pockets*
Prepare the Mushroom *Duxelles* according to the recipe, and set aside. Using any type of light pasta dough, roll out the dough to a thickness of ⅛ to 1/16 inch; this is very thin. Cut out about 20 rounds of dough, using a 2½-inch-diameter cookie cutter or a glass. To make the pockets, moisten the edges of each dough round with water, place 1 teaspoon of *duxelles* mixture on one half of the round, fold the other half over to make a half circle, and seal the edges securely. Bring

a large saucepan of water to a gentle boil, add a pinch of salt and 1 tablespoon of cooking oil. Boil half the batch of pockets in the water (gently, so they will not open up) for about 5 or 6 minutes. Remove with a slotted spoon and cook the next batch. These little turnovers may be served as an appetizer or as a garnish for clear soup.

Canapés

*T*he French word *canapé* means "cushion" or "sofa." The medieval Latin word is *canapeum*. In kitchen parlance, it is an appetizer made up of a small piece of food that rests on a base that may be square, round, triangular, or oval. The base is usually a thin piece of toast or cracker spread with any of a variety of foods including vegetables, fish, spreads, minced eggs, sardines, anchovies, cheese, and so on. They are usually served on a tray before the first course.

The canapé was first mentioned in America in 1890; it was described as a tidbit served with anchovies. Small frankfurters wrapped in pastry (called "pigs-in-a-blanket") and oysters wrapped in bacon (an English canapé known as "angels on horseback") stretch the definition of the traditional canapé but still qualify.

Canapés are the classic presentation of "spreads on breads." There are hot and cold canapés, thick and thin canapés. This recipe describes a technique rather than offering a formula. For my entirely vegetarian canapés, I use various vegetable pates that may be piped or spread. Thin slices of tofu could be used or small quantities of Mushroom *Duxelles* (page 51).

The Canapé Base

*P*resliced bread may be used, but an unsliced loaf of bread makes more elegant canapés. Slice a large loaf of sandwich-type bread horizontally about ½ inch thick and remove the crusts. Next, toast the bread (under the broiler) on one side only. In the final assembly, the toasted side of the bread should be facing downward and the spread placed on the untoasted side. If you cut a 3-pound pullman loaf of bread into twelve slices, with each slice yielding twenty ½-inch canapés (or twelve 1-inch canapés), the entire loaf will yield about 240 canapés.

The Spread

*F*or hot canapés, use the Mushroom *Duxelles* or similar spread. You can pipe the *duxelles* mixture onto the canapé bases or spread it. Serve the hot canapés immediately.

For cold canapés, use any tasty vegetable pâté or hummus. Be careful, though, because soggy canapés taste terrible! If you are using a wet spread, use a buffer such as soy

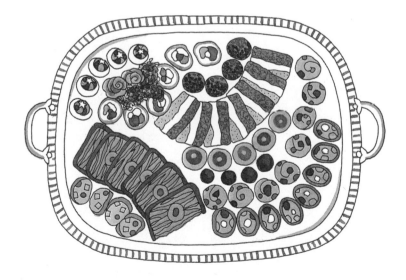

mayonnaise, tahini, tofu, or margarine first. (The oils keep the moisture at bay.)

The vegetable pâté recipes given in this book (pages 46–47) are low in oil but dry enough that they do not need a buffer. Using the star attachment on a pastry bag, pipe the vegetable pâtés onto the bread, or simply spread the pâté on the bread. Cut the canapés into the desired shapes and garnish.

Cold canapés should be served within 24 hours; when they oxidize, they lose their luster. Aspic-glazed canapés will keep a while longer. Always cover canapés with plastic wrap to keep them fresh.

Use a variety of colors and tastes on a canapé tray. It is acceptable to use only one type of canapé per tray, but this presentation is rather boring. If you have used the same spread on all canapés, be creative with the garnishes.

Garnishes

*H*ere are some suggestions for garnishes on cold canapés:

- Stir some dried mustard into a firm soy mayonnaise. Pipe a border of this mayonnaise around the edge of the bread.
- Make an agar aspic to spread over the canapés. Simmer 2 cups of water with 4 teaspoons of agar flakes until the agar is dissolved. When the solution begins to cool, glaze the canapés and chill them. (The aspic will also keep the canapés from oxidizing.)
- Stir a little of the aspic solution into horseradish or catsup. Pipe this mixture over the canapés.
- Sprinkle chopped herbs or chopped tofu around the edges as a border or lightly over the entire canapé.
- Spread halved and thinly sliced red radishes over the canapé.

Soups

When I think of lunch, I immediately think of soup. With a salad or a sandwich, a cup of soup makes an excellent small meal. A bowl of warm, hearty soup, along with a salad and fresh bread, is a wonderful dinner, especially in winter. Many lighter soups are appropriate served before the main course.

I believe that soup must be in harmony with the whole menu. For macrobiotics, soup usually is a lightly salty miso soup, served before the main course and intended to stimulate the appetite. In that sense, soup contracts our energy. Not only should the soup be in balance with the menu, but it also should correspond to the season. Winter soups are hearty and warming. Summer soups are lighter and sometimes are served cold.

One way to balance the soup in relation to the whole menu is to focus on the main nutritional elements of the planned meal. For example, if the main course consists of a seitan dish with a tofu-based sauce, you may want to begin with a light vegetable soup, perhaps one in which the vegetables can be identified. Likewise, you probably would want to avoid serving a creamy soup. You can also choose a soup that breaks the monotony of flavors or colors of the main course.

This chapter offers a variety of soup recipes. There are broth-based soups, bean soups, vegetable soups, cream soups, fruit soups, and other types of soups. This introduction provides information on these various types of soups. All of the recipes—including the cream soups—are vegan.

The soups in this chapter are versatile and have many uses. Try serving the cream soups as sauces over grains or pasta. Some of the cream soups are excellent as toppings over oatmeal or other breakfast cereals. Heartier vegetable or bean soups can be used as a base for casseroles, stews, and other entrées. Chilled fruit soups can be served between courses to cleanse the palate. Or they can be served for dessert, alone or as a complement to fruit or cake.

Soup Stock

Usually, a recipe begins with vegetable stock. You can use either vegetable soup cubes (compressed and packaged in small cubes) or a powdered stock base, available in bulk or in packages. I recommend Vogue Vegy Base because it is low in sodium, but you can try other types of stock base. At times, you may wish to make your own stock. (See page 162 for a recipe for vegetable stock.)

When making stock, season the liquid slightly and let the stock simmer. Don't boil it. If you are making a soup that features a particular vegetable, make a stock using that vegetable and other complementary vegetables. For example, to make broccoli soup you might use the broccoli stems in the stock, along with a carrot, a celery stalk, and a leek. An appropriate ratio would be four parts of the main vegetable to one part of the other vegetables. Avoid using vegetables that would offset the flavor of the main vegetable.

Soup Seasonings

When using whole herbs and spices, place them in a small piece of clean cheese-cloth, tied with a string. Place the bag in the cooking liquid when you begin to make the soup. Add finely ground spices or salt later because their flavor dissipates quickly. White pepper builds on the taste buds, so you are better off using black pepper, unless a recipe calls for white pepper. Use curry powder with caution because it burns easily.

Pea, bean, cream of tomato, and potato soups often have a smokey flavor. To achieve this, use smoked yeast, available from natural food stores. Or use a natural liquid smoke flavoring, available at most supermarkets.

Vegan Cream Soups

Cream soups generally are rich in saturated fats and cholesterol because they contain large amounts of heavy cream. The recipes in this chapter, however, use soy milk in place of dairy milk or cream. Some recipes use nut milks—liquid blended with cashews or other nuts—to create smooth, creamy soups. Because soy milk has a high fat content, you may wish to substitute water for half of the milk.

Traditionally, cream soups are made by adding a thickening agent to a flavorful stock and then adding warm milk or cream. I use puréed cooked vegetables, such as carrots or potatoes or other starchy vegetables, as the thickening agent. This enhances the flavor of the soup and improves its nutritional value. After cooking, strain the soy milk as you pour it into the puréed vegetables. This way, you can avoid pouring in any of the "skin" that develops over the heated milk.

Soy milk (or other bean milk) can curdle when a souring agent such as wine or vinegar is added to it. For this reason, you should add the milk to the soup, thicken it, and then add the souring agent. If the soup is thickened, the milk will be less likely to curdle. It will also be more likely to retain the luster of a smooth creamy soup.

Some Helpful Hints for Soup Making

- Never peel vegetables, unless the recipe states otherwise.
- Cutting all vegetables to a uniform size will ensure even cooking.
- With soups that contain macaroni or rice, it's a good idea to keep some stock in reserve because the pasta or grain will absorb the broth. Or you could precook the pasta and refrain from adding it until just before serving.
- Potato flour is a good thickening agent for soups; it gives the soup a creamy texture.
- To develop their flavors properly, beans should be cooked slowly, regardless of presoaking. (Check the table on page 99 for quantities and soaking times of various beans.) Ideally, you should soak beans overnight and discard the soaking water. This helps eliminate the enzymes that cause gas.
- To make your soups even more nutritious, add vitamin-rich vegetables such as kale, collards, and spinach. Stir in these chopped vegetables just a few minutes before serving the soup. This way you will add texture as well as the delicious crunch of fresh leafy vegetables.

Creamy Lima Bean Soup

YIELD: *6 servings*
TIME: *several hours or overnight for soaking beans; 1½ hours for cooking beans; 30 minutes for preparing and cooking the soup*

1½ cups lima beans, washed
6 cups water
1 strip kombu, about 7 inches long (optional)
2 cups peeled and finely diced onions
1 cup peeled and coarsely grated carrots
2 tablespoons coarsely chopped garlic
2 tablespoons olive oil
¼ teaspoon black pepper
½ cup finely diced green bell pepper
1 tablespoon sea salt
¼ teaspoon ground coriander
finely shredded scallions, for garnish

*T*his is a very hearty winter soup.

To prepare the beans, bring the water to a simmer in a large saucepan and add the beans and the kombu. Immediately remove from heat, let the mixture cool, and refrigerate for several hours or overnight. Remove the kombu, cut it into strips, and set aside. Cook the beans in the soaking water, covered, over medium heat until tender (about 1½ hours).

To make the soup, sauté the onions, carrots, and garlic in a 2-quart saucepan with the oil and black pepper over medium heat until the onions are translucent.

In a blender, purée 2 cups of cooked lima beans with 2 cups water. Add this purée to the sautéed vegetables. Add the remaining 1 cup of cooked lima beans, keeping them whole. Then add the bell peppers, salt, coriander, and kombu strips to the bean mixture and cook for a few minutes to blend the flavors.

Serve hot with a garnish of finely shredded scallions.

VARIATION: *Succotash Soup*
Add 1 cup of fresh or frozen whole-kernel corn and 1 teaspoon ground cumin while sautéing the other vegetables.

Michigan Navy Bean Soup

YIELD: *6 cups; 6 servings*
TIME: *40 minutes if using precooked or canned beans*

2 ½ *cups precooked navy beans (two 15-ounce cans navy beans, drained)*
2 *tablespoons canola oil or other vegetable oil*
½ *cup peeled and sliced carrots*
½ *cup peeled and diced onions*
½ *cup diced celery*
¼ *cup washed and sliced leek tops*
2 *teaspoons minced garlic*
1 *teaspoon chopped basil*
1 *teaspoon marjoram*
1 *teaspoon salt*
½ *teaspoon black pepper*
1 *tablespoon Vogue Vegy Base*
1 *tablespoon smoked yeast*
1 *strip kombu, about 7 inches long, soaked and chopped*
2 *medium tomatoes (blanched, peeled, seeded, and chopped to yield 1 cup)*
4 *cups water*
3 *tablespoons white miso*
finely chopped scallions, for garnish

*M*ichigan is well known for the navy beans it produces. Being a native of Michigan, I appropriately dedicate this soup to the state.

Sauté the beans, carrots, onions, celery, leek tops, and garlic in the oil with the basil, marjoram, salt, pepper, and soup base in a 2-quart saucepan or soup pot over medium heat for about 5 minutes.

Add the yeast, kombu, tomatoes, and water to the sautéed vegetables and let the soup simmer over medium heat for about 20 minutes. Dissolve the miso in about half a cup of the soup, add the mixture back to the saucepan, and continue simmering for another 10 minutes. Serve hot; garnish with the chopped scallions.

Aduki Bean Soup

YIELD: *5 servings*

TIME: *20 minutes preparation; about 2 hours cooking*

1 cup aduki beans
5 cups water
1 strip kombu, about 7 inches long
½ cup peeled and diced onions
½ cup peeled and diced carrots
½ cup diced celery
1 cup peeled and diced butternut squash
1 tablespoon sesame oil
1 tablespoon minced garlic
1 tablespoon peeled and finely chopped fresh ginger
1 tablespoon rice vinegar
½ teaspoon black pepper
2 bay leaves
2 teaspoons chopped savory (or 1 teaspoon dried savory)
1 tablespoon molasses
2 tablespoons barley miso
chopped chives, scallions, or parsley, for garnish

Wash the beans and place them in a 2-quart pot with the water and kombu. Simmer for about 2 hours. Meanwhile, you can prepare the vegetables and seasonings.

Sauté the onions, carrots, celery, and squash in the oil over medium heat for about 10 minutes. Add to the cooking beans. Stir in the garlic, ginger, vinegar, pepper, bay leaves, savory, and molasses, and continue cooking until the beans are soft (about 1 hour). When the beans are cooked, dissolve the miso in about ½ cup of the soup and return the mixture to the saucepan. Simmer the soup for 3 to 5 minutes after adding the miso. (For a more full-bodied soup, purée about 2 cups of the soup mixture in a blender and stir this back into the remaining soup.) Serve hot, garnished with the chopped chives, scallions, or parsley.

Hearty German Soup

YIELD: *5 to 6 servings*
TIME: *20 minutes preparation; 30 minutes cooking*

5 tablespoons diced carrots
5 tablespoons diced red or
    green cabbage
5 tablespoons diced potatoes
½ small onion, finely minced
2 teaspoons minced garlic
2½ teaspoons caraway seeds
2 tablespoons sesame oil or
    soy oil
1½ teaspoons brown rice
    vinegar (or cider vinegar
    for a stronger flavor)
½ cup vegetarian ''ham'' or
    ''bacon'' bits, ground
    seitan, or soy grits
¾ cup tomato sauce
5 cups water
1½ tablespoons barley miso
⅛ teaspoon black pepper
¾ teaspoon sea salt

*T*his recipe was created at the Renaissance Restaurant, where I was executive chef. It is a good winter soup and reflects the hearty foods of Germany without any of the heavy meats associated with traditional German cuisine.

Sauté the carrots, cabbage, potato, onion, and garlic with the caraway seeds in the oil until almost soft. Add the vinegar, ''ham'' bits, tomato sauce, and water. Cover and simmer for 10 minutes. Dissolve the miso in about ½ cup of the soup and add this mixture back into the soup, together with the pepper and salt. Simmer very gently for 5 more minutes to cook the miso. Serve hot.

VARIATION: *German Lentil Soup*
Omit the potatoes and substitute ½ to ¾ cup cooked lentils. Add the lentils during the last ten minutes of cooking. Reserve the water from cooking the lentils, and add this, along with enough water to make the 5 cups called for in the recipe.

Rice Soup Florentine

YIELD: *5 servings*
TIME: *30 minutes*

1 cup basmati rice
4½ cups water
pinch of salt
½ cup chopped leek tops (the dark green part)
1 cup chopped scallions
4 teaspoons minced garlic (or 2 teaspoons garlic powder)
1 tablespoon olive oil
5 teaspoons Vogue Vegy Base
1 teaspoon salt
½ teaspoon black pepper
1 cup chopped spinach, packed (or about 5 ounces frozen spinach, thawed)

*Y*ou may wish to serve this soup with a little Parmesan cheese. Without the cheese, of course, the soup is entirely vegetarian.

Cook the rice, with a pinch of salt, in 1½ cups of water. Once the rice has cooked for about 10 minutes, you can begin making the soup.

Sauté the leek tops, scallions, and garlic in the oil, along with the seasonings, for 10 to 15 minutes. Add the spinach, remaining 3 cups of water, and cooked rice and heat thoroughly. Serve hot.

Doukabar Vegetable Soup

YIELD: *4 servings*
TIME: *30 minutes prepara-*
tion; 30 to 40 minutes
cooking

1 medium-sized raw beet,
  unpeeled (or one 16-ounce
  can whole beets)
1 large unpeeled potato,
  julienned
1 medium carrot, peeled and
  diced
half a large onion, diced
1 small wedge (½-inch) green
  cabbage, shredded
⅓ of a medium green bell
  pepper, seeded and diced
2 tablespoons oil
⅓ cup tomato paste mixed
  with ⅓ cup water
1½ to 2 cups water
1 teaspoon dill weed
1½ teaspoons minced garlic
1 teaspoon sea salt
¾ teaspoon ground caraway
  seeds
Vegan Sour Cream (page 90)
chopped fresh dill, for garnish

*T*his soup recipe was created originally by Russian emi-
grants who settled in Canada. They wanted a soup of the
same nature as borscht that would be hearty and warm. Normally, this is a dairy soup; my version is vegan. Unlike the
original borscht, this very hearty winter soup is served hot.

Cut the unpeeled beet into julienned pieces. (If you are using
canned beets, drain, reserve the liquid, and set aside three of
the beets for another use. Cut the remaining beets into julienned pieces. Measure the juice, add water to make 2½
cups, and set aside for the soup.)

Sauté the vegetables in the oil for about 5 minutes over
medium heat. Add the tomato paste mixture and the water
(or beet juice and water mixture). Add and stir in the dill
weed, garlic, salt, and ground caraway seed. Cover and simmer for about 30 minutes.

Serve the soup hot. Add a small dollop of Vegan Sour
Cream to each small bowl. Garnish with fresh dill. (As an
alternative, you could stir the sour cream into the soup before serving; use 3 tablespoons for the entire recipe of soup.)

Butternut Squash Chowder

YIELD: *6 servings*
TIME: *1 hour*

*2 cups butternut squash
(peeled, diced, and steamed
until soft)*

*1 cup sweet potato (peeled,
diced, and steamed)*

*1 cup carrots (peeled, sliced,
and steamed)*

*3 cups water (including water
left over from steaming the
vegetables)*

½ cup diced red bell pepper

½ cup diced onion

1½ to 2 teaspoons sea salt

1½ teaspoons minced garlic

1½ teaspoons chopped basil

*¾ teaspoon chopped
rosemary*

½ teaspoon chopped thyme

*2 teaspoons sesame oil, olive
oil, or other cooking oil*

½ cup diced celery

*½ cup diced green bell pepper
or diced zucchini*

5 teaspoons Vogue Vegy Base

*¼ teaspoon paprika
(preferably Spanish,
because it is hotter than the
sweeter Hungarian paprika
and is added to counter the
sweetness of this soup)*

T his soup is rich, nonfattening, and delicately sweet, with mild herbs to emphasize the squash flavor. The garlic comes across as a subtle accent. Serve the soup with a crisp, colorful salad and whole wheat crackers. This recipe also makes a superb sauce to be served over rice for a light lunch.

Blend the squash, sweet potatoes, and carrots with the water until smooth, and set aside.

Sauté the red bell pepper, onion, salt, garlic, basil, rosemary, and thyme in the oil over medium heat for 5 minutes. Now add the remaining ingredients and sauté for another 5 minutes. Add the puréed vegetable mixture, cook for another 5 to 10 minutes, and serve hot.

VARIATION: *Hokkaido Squash Chowder*
Use Hokkaido squash in place of butternut squash. Hokkaido squash, also called *kobocha*, looks similar to an acorn squash. It is a sweet, mellow squash that has a very high sugar content. This squash gets its name from the Japanese island of Hokkaido. Actually, the plant is native to the Boston area and was sent to Japan. Now, it is mainly brought into the United States from Japan.

VARIATION: *Vegetable Chowder*
Replace the 2 cups of squash with 1 more cup each of the carrots and sweet potatoes.

Zucchini Bisque

YIELD: *6 servings*
TIME: *25 to 30 minutes*

2 medium onions, peeled and
*   coarsely chopped*
5 to 6 cups (about 3 pounds)
*   sliced zucchini*
1 cup thinly sliced carrot
4 teaspoons olive oil (or other
*   cooking oil)*
4 teaspoons sea salt
5 cups water (or 1 cup white
*   wine and 4 cups water)*
4 tablespoons Vogue Vegy
*   Base*
¼ teaspoon finely ground
*   black pepper*
16 ounces tofu, preferably
*   silken tofu*
chopped parsley or scallions,
*   for garnish*

*T*raditionally, bisques are thick soups made from shellfish and other seafood. Originally, however, the name was given to any thick, creamy soup, regardless of the ingredients. My recipe is rich-bodied, creamy, and completely vegetarian. I hope it is the start of a new tradition. Maybe in the next century, vegetarian bisques will be the norm.

In a large soup pot, sauté the onions, carrot, and zucchini in the oil, together with the salt, for about 5 minutes over medium heat. Add the water (and wine, if you are using it), soup base, pepper, and tofu, and cook for another 5 minutes. Blend the ingredients until smooth, return to the heat, and cook for a few more minutes. Garnish with finely chopped fresh parsley or scallions.

Divine Corn Chowder

YIELD: *4 to 6 servings*
TIME: *30 minutes*

*2 tablespoons corn oil (or
    sesame oil)*
2 cups chopped onion
*¾ cup finely diced red bell
    pepper and ¼ cup finely
    diced green bell pepper (or
    1 cup finely diced bell
    pepper of one type)*
3 or 4 cloves of garlic, minced
*1 cup whole-kernel corn,
    fresh or frozen*
1 teaspoon sea salt
1 teaspoon ground cumin
¼ teaspoon white pepper
*1 teaspoon chopped thyme (or
    ½ teaspoon dried thyme)*
½ teaspoon curry powder
*2 teaspoons Vogue Vegy Base
    (optional)*
*chopped parsley or scallions,
    for garnish*

*T*his soup has a superb flavor that reminds me of walking through my father's corn patch in northern Michigan. It calls up memories of those midnight raiders, the raccoons; the sweet aromas of cooked corn coming from the kitchen; and then the heavenly taste of sweet, freshly picked, cooked corn with butter. The simple pleasures of life are really divine.

Heat the oil in a large saucepan. Sauté the onion, bell pepper, garlic, and ½ cup of the corn for about 5 minutes. Add the salt, cumin, pepper, thyme, curry powder, and soup base, and sauté for another 5 minutes.

Steam or boil the remaining corn until it is soft and sweet to the taste (5 to 10 minutes). Drain the corn, reserving the liquid, if there is any. Add enough water to make up 1 cup. Blend the corn with the liquid and add this purée to the sautéed vegetables. Mix all of the ingredients, heat through, and serve. Garnish with chopped parsley or scallions.

Chili con Seitan

YIELD: *7 servings*
TIME: *30 minutes; allow an additional 3 hours to soak and cook the beans, if necessary*

1 cup peeled and finely diced onion
½ cup finely diced celery
½ cup finely diced green bell pepper
3 tablespoons minced garlic
1 tablespoon olive oil or sesame oil
1 tablespoon chili powder
1 teaspoon ground cumin
1 tablespoon dark soybean miso (hatcho)
2 tablespoons tomato paste
4 cups fresh tomatoes (blanched, seeded, and chopped)
1½ tablespoon barley malt syrup
1 cup (or one 15-ounce can) red kidney beans or pinto beans
1 cup drained and chopped seitan

O f all the chilis, both meat and meatless, that I have tasted in my life, this is the best. I developed this recipe when I was home on vacation during the summer of 1986. It is very easy to make, especially since it calls for canned, precooked kidney beans.

In a heavy soup pot, sauté the onion, celery, bell pepper, and garlic in the oil, along with the seasonings, over medium heat. Sauté for about 10 minutes, stirring occasionally to prevent burning.

Dissolve the miso and tomato paste in the chopped tomatoes and add to the sautéed vegetables. Add the barley malt syrup and stir well. Finally, stir in the cooked beans and chopped seitan. Cook for about 10 minutes over medium heat. Serve alone, over brown rice, or over spaghetti squash.

Burgundy Soup

YIELD: *4 servings*

TIME: *30 minutes*

*2 tablespoons soy oil (or
    sesame oil)*
1½ cups diced onion
¼ cup diagonally sliced celery
¾ cup sliced mushrooms
1 teaspoon minced garlic
*1½ teaspoons chopped basil
    (or ½ teaspoon dried basil)*
⅓ teaspoon black pepper
½ cup dry red wine
¾ cup tomato purée
1 cup flaked seitan
1½ cups water
1 tablespoon barley miso
½ teaspoon salt (optional)
*1 red radish, shredded, or
    chopped parsley, for
    garnish*

*T*his soup was inspired by Boeuf Bourguignon. It tastes like a wild game (hare) soup, a flavor made up of wine, tomato, spices, and miso.

Sauté the onion, celery, and mushrooms in the oil, together with the garlic, basil, and pepper, until the onion becomes translucent. Add the wine and simmer for 2 minutes. Add the tomato purée, seitan, and water. Continue to simmer, covered, over low heat for 30 minutes.

Dissolve the barley miso in 3 tablespoons of water and add to the soup. Simmer over very low heat for 5 minutes more and serve. Garnish with shredded red radish or chopped parsley.

Andalusian Vegetable Cream Soup

YIELD: *4 servings*

TIME: *20 minutes preparation; 30 minutes cooking*

*2 cups peeled and finely diced
    potato*
*1 cup peeled and finely diced
    onion*
2 medium tomatoes,

*T*his soup was developed from Henri Paul Pellaprat's *Great Book of French Cuisine*. It has been a five-star soup in every establishment in which I have served it.

Sauté the potato, onion, tomato, and garlic in the oil, with the salt and pepper, for about 5 minutes, stirring occasion-ally. Sprinkle on the flour and cook until the mixture has thickened and the flour is cooked (about 5 minutes).

blanched, seeded, peeled
and diced into ½-inch
pieces
½ teaspoon minced garlic
2 tablespoons soy oil (or
sesame oil)
½ teaspoon sea salt
⅛ teaspoon white pepper
2 tablespoons unbleached
flour (or 4 tablespoons
whole wheat flour)
¼ cup tomato juice (or 1
tablespoon tomato paste
mixed with 3 tablespoons
water)
2 tablespoons barley miso (or
2 vegetable soup cubes)
3 cups plain soy milk
¼ cup cooked brown rice
1 or 2 scallions, sliced
diagonally, for garnish

Dissolve the miso in the tomato juice and add it to the vegetable mixture. Then add the soy milk and cook, stirring constantly to prevent the vegetables from burning, until the soup thickens. Stir in the rice. Serve the soup hot with a garnish of scallions.

Cream of Red Pepper Soup

YIELD: *2 to 4 servings*
TIME: *15 minutes prepara-tion; 30 minutes cooking*

2 tablespoons olive oil
1 medium-sized red bell
pepper, seeded and chopped
½ cup chopped onions
¼ cup diced celery
½ cup diced potatoes

*T*his soup has a very delicate flavor. If you want a more fla-vorful soup, you can add up to twice as much of the sea-sonings; be careful, though, that the seasonings don't over-power the naturally delicate flavor of the red pepper.

Heat the oil in a medium-sized saucepan. Sauté all of the vegetables, along with the seasonings, on medium heat for about 5 minutes. Add the soy milk and water. Simmer, cov-ered, for about 20 minutes.

½ teaspoon whole rosemary
½ teaspoon whole fennel
    seeds
½ teaspoon paprika,
    preferably Hungarian
    paprika
½ teaspoon salt
scant ⅛ teaspoon white
    pepper
1½ cups soy milk
½ cup water
2 tablespoons white miso
½ cup julienned carrots
2 teaspoons chopped fresh
    parsley, for garnish

Add the miso directly into the soup. Purée the soup in a blender until smooth. Pour the soup back into the saucepan, add the carrots, and cook at a medium heat for an additional 5 minutes. Serve hot, garnished with parsley.

VARIATION: *Cream of Yellow Pepper Soup*
Substitute a yellow bell pepper for the red bell pepper.

Cream of Avocado and Cucumber Soup

YIELD: *4 servings*
TIME: *15 minutes*

1¼ cups avocado pulp, tightly
    packed
2¼ cups peeled, seeded, and
    diced cucumber
2 tablespoons fresh lime juice
    or lemon juice
1 cup soy milk
⅛ to ¼ teaspoon white
    pepper
2 teaspoons minced garlic
5 tablespoons white miso
2 teaspoons dill weed
thinly sliced scallions, for
    garnish

Avocados are high in calories—but these are high-quality calories, which means that they are loaded with nutrition. I enjoy eating a few avocados each month. In his book, *The Encyclopedia of Fruits, Vegetables, Nuts, and Seeds of Healthful Living*, Joseph M. Kadans, Ph.D., N.D., suggests that avocados are good for anyone with ulcers.

Put all of the ingredients except the scallions into a blender and blend until smooth. Cool and serve, garnished with the scallions. If ingredients are cold to start with, the soup may be served immediately. If the soup is left in the refrigerator for long, the surface may oxidize and turn dark. If it does, simply skim off the surface and use the rest. The flavor is not affected by the oxidation, but the soup does not look as appetizing.

Chilled Pear Soup

YIELD: *4 servings*
TIME: *30 minutes*

*8 pears (peeled, cored, and
    diced)*
2 cups water
¼ teaspoon sea salt
*4 tablespoons brown rice
    syrup*
*½ teaspoon peeled and finely
    minced ginger (or ½
    teaspoon powdered ginger)*
*¼ teaspoon anise extract
    (optional)*
*mint leaves or fresh
    strawberries, for garnish*

Bring the pears, water, and salt to a simmer. Add the rice syrup and ginger (and the anise extract, if you wish). Simmer for 3 more minutes. Allow the mixture to cool. Then purée the mixture and chill. Serve garnished with mint leaves or strawberries.

Salads and Dressings

*S*alads are very versatile: they can be used for appetizers, entrées, or as a traditional accompaniment to an entrée. Our word for salad comes from the Latin, *sal*, meaning "salt," because the Romans dressed their leafy green vegetables with little more than simple salt. In Middle English, the word became *salade* and, throughout the nineteenth century, the spelling *salat* was often used in American cookbooks. Americans in general, however, had very little interest in salad for most of their history. After the Civil War, a salad consisted primarily of a lot of poultry or seafood and a little green lettuce or a few vegetables. Then the wealthy began enjoying European-style salads that were being served in the new restaurants opening in the large cities, especially in New York, where Delmonico's restaurant specialized in the then-novel salad dressings. The Waldorf salad, developed at the Waldorf-Astoria, became an instant success.

In composing a salad, you might keep in mind a number of factors, including:

- *Quality of ingredients:* Choose fresh, wholesome, and, if possible, organic produce.
- *Eye appeal:* Use colorful produce and interesting shapes.
- *Simplicity:* Do not overgarnish.
- *Neatness:* Arrange the ingredients properly, do not slop on the dressing.
- *Contrast and harmony:* Do not put solid and soft ingredients together.
- *Compatibility of ingredients:* Oranges, anchovies, sour cream, and dill pickles do not go together!
- *Temperature:* Salad loses its flavor when chilled too much.
- *Dryness:* The salad ingredients should be drained properly; this will keep the vegetables firm and allow the dressing to cling to them.
- *Texture:* Do not overcook salad ingredients; the vegetables should be tender-crisp.
- *Consistency:* Cooked vegetables should be cut and cooked separately so that each ingredient is cooked appropriately.
- *Definition:* All ingredients in the salad should be identifiable.

Most salads have four basic parts: the base, usually consisting of lettuce, which provides bright color or contrast; the body, which is the principal ingredients; the dressing, which should complement the salad; and the garnish, which should give the salad eye appeal. Transparent dressings, such as vinaigrette, should be used on beautifully arranged salads so they are not masked.

Tips on Working with Lettuce

Contrary to popular opinion, head lettuce should not be too solid or hard. It should respond to pressure with a certain springiness that indicates the presence of air pockets between the leaves—proof that the lettuce is at the right stage of development.

To clean head lettuce most efficiently, cut out the stem to a depth of about one inch and allow cold water to run briskly into the hollow. Slamming the core will loosen it but will make the lettuce limp. Drain the lettuce cored-end down. Romaine, escarole, and other varieties of leaf lettuce should be pulled apart and then washed and patted dry. A salad spinner may be used to dry the less fragile greens quickly. But softer lettuces, such as Boston lettuce, are too delicate to be spun dry. It is important to eliminate as much water as possible, because excess moisture tends to dilute the dressing.

Wrap washed and dried leaves in a towel and larger quantities in a pillow case that will allow the lettuce to breathe and the water to be absorbed. Tear lettuce, rather than cutting it, to prevent the edges from browning. Leafy lettuce should be torn into larger than bite-sized pieces that may be folded into a fork. Remove the coarse center ribs from the larger leaves of romaine lettuce. When it comes to tossing a salad, the human touch is best: wash your hands and gently toss the lettuces to coat them with the dressing or to mix the salad ingredients.

Salad Dressings

Salad dressings add character to the salad if used properly and if the dressing is chosen to complement the salad. Unfortunately, salad dressings, nutritionally speaking, are probably the most offensive elements in a salad. Why? They include excessive quantities of oils, chemicals, sugars, and salts. That need not be the case, but frequently it is. Lying in ambush on supermarket shelves and salad bars are numerous salad dressings that are among the world's most notorious fat traps. Restaurant salad dressings are generally of poor quality unless the establishment is particularly conscientious.

In general, natural foods dressings are free of flavor enhancers, chemicals, and preservatives. However, they contain highly refined oils—more refined than oils sold separately but less refined than oils contained in mainstream bottle dressings.

Refined oils have a longer shelf life, which helps reduce the cost of these dressings. Most mainstream salad dressings contain soybean oil, which, in its unrefined state, has a strong, fishy taste and so must be refined and deodorized by a process in which steam is forced through the oil under a vacuum. Natural salad dressings, on the other hand, usually contain milder oil that lets the taste of the natural ingredients come through.

Edible Flowers in the Salads

Flowers have long been a delicacy of the animal kingdom and have now begun to be appreciated by the rest of us. They add color to the plate that rivals that of the most elegant vegetables. Some even accentuate the principal ingredients in the dish.

I have seen edible flowers for sale in some supermarkets, but all you need to do is be able to identify them in your flower garden or windowsill and pick them for your salad when you are ready to assemble it. Beware of the use of pesticides on the flowers. In some areas of the country edible flowers are grown hydroponically and are therefore available year-round. With salads that feature flowers, I prefer to use a transparent dressing, such as a vinaigrette. I would suggest that, if you are using a creamy dressing, you place the flowers on the salad after the dressing has been added. Here are some descriptions of a few of the edible flowers and a simple salad using them. You can safely use up to three different types of flowers in a single salad; more may be overdoing it.

HOLLYHOCK   (*Alcea rosea*, also called pastel flowers): They are very delicate and have a slightly sweet flavor that makes any dish look and feel light.

LAVENDER (*Lavandula*): Related to the mint family, lavender is rapidly becoming a very popular culinary herb. The purplish flowers are used for stews, punches, marinades, and jellies. By itself, a spray makes a classic garnish.

MARIGOLD (*Calendula officinalis*): These flowers come in a variety of yellow and orange. The taste may vary a great deal. Flower petals are used as a saffron substitute in coloring soups and stews and also as a flavoring agent. The taste is similar to that of tarragon.

NASTURTIUM (*Tropaeolum majus*): These flowers come in a wide variety of yellow, orange, red, rust, mahogany, and so on. They are exciting in appearance and absolutely beautiful. They have a hot, peppery taste, similar to that of horseradish. Add a few of these flowers to your salad to create a brilliant sight. Their fuzzy leaves are also edible and add texture to salads.

OREGANO (*Origanum majorana, O. vulgare*): The tiny, mauve flowers of the well-known herb have a very mild taste. A flowering sprig makes a lovely garnish.

PANSY (*Viola*): Pansies are large and colorful flowers; you can also use violas (johnny-jump-ups) and violets, which are smaller.

PINEAPPLE SAGE (*Salvia elegans*): Pineapple sage flowers smell so strongly of fresh-cut pineapple that you can almost taste it. These flowers make any dish exciting. Sprinkled over a fruit cup, they are absolutely perfect.

Try the following recipe: Make a salad base of watercress (or any combination of salad greens and assorted shredded vegetables), add marinated mushrooms and marinated seitan (about ¼ cup each per person), scatter edible flowers on top, and dress with leftover marinade or Basic French Dressing (page 93).

Cucumber and Lemon Cream Salad

YIELD: *4 servings*
TIME: *25 minutes
preparation; 2 hours to stand*

*2¼ cups cucumbers, peeled,
   cut in half horizontally,
   seeded, and cut into ⅛- to
   ¼-inch slices*
½ teaspoon sea salt
*1 cup Lemon Cream Dressing
   (page 92)*
*1 tablespoon fresh chopped
   dill*
Bibb lettuce (or other lettuce)
*tomato and yellow squash,
   for garnish*

*T*his salad is also suitable as an appetizer.

Mix the cucumber and sea salt well. Let stand for at least 2 hours to draw out the water. While the cucumber is standing, make the dressing and set aside. Rinse and drain the slices and press them moderately to dry them. (The cucumbers must be dry or they will make the dressing runny.) Add the dressing and the dill to the cucumbers and mix in well.

   To serve, arrange a leaf of Bibb lettuce or other lettuce on the plate, half a cup of salad on the lettuce, and garnish with a slice of tomato and a slice of yellow squash each cut in half and placed on either side of the salad.

2 tablespoons mirin
2 tablespoons tahini
2 tablespoons brown rice
    vinegar or 1 tablespoon
    cider vinegar and 1
    tablespoon water
2 tablespoons white miso

VARIATION: *Dilled Sour Cream Cucumber Salad*
Prepare the cucumbers according to the recipe above. Use this dressing instead of the Lemon Cream Dressing.

Mix the ingredients together to form a smooth paste. Combine with the prepared cucumbers. Stir in ½ cup thinly sliced scallions and 1 teaspoon fresh chopped dill. Refrigerate until ready to use. To serve, place a portion of salad on a lettuce leaf and garnish with a slice of tomato.

Salad à la Russe

YIELD: *5 servings*
TIME: *40 minutes*

2 medium potatoes
1 cup peeled and julienned
    carrots
1 tablespoon soy oil
1½ teaspoons minced garlic
¼ teaspoon black pepper
1 cup frozen green peas
½ cup soy mayonnaise
1 cup peeled and diced onions
5 medium tomatoes
5 pitted black olives

*T*his is a hearty salad but not strictly a potato salad. It is best to let the salad set overnight to let the onions mellow out the flavor. The raw onions, like any raw vegetable, lighten the salad.

Cook and peel the potatoes. When cool, cut them into thick strips. Set aside.

Sauté the carrots in the oil with the garlic and pepper over medium heat for about 5 minutes. After 2 minutes add the peas, which will continue to cook in the hot mixture.

Mix the potatoes with the mayonnaise and the carrot mixture. Add the diced onions.

Cut the top off the tomatoes and hollow out the centers. Fill the tomatoes with the mixture and serve on a plate lined with lettuce leaves. Garnish the salads with the olives. Refrigerate until ready to serve.

VARIATION: *Salade à la RizCous*
Substitute 1 cup cooked RizCous for the potatoes. Add 2 teaspoons each of fresh mint and fresh cilantro.

To serve, arrange the salad on a leaf of lettuce with two slices of tomato. Garnish with olives, fresh oregano leaves, and diced jicama on the side. Serve cold.

Dijon Potato Salad

YIELD: *6 servings*
TIME: *40 minutes*

*4 or 5 medium boiling
    potatoes*
*3 tablespoons Dijon-style
    mustard*
*1½ cups French or Italian
    dressing*
*1 cup peeled and finely diced
    onions*
*1 cup peeled and finely
    chopped carrots*
½ teaspoon sea salt
¼ teaspoon black pepper
*1 tablespoon dry arame,
    crumbled fine*
1 cup coarsely grated celery
*1 cup broccoli pieces, stems
    and florets*

*T*his spicy salad is appropriate for a picnic or with a luncheon sandwich. You could use this dish as a dinner salad if you are serving a bright entrée.

Peel and dice the potatoes and place them in a saucepan with water to cover. Bring to a boil, then simmer the potatoes, half-covered, for 20 minutes, until the potatoes are tender. Drain and set aside.

Mix the mustard into the dressing. Sauté the onions, carrots, and celery in ½ cup of the dressing mixture, with the salt and pepper, over medium heat for 5 minutes. Add the cooked potatoes and arame and sauté for another 2 minutes. Remove from heat, add the remaining dressing, and let cool. Then refrigerate until the potatoes are cold.

Blanch the broccoli pieces and set aside to cool. Add the broccoli just before serving. (If you add the broccoli earlier, the vinegar will turn the broccoli an unappetizing gray-green color.)

VARIATION
You can also serve this salad warm, like a warm German potato salad. While sautéing the vegetables, stir in about 1 to 2 teaspoons of smoked yeast.

Excelsior Salad

YIELD: *2 servings*
TIME: *15 minutes*

*1 large Red Delicious apple
finely chopped celery
finely chopped pineapple*

*S*pecific measurements for this recipe are hard to gauge because it depends on the size of the apple. I recommend using a plain soy mayonnaise that does not have any spices. If you are using the Soy Mayonnaise recipe on page 90, omit the mustard, garlic, and onion.

soy mayonnaise
⅛ teaspoon vanilla extract
bed of lettuce
2 teaspoons chopped nuts for
    garnish
2 strawberries for garnish,
    sliced up to the stem and
    fanned out

Cut the apple in half and remove the seeds and core. Scoop out the flesh of the apple, leaving a wall of apple peel about ⅛-inch thick. Chop the apple flesh into small pieces and measure it. Measure out an equal amount of chopped celery. Then measure out the same quantity of pineapple.

Mix the chopped fruit together with enough mayonnaise to bind it (about 6 to 8 tablespoons). Add the vanilla extract. Fill the 2 apple halves and place each one on a bed of lettuce. Garnish with nuts and a strawberry.

Cucumber Almond Couscous Salad

YIELD: *6 servings*
TIME: *20 minutes*

2 cups water
1½ teaspoons sea salt
¾ cup, plus 2 tablespoons,
    uncooked couscous
1 cup slivered almonds
1 tablespoon canola oil (or
    olive oil)
3 cups cucumbers (peeled,
    seeded, and diced before
    measuring)
½ cup thinly sliced scallions
3 tablespoons olive oil
3 tablespoons lemon juice
2 teaspoons dried oregano
½ teaspoon black pepper

Bring the water to a simmer in a small saucepan. Add ½ teaspoon salt and the couscous. Cover and let simmer for 4 to 5 minutes. Then remove from heat and set aside. (If you want to serve the salad right away, transfer the cooked couscous to a bowl and set that bowl inside a pan of ice. This will cool the grains quickly.)

Sauté the almonds in the oil until lightly browned, stirring constantly to prevent burning. Immediately transfer the almonds to a dish to stop their cooking. Set aside.

In a large bowl, combine the cucumbers, scallions, olive oil, lemon juice, oregano, pepper, and remaining 1 teaspoon salt. Add the cooked couscous and almonds. Chill and serve.

Tofu Wakame Salad

YIELD: *2 servings, as a main course*
TIME: *45 minutes*

1 cup garbanzo flour
1 teaspoon sea salt
1 teaspoon curry powder
1 teaspoon garlic powder
12 ounces tofu, cut into 6 equal triangles
5 tablespoons olive oil
several leaves of Bibb or butter lettuce
1 cup diced onion
½ teaspoon black pepper
1 teaspoon minced garlic
1 cup cucumbers (peeled, cut in half lengthwise, seeded, and sliced)
¼ cup dry wakame
1 cup Millet ''Mashed Potatoes'' (see page 198) or 1 cup any type of cooked grain
¼ cup Curry-Flavored Mayonnaise (page 91)
shredded red radish, for garnish

*T*his salad has a delicate combination of flavors and textures. It is perfect for a cool spring or fall menu when you might want a fresh salad with a little more substance. The optional Millet ''Mashed Potatoes'' complements the salad quite well. You could use any other grain as a substitute for the millet dish.

Mix the garbanzo flour, ½ teaspoon salt, curry powder, and garlic together and set aside.

Wet the tofu pieces and let them drain for a few minutes. Dredge them in the seasoned garbanzo flour and sauté in 3 tablespoons of olive oil until lightly brown on both sides.

Arrange a bed of lettuce on each serving plate and keep them cool until you are ready to assemble the salad.

Sauté the onion in the remaining 2 tablespoons of oil, with the pepper, garlic, and remaining ½ teaspoon of salt, over medium heat for 4 to 5 minutes. Add the cucumber and wakame and sauté for another 4 to 5 minutes.

To assemble the salad, place ½ cup Millet ''Mashed Potatoes'' or other grain in the center of each plate. Put ¾ cup cucumber mixture around the millet. Arrange three pieces of tofu on each plate. Place a small amount of Curry-Flavored Mayonnaise on each plate and garnish the salad with the shredded radish.

Manhattan Salad

YIELD: *2 servings, as a main course*
TIME: *30 to 45 minutes*

2 tablespoons olive oil
1 cup diced zucchini
1 cup peeled and diced onions
4 teaspoons minced garlic
1 cup diced eggplant
½ cup chopped celery
¼ cup diced green bell peppers
½ cup quartered mushrooms
½ cup cooked garbanzo beans
¼ cup chopped black olives
1 teaspoon chopped basil
1 teaspoon chopped marjoram
1 teaspoon chopped savory (optional)
¼ teaspoon white pepper
½ cup tomato paste
1 cup water
4 tablespoons white miso
4 cups shredded lettuce
1 cup cooked brown rice
2 slices cucumber, scored, for garnish
2 whole black olives, for garnish

*T*his substantial entrée salad may be served cold or hot. If you are serving it cold, be sure to allow time to refrigerate it. This is a great recipe for using leftover rice.

Heat the oil in a large ovenproof pan, if possible. Sauté the zucchini, onions, garlic, eggplant, celery, bell peppers, mushrooms, garbanzo beans, and diced olives, together with the herbs and white pepper, until half-cooked (about 10 to 15 minutes).

Mix the tomato paste, water, and miso and add to the vegetables. If your sauté pan is not ovenproof, place the vegetables in a baking dish that has a lid. Cover and bake in a preheated oven at 350 degrees F for 20 minutes. Remove from the oven and let the mixture cool until pleasantly warm.

To assemble the salad, make a bed of lettuce on each of two plates. Put half of the rice on each plate. Then divide the vegetables evenly over the two mounds of rice. Garnish each salad with a cucumber slice and a whole olive.

Cucumber and Wakame Salad

YIELD: *4 to 5 servings*
TIME: *20 minutes prepara-*
tion; several hours to stand

3 medium cucumbers
½ teaspoon salt
½ cup chopped wakame
½ cup water
6 tablespoons rice vinegar
2 tablespoons mirin
2 tablespoons olive oil
¾ teaspoon ginger juice (or ¼
   teaspoon ground ginger)
¼ cup chopped scallions
¼ cup thinly sliced red
   radishes
1 teaspoon minced garlic
¼ teaspoon black pepper
several lettuce leaves
parsley and/or tomato-peel
   rose, for garnish

Score and slice the cucumbers. (If the cucumbers have been waxed, you probably should peel them instead of scoring them.) Add all of the ingredients, except the lettuce and garnish, to the sliced cucumbers. Refrigerate the salad, covered, overnight. Serve the salad on a bed of lettuce and garnish.

Roasted Vegetable Salad

YIELD: *4 to 6 servings*

TIME: *1 hour; 2 hours to chill*

1½ cups carrots, peeled, cut in half lengthwise, and sliced

1½ cups parsnips (peeled, cut in half lengthwise, and sliced)

1½ cups sliced jerusalem artichokes

2 cups peeled and diced rutabaga

1½ cups Spanish onion, peeled and diced

1 tablespoon minced garlic

3 tablespoons olive oil

½ teaspoon salt

½ teaspoon black pepper

1½ cups Baked Squash (recipe follows)

2 cups Basic French Dressing (page 93)

1 head leaf lettuce

2 tomatoes, for garnish

*F*or this salad, you can substitute a different type of root vegetable for any of those listed in the recipe. In making substitutions, use the same amount as for the original vegetable.

Place the prepared vegetables in a roasting pan with the oil and seasonings and shake them well to make sure that all of the vegetables are well coated. Cover the pan with a lid or aluminum foil and place it in a preheated oven at 375 degrees F. Roast the vegetables for about 25 minutes or until they are soft but firm. Remove from oven and set aside to cool.

When the vegetables are cool, toss them gently with the dressing. Refrigerate. Serve the salad cold on a bed of lettuce garnished with wedges of tomato.

Baked Squash

You will need half of a large butternut squash or 1 small acorn squash. If you are using a whole squash, cut it in half lengthwise and scrape out the seeds and the stringy part. Rub the inside of the squash with 1 teaspoon of olive oil and sprinkle it with a little salt. Bake uncovered in the oven while the other vegetables are roasting. The squash should take 30 to 45 minutes to bake. It should be tender but still fairly firm. Allow the squash to cool. Then peel and dice it. Measure out about 1½ cups for the salad.

Aduki Bean Aspic

YIELD: *4 servings*
TIME: *20 minutes preparation; 2 hours to chill; allow several hours to soak the beans and about 2 hours to cook them*

1 cup dried aduki beans
2 cups water
1 small piece kombu, about 2
   inches long
1 cup sliced onions
1 tablespoon minced garlic
¾ cup thinly sliced carrots
1 tablespoon roasted sesame
   oil
1 tablespoon minced ginger
1 tablespoon barley miso
½ teaspoon black pepper
3 tablespoons agar flakes (or
   1½ tablespoons agar
   powder)
¼ cup chopped dried arame
2 teaspoons smoked yeast
1 cup chopped fresh fennel
2 cups water

Soak the beans for several hours in water to cover. Drain and place in a large saucepan with 2 cups of fresh water and the kombu. Simmer, partially covered, until the beans are soft (about 2 hours). Add more water if necessary to prevent the beans from burning. When the beans are cooked, drain them (reserving the liquid for soup, if you wish), and set aside. Chop up the kombu and either add it to the aspic or use it in another dish (soup, sandwich, and so on).

Sauté the onions, garlic, and carrots in the oil with the ginger, miso, and pepper, until the onions are translucent and the miso is dissolved.

In a separate pan, mix the agar, arame, yeast, and fennel with 2 cups of water, and simmer until the arame is cooked (about 10 minutes; 5 minutes if using agar powder). Add the cooked beans and the sautéed onion mixture. Mix well and heat through. Pour the mixture into a 1½-quart mold and refrigerate until the aspic is cold and the agar has set (about 2 hours). To serve, turn out onto a chilled plate.

Melon Aspic

YIELD: *6 servings*
TIME: *30 minutes preparation; 30 minutes to set and chill*

4 cups watermelon chunks, peeled and seeded
half a honeydew melon (peeled, seeded, and diced)
half a cantaloupe (peeled, seeded, and diced)
1 tablespoon agar powder*

*If you prefer a firmer aspic, you can add up to 1½ teaspoons more agar powder. If you are using agar flakes instead of powder, use 3 tablespoons of flakes for 1 tablespoon of powder; simmer the flakes in about ½ cup of water for 8 to 10 minutes to dissolve.

*T*his fruit aspic is particularly suitable as a salad for a late summer meal, when melons are at their peak and it is almost too hot to eat. It also makes a nice dessert: serve it with fresh pineapple or strawberries; with a scoop of lemon, papaya, or passion fruit sorbet; or with a fruit sauce—a strawberry or apricot fruit sauce would be wonderful.

The quantities given in the recipe are approximate because fruit varies in size. You will need enough to yield two cups of each type of purée: watermelon, honeydew, and cantaloupe. (One tablespoon of agar powder will gel six cups of melon purée.) It is important that the purées are at room temperature. If they are chilled, the agar will gel before it can be mixed thoroughly into the melon.

Lightly oil a 6-cup mold (or six 1-cup molds). Set aside.

Purée each type of melon, separately, using a food processor or a sieve, using enough fruit to yield 2 cups of each purée. Set aside, unrefrigerated.

Combine the agar powder with 1 cup of the watermelon purée. Stir until the agar is dissolved, and cook over medium heat until the mixture thickens. Remove from heat and, while the mixture is still warm, add the remaining cup of watermelon purée, 1 cup of honeydew purée, and 1 cup of cantaloupe purée, blending them well.

Turn the remaining 2 cups of melon purée into a bowl, pour in the heated mixture, and whip vigorously for about 1 minute—stirring 20 seconds in a clockwise direction, 20 seconds counterclockwise, and 20 seconds clockwise again. Pour into the prepared mold and refrigerate until set (about 30 minutes). To serve, turn out onto a chilled plate.

Broccoli and Arame Salad

YIELD: *4 servings*
TIME: *25 to 30 minutes*

1 cup dried arame
1 cup water
5 tablespoons rice vinegar
2 tablespoons shoyu
1 cup halved, sliced onions
2 tablespoons roasted sesame oil
2 cups broccoli florets, steamed and cooled in ice water
leaf lettuce

*W*hen this salad is made it should be eaten immediately because the vinegar will cause the broccoli to turn gray-green. This salad is a macrobiotic dish.

Mix the arame in the water, bring to a simmer over medium heat, and cook for 4 to 5 minutes. Remove from heat, add the vinegar and shoyu, and mix well.

Sauté the onions in the oil over medium heat until the onions are translucent. Add them to the arame mixture. Set aside to cool. Drain the broccoli and add it to the arame mixture. Arrange the salad on a bed of fresh leaf lettuce. Serve the salad cold.

Princess Salad

YIELD: *4 servings*
TIME: *15 to 20 minutes preparation; 1 hour to chill*

leaf lettuce
8 thin slices medium tomatoes
12 asparagus spears, peeled and steamed al dente
8 thin strips red pimiento
1 cup Oil-less Sesame Dressing (page 96), Basic French Dressing (page 93), or a vinaigrette dressing of your choice

Divide the lettuce among four plates and top with two slices tomato for each plate. Place three pieces of asparagus on the tomato and the pimiento strips crosswise on the asparagus. Refrigerate until cool. Pour the dressing over the salad when ready to serve.

Tofu "Cottage Cheese"

YIELD: *3 servings*
TIME: *20 minutes*

½ cup finely chopped onion
1½ teaspoons sesame oil (or olive oil)
¼ teaspoon dill weed
¼ teaspoon sea salt (optional)
1 cup firm tofu, crushed by hand
½ cup soy mayonnaise
2 tablespoons chopped chives

T his bears a remarkable resemblance to regular cottage cheese. It has a delicate flavor accented by the dill weed.

Sauté the onions in the oil, along with the dill weed and salt, if you wish. Set aside to cool. Add the tofu, soy mayonnaise, and chives.

DRESSINGS

Vegan Sour Cream

YIELD: *1 cup*
TIME: *10 minutes*

¾ cup soy milk
1 cup raw cashew nuts
1½ teaspoons cider vinegar or
  lemon juice

Blend the soy milk and cashews until smooth and creamy. Add more nuts if necessary. Then blend in the vinegar.

Soy Mayonnaise

YIELD: *2½ cups mayonnaise*
TIME: *15 minutes*

12 ounces firm tofu
6 tablespoons oil
1 tablespoon cider vinegar
½ cup water
1½ teaspoons prepared
  yellow mustard
1 teaspoon minced garlic
4 tablespoons minced onion
¼ teaspoon white pepper
1¼ teaspoons sea salt
1 tablespoon lemon juice
1 tablespoon very finely
  ground cashew nuts
  (optional)

*T*his is a basic, all-purpose mayonnaise that will keep, refrigerated, for 8 to 12 weeks. If you are using the cashew nuts, make sure that they are blended until they turn into a fine meal, or your mayonnaise will feel gritty. The same mayonnaise, with the garlic, onion, and mustard omitted, may be used for fruit salads.

Place all ingredients in a blender and blend until smooth and creamy. Refrigerate until cool.

¾ cup finely diced onions
¾ cup chili sauce
2 tablespoons chopped capers
6 tablespoons chopped dill
  pickles
¾ cup finely diced tofu
¾ cup finely diced green bell
  peppers
1 tablespoon finely chopped
  parsley
¾ cup natural catsup

VARIATION: *Thousand-Island Dressing*
This dressing yields about 4½ cups of dressing. To the previous recipe, add these ingredients. Mix all ingredients together, place in a sealed container, and refrigerate until cool.

Silken Tofu Mayonnaise

YIELD: *1½ cups mayonnaise*
TIME: *15 minutes*

10½ ounces (1 box) firm
  silken tofu
2 tablespoons granulated
  lecithin
1 teaspoon granulated garlic
1 teaspoon prepared yellow
  mustard
2 tablespoons rice vinegar
1 tablespoon lemon juice (or 2
  tablespoons cider vinegar)
¼ cup canola oil
1 teaspoon sea salt
⅛ teaspoon white pepper

*T*his is an easy mayonnaise to make. It has a light texture
and a delicate flavor. You can increase or decrease the seasonings according to your taste. It may also be used as a base for
cold sauces, such as caper mayonnaise, curry mayonnaise,
and so forth.

Blend all of the ingredients together until the mixture is
smooth. Pour into a container and set aside for about 30
minutes until the lecithin sets.

VARIATION: *Curry-Flavored Mayonnaise*
To the above recipe, add ½ teaspoon curry powder and ½ teaspoon powdered ginger.

Lemon Cream Dressing

YIELD: *2¼ cups dressing*
TIME: *15 minutes*

½ cup tahini
8 ounces firm tofu (or firm
silken tofu)
zest and juice from 1 lemon
¼ cup cider vinegar
1 clove garlic, minced
¼ cup brown rice syrup (or ⅓
cup honey)
2 tablespoons white miso
½ cup water

Place all ingredients in a blender and blend until the mixture is smooth. Cool and use as desired.

Mirin Salad Dressing

YIELD: *1 cup dressing*
TIME: *5 minutes*

⅓ cup mirin
⅓ cup red wine vinegar
⅓ cup olive oil
about ⅛ teaspoon salt

This is a good dressing for a salad of field greens, red-leaf lettuce, red peppers, tomatoes, green onions, and carrots. If the mirin you use is unsalted, simply add a little more salt to the dressing.

Place all ingredients in a jar. Shake the jar vigorously to blend the ingredients.

Basic French Dressing

YIELD: *3 cups dressing*
TIME: *30 minutes*

1½ cups canola oil
1¼ cups cider vinegar that
   has 5 percent acidity
¼ cup finely diced onion
2 teaspoons minced garlic
1½ tablespoons tamari
1 tablespoon chopped basil
1⅛ teaspoons black pepper
2 tablespoons (about 1 ounce)
   tofu, crushed by hand
1½ tablespoons minced red
   pepper or pimiento
2 tablespoons minced pickles
2 tablespoons minced green
   bell peppers
1 tablespoon finely chopped
   scallions or chives
1½ tablespoons finely
   chopped parsley
1 tablespoon finely chopped
   black olives
1½ teaspoons salt

Mix all ingredients together and refrigerate until cool. Mix well before using.

¾ cup chili sauce
¾ cup natural catsup
¼ cup horseradish
¼ cup chopped parsley

VARIATION: *Lorenzo Dressing*
This recipe yields 2½ cups of dressing. Begin with ¾ cup of Basic French Dressing. Add these ingredients. Place all ingredients in a blender and blend until smooth. Refrigerate until cold.

Poppy Seed Dressing

YIELD: *4 cups dressing*
TIME: *10 to 15 minutes*

¼ cup finely diced onions
1 tablespoon minced garlic
6 tablespoons rice vinegar (or
  3 tablespoons cider vinegar
  and 3 tablespoons water)
¼ cup lemon juice
6 tablespoons celery seed
2 teaspoons sea salt (or 4
  teaspoons celery seed salt)
1 tablespoon Spike seasoning
  (or other natural, all-
  purpose seasoning)
1 tablespoon dry mustard
¼ cup honey
½ cup tahini
2 cups soy oil
4 tablespoons poppy seeds

One of the best features of this dressing is that it doesn't separate; it is creamy by nature. It may also be used as a sauce for cold appetizers.

Place everything except the soy oil and the poppy seeds in the blender and blend until smooth. Add the oil gradually to prevent it from separating. (You could also add the oil all at once and then agitate rapidly; this method will also prevent separation.) Stir in the poppy seeds. Refrigerate until cold.

Creamy Ginger Dressing

YIELD: *2½ cups dressing*
TIME: *20 minutes*

*1½ tablespoons peeled and
     chopped ginger*
*½ cup peeled and chopped
     carrots*
¼ cup chopped celery
*½ cup peeled and chopped
     onion*
½ cup canola oil
½ cup cider vinegar
¼ cup white miso
2 tablespoons tomato paste
1 tablespoon Sucanat
3 tablespoons lemon juice
¾ teaspoon dried basil
*¼ teaspoon Szechuan
     peppercorns*

*T*his dressing is good on any mixed green salad. The basil and peppercorns (which are not extremely hot, and are also a little sweet) add body to the flavor of this dressing.

Place all ingredients in a blender and blend until the dressing is smooth. This will take about 5 minutes.

Store spices in a cool, dark place. (Unfortunately, most kitchens don't have many cool, dark places!) Ultraviolet rays will draw the flavor from spices and therefore weaken them.

Oil-less Miso Dressing

YIELD: *2½ cups dressing*
TIME: *25 minutes*

*½ cup peeled and thinly sliced
   carrots*
1 cup soy milk
*5 ounces (½ package) firm
   silken tofu*
½ cup white miso
*¼ cup rice vinegar (or 2
   tablespoons cider vinegar
   and 2 tablespoons water)*
½ teaspoon ginger powder

*T*his dressing can be used immediately, but it is much better if it is left refrigerated for a few days. That way the flavors will have a chance to develop.

Steam the carrots until they are soft. Drain and transfer the carrots to a blender. Add the remaining ingredients and blend until smooth (about 90 seconds). Refrigerate until cool.

Oil-less Sesame Dressing

YIELD: *2⅔ cups dressing*
TIME: *25 minutes*

1½ cups sesame seeds
¼ cup umeboshi vinegar
½ cup mirin
¼ cup tamari
1 cup water
½ cup brown rice vinegar

*T*his versatile dressing is great on any salad. It is superb on the Princess Salad (page 88). You can also use this dressing to marinate vegetables or tofu.

Wash and drain the sesame seeds and roast them in a skillet over medium heat, stirring occasionally to prevent their burning. When the seeds begin to pop and turn a light brown, they are finished and must be removed from the pan immediately or they will burn.

Put all of the ingredients into a blender and blend until the seeds are mealy. Or, grind the seeds in a suribachi and then whip all the remaining ingredients together with them.

Entrées

*I*n the traditional American diet, meat is the focus of the main course. Even in a meat dish, though, it is usually the herbs, spices, sauces, and incorporated vegetables that make the dish a good entrée: meat alone is not very exciting. Therefore, removing meat from the menu is not difficult at all, and there are many protein substitutes available. It is my philosophy to blend as many vegetables as possible into the entrée dish.

The entrée recipes in this chapter feature protein foods such as beans, tofu, tempeh, and seitan (wheat gluten, also called kofu). Some of the dishes should seem familiar. There are some old favorites, like pizza, vegetable pies, and moussaka, adapted to a vegan eating style. You will also find some more unusual recipes, especially those featuring seitan. Use this introduction to the entrée recipes as a resource in preparing the foods.

Beans

Beans have a rich history in our country and the world. They have been a staple for humans from the beginning of time. Nutritionally speaking, beans are nearly flawless: they are high in complex carbohydrates and fiber and, except for soybeans, are very low in fat. They are extremely versatile and easy to prepare. They do require a long time to cook, but this only means you have to plan ahead when cooking dried beans; they generally don't require any attention while they are being cooked. In a pinch, you can use precooked, canned beans. In addition, some natural foods companies produce high-quality instant refried bean mixtures that are very convenient to use.

You can cook beans by boiling them on the stove, using a Crock Pot, or using a pressure cooker. I actually prefer the slow-cooking method of the Crock Pot, since it enhances the flavor. I seldom use this method, however, because it is time-consuming. Pressure cookers are much faster than either of the other methods.

When using a pressure cooker, cook the beans with the lid off until a film appears on the surface; then skim off the film, place the lid on the cooker, and seal it. Otherwise, the film that surfaces may jam the release valve and the pressure that accumulates inside the cooker may cause the safety valve to explode. Needless to say, this will make a mess in your kitchen.

In cooking beans, I have adopted the macrobiotic procedure of using kombu, a sea vegetable that is rich in minerals. Kombu usually comes in 7- to 8-inch strips. You can use a small piece of kombu (2 to 3 inches) for a smaller batch of beans, or the entire strip of kombu for a larger batch, or if you like the flavor of this sea vegetable in your food. Kombu helps tenderize the beans and enhances the nutritional density of this food.

In general, one cup of dried beans or peas (6 to 7 ounces) yields about 2 cups of cooked legume. Amounts vary, of course, depending on the type of legume. Likewise, cooking time varies, depending on the type of bean or pea. The following table shows the quantity of water to use in cooking various legumes, the different cooking times, and the yields per one cup of dried legume. Cooking times will vary if you are using a pressure cooker.

	WATER	COOKING TIME	YIELD
Per one cup dried beans or peas:			
Aduki beans	3¼ cups	45 minutes	3 cups
Anasazi beans	2 cups	2 hours	2 cups
Black beans	3 cups	1½ hours	2 cups
Black-eyed peas	3 cups	60 minutes	2 cups
Garbanzo beans	4 cups	3 hours	2 cups
Great northern beans	3½ cups	2 hours	2 cups
Kidney beans	3 cups	1½ hours	2 cups
Lentils and split peas	3 cups	45 minutes	2¼ cups
Lima beans, baby*	2 cups	1½ hours	1¾ cups
Navy beans (small white beans)	3 cups	2½ hours	2 cups

	WATER	COOKING TIME	YIELD
Per one cup dried beans or peas:			
Pinto beans	3 cups	2½ hours	2 cups
Red beans	3 cups	3 hours	2 cups
Soy grits	2 cups	15 minutes	2 cups
Soybeans	4 cups	3 to 3½ hours	2 cups

*Large lima beans differ only in that they yield 1¼ cups of cooked beans.

You can use the following guidelines in cooking beans or peas:

1. Sort the beans or peas. Throw away any rocks or other foreign matter and any discolored beans or peas.
2. Rinse the beans or peas in cold water.
3. Cover the beans or peas with three to four times their volume of water. (If you use hot water, it should reduce the soaking time. Let the water cool to room temperature.)
4. Soak them for several hours (or overnight) in the refrigerator. As an alternative, bring the beans or peas to a boil, boil for two minutes, and remove from heat. Cover and let soak for one hour.
5. Discard the soaking water, if you wish, and add fresh water. (With soybeans, you should always discard the soaking water.) Bring to a boil, lower heat, and simmer (partially covered).
6. Add water as needed to keep beans or peas covered. Do not add salt, oil, or other seasonings until beans or peas are tender.
7. Add salt toward the end of cooking, because salt will toughen beans and peas, causing a longer cooking time. As a rule of thumb, use ½ teaspoon salt per cup of raw beans.
8. If you wish, add a very small amount of vinegar (preferably rice vinegar) toward the end of the cooking time. This may help retain the color of the beans.

Tofu

Tofu is ready to eat out of the package. It can be grilled, dried, baked, steamed, boiled, scrambled, barbecued, marinated, or crumbled raw into salads. It can be used in sauces or soups, or as a substitute for cottage cheese, sour cream, or yogurt. It has a mild flavor and quickly picks up the flavor of surrounding foods and spices.

Eight ounces of tofu has 147 calories and 27 percent of the daily need for protein. It is low in sodium and fat. It is a good source of calcium, iron, potassium, phosphorus, choline, and vitamins E and B and it is easily digested.

You should use tofu within two to five days. Refrigerate it in water, and change the water every other day. For a firmer texture, drain the tofu by storing it out of water for two to twelve hours. Frozen tofu, when thawed and squeezed dry, has a chewy, meat-like texture. It is excellent in casseroles.

If you are planning to use tofu uncooked, you should boil it for at least three minutes, or steam it for eight to ten minutes, to kill any bacteria. If it is simmered for too long, though, it will become hard. Tofu that is aseptically packaged does not need to be boiled or steamed.

Tofu is sold in several forms: soft, firm, extra firm, silken soft, silken firm, and silken extra firm. The type to buy depends on the use. Softer tofu tends to be better for soups and quiches; firmer tofu tends to be better for shish kebabs or fried tofu; silken tofu is more appropriate in desserts or sauces. Dry tofu is sold commercially but is not widely available; it does not in any way resemble fresh tofu. When purchasing tofu at the supermarket, always check the expiration date. Fresh tofu is best and should be used before the expiration date.

As I mentioned, tofu is a good source of calcium, but it is especially good if it has been curdled with calcium sulfate. If it is curdled with nigari, the calcium content will not be as great. Calcium sulfate-stabilized tofu tends to draw in moisture, so it is very successful for marinated tofu; the marinade permeates the surface of the tofu more thoroughly. Nigari-stabilized tofu will not draw in moisture, so marinating it will not be as successful. The nigari tofu also tends to be sweeter.

Silken tofu is a rich soy milk that has been transformed into a deliciously firm and smooth tofu right inside its aseptic package. As long as the package is kept intact, the tofu will last for several months without refrigeration. Note the expiration date. Silken tofu comes in three varieties: soft, firm, and extra firm. Firm silken tofu contains soy isolates.

Tempeh

Tempeh is a cultured soy product that has its roots in Indonesia. The process for making tempeh involves splitting the soybeans, cooking them, removing the hulls, and incubating the beans. Tempeh is considered "meatier" than tofu. It is appropriate for use in making burgers and other dishes that call for large pieces of meat substitute.

In general, tempeh has a mild flavor. If it has a strong flavor, it may have been incubated too long, or it may have been cooled or frozen in such a way that the culture was allowed to continue developing. (Unless the culture is radically stopped, it continues to work and, in so doing, imparts a strong flavor.)

Color is another indicator of the quality of tempeh. Tempeh should be white with perhaps a few fairly dark gray spots. Too many spots, or spots that are very dark in color, indicate that the tempeh has been overincubated and will have a stronger taste. A strong tasting tempeh probably will not be as appetizing. Finally, good quality tempeh will be firm but somewhat bendable.

Tempeh usually is sold frozen. If it is not pasteurized before freezing, it will spoil much faster. It's safest to treat tempeh in the same way you would treat meat. Try to cook fresh tempeh right away to avoid spoilage.

Seitan

If there is one single "friendly food" you should become acquainted with, it is seitan, often called "wheat meat" or kofu. Seitan was originally developed in ancient China and is now enjoyed in Japan, Korea, Russia, the Middle East, and elsewhere. The Japanese introduced it to America, and here it is used frequently by Mormons, Seventh-Day Adventists, and vegetarians. In Chinese restaurants, it is sometimes called "Buddha food," because it is also believed to have been developed by Buddhist monks about 500 years ago.

Whatever its origins, it is an excellent substitute for meat. Basically a gluten dough that is cooked with ginger root, kombu, and tamari in water, seitan is substantial enough that it fills the stomach in much the same way that meat does. It is a high-protein, low-fat food that can be cooked in a number of ways. I first tasted it in Vancouver, British Columbia, and didn't care for the soggy-bread texture I was confronted with. I tasted it again, in Miami, in a dish prepared in a macrobiotic fashion. This version was much better, with a meaty texture, a good taste, and an appealing appearance. I could appreciate its potential as a transitional food for those who enjoy red meat but need to eat less of it.

Some people, especially food purists, are reluctant to eat seitan because it is a refined product. Most of the starch and all the bran are, indeed, washed out of the dough. But they both can be collected and used in other dishes. Perhaps it is not even necessary to do so if you are eating a diet of whole foods and regard seitan only as a source of protein. Pound for pound, it is far better as a protein source than beef. For a low-cholesterol diet, it may be the best food.

Nutritionally, 2⅔ ounces (a reasonable serving) of seitan will provide 70 calories and 12 grams of protein. A little over 5 ounces will provide 92 percent of the minimum daily requirement of protein for an adult. To get the same quantity of protein from sources that are more common in the American diet, you would have to eat hamburger meat or tofu (and consume 167 calories), pot roast (105 calories), eggs (93 calories), or hot dogs (87 calories).

Seitan is available commercially and is sold in health food stores and natural foods stores. It is sold in jars and, like tofu, in 12- to 16-ounce packages and in a salt solution. In addition, seitan is just becoming available in an instant form. Cheaper than commercial seitan, it is a powdered gluten from which the starch and bran have been removed. To use it, just add water, allow the dough to rest, and proceed to cook it according to the methods followed for traditional seitan.

You can also make your own seitan from scratch. There are two methods provided here in this chapter for making your own seitan. Because of the number of different steps, the recipe looks complicated. However, the procedures—kneading, rinsing, and simmering—are not difficult. You could make enough in one afternoon to last a whole month. A regular batch (the quantities yielded by the first recipe, for instance) can be prepared in 30 minutes. It will take between two and three hours to cook but certainly does not require constant supervision. The advantages of making your own seitan are that it will have considerably less sodium in it (salt is added to commercial seitan to give it a longer life), you will be able to use it raw as well, if you like, and it is considerably cheaper. In 1990, a pound of commercial seitan costs about $7.00; homemade, that same pound costs about $2.25.

The basic ingredient of seitan is a high-gluten wheat flour. Always use hard-wheat flour (sometimes called bread flour) to make seitan. All-purpose, cake, or pastry flours sold in the U.S. will not work because they do not contain enough gluten. To improve the yield of a recipe, I often add pure gluten flour (in the proportions of 2 ounces gluten flour to 14 ounces regular flour). If you are planning to serve the seitan in slices or "cutlets," precook the dough (in the tamari stock) in large pieces, at least four inches in diameter. This firms up the seitan pieces.

I highly recommend the book *Cooking with Seitan*, by Lenny Jacobs and Barbara Jacobs (Japan Publications, 1986). It covers many of the traditional techniques of making and using seitan, gives directions for basic preparations, and offers numerous ideas for using it.

Soysage

YIELD: *3 cups; 4 servings*
TIME: *2 hours; allow several hours to soak the soybeans and 4 hours to cook them*

1 cup dried soybeans (this will yield 2 cups of cooked soybeans)
1 piece kombu, about 2 inches long
2 tablespoons stone-ground whole wheat flour
¾ cup rolled oats
3 tablespoons canola oil
5 tablespoons soy milk
2 tablespoons nutritional yeast
¼ teaspoon ground fennel seeds
¼ teaspoon black pepper
1 tablespoon tamari
¾ teaspoon dried oregano
½ teaspoon salt
⅛ teaspoon cayenne pepper
2 to 3 teaspoons minced garlic
half of an onion, finely chopped
¾ teaspoon Dijon-style or other prepared mustard
1½ teaspoons dried sage or ground allspice
¼ cup water
¼ cider vinegar
4 to 8 tablespoons gluten flour

*T*his is a small recipe, but it can be made in larger quantities and frozen in small batches. I would recommend making about four or five times the recipe for future use. Soysage—a vegetarian sausage substitute—makes excellent breakfast patties, "meatballs," and filling for other dishes in which you might use sausage.

Soak the soybeans in water overnight. Discard the water. Then cook the soybeans with the kombu in about 4 cups of fresh water for about 4 hours. The soybeans should be soft. Drain them.

Coarsely chop the cooked soybeans and the kombu, if you wish. Then mix all of the ingredients together until the mixture binds and is of a medium-stiff consistency. Pack the mixture tightly into a stainless steel, ceramic, or ovenproof glass bowl and cover it tightly with foil, sealing the edges carefully.

Invert a shallow bowl in the bottom of a large pot and fill the pot with just enough water to cover the inverted bowl. Place the bowl of soysage mixture onto the inverted bowl. Cover the pot, bring the water to a simmer, and steam the soysage for 1½ hours. You may need to adjust the water level during this time. Remove the pot from the heat, let it cool, and then remove the foil.

Cuban Black Bean Stew

YIELD: *5 servings*

TIME: *30 minutes; allow a few hours to soak the beans and 1½ hours to cook them*

¾ *cup dried black beans*

2½ *cups water*

1½ *cups diced onions*

1 *cup diced carrots*

½ *cup diced red bell pepper and ½ cup diced yellow bell pepper (or use 1 cup diced bell pepper of any color)*

4 *teaspoons minced garlic*

2 *tablespoons sesame oil*

1 *teaspoon salt*

3 *tablespoons thyme leaves (or 1 tablespoon dried thyme)*

1 *teaspoon coarsely ground black pepper*

1 *tablespoon ground cumin*

1 *tablespoon smoked yeast (optional)*

2 *tablespoons tamari (or less if you desire)*

2 *cups water*

1 *cup diced seitan*

2 *tablespoons arrowroot or cornstarch, dissolved in 3 tablespoons water*

*T*ypically, Cuban people like to serve rice with black beans or lentils. The combination is an excellent source of carbohydrates and protein. If you plan to serve the stew over rice, other grain, or pasta, make your stew a little spicier, because the starches will tone down the flavor.

Soak the black beans in water for a few hours. Discard the water and cook the beans in 2½ cups of fresh water for about 1½ hours.

Sauté the onions, carrots, peppers, and garlic in the oil, along with the seasonings and the tamari, for about 5 to 7 minutes, stirring occasionally. Add the cooked beans, 2 cups of water, and the seitan. Continue to cook in a covered pot for another 10 to 15 minutes. (During this time, prepare the grain or pasta if you plan to serve it with the stew.) Add the arrowroot mixture to the stew and stir rapidly to make a smooth sauce. Cook until thickened, about 3 minutes, and serve.

"Meatballs"

YIELD: *6 cups; 9 to 10 servings*
TIME: *40 minutes; allow several hours to soak the soybeans and 2 to 3 hours to cook them*

2 cups dried soybeans
8 cups water
1 cup coarsely chopped
   walnuts
1 cup peeled and chopped
   carrots
1 cup peeled and chopped
   onions
2 cloves garlic, minced
¼ cup corn oil
¼ cup tamari
1 teaspoon black pepper
½ cup gluten flour
½ cup stone-ground whole
   wheat flour
½ cup oat bran
½ cup cooked RizCous
1 cup chopped nuts (optional)
1 cup finely chopped seitan
   (optional)
1 cup roasted sunflower seeds
   (optional)

*R*izCous is a packaged product that is much like couscous; because it is made from rice, it is light and easy to digest. To make the RizCous, follow the cooking directions on the package. This recipe makes a large quantity; the mixture is versatile, though, and can be used in numerous dishes.

Soak the soybeans for several hours. Discard the water and cook the beans in 8 cups of fresh water for 2 to 3 hours.

Coarsely chop the cooked soybeans, using a food processor if possible, and mix them with the walnuts. (Be careful not to overprocess the beans.)

Sauté the carrots, onions, and garlic in the oil over a medium heat until the onions are translucent. Add the sautéed vegetables to the soybeans and mix in well. Then add the tamari and pepper. Combine the two flours and add them to the soybean mixture, mixing well. Add the oat bran, the cooked RizCous, and any of the optional ingredients.

Form the mixture into round shapes of about 1 inch in diameter. Steam them on the stove, using a covered steamer, for about 20 minutes. You can also bake-steam the meatballs in the oven as follows: place them in a baking dish, tightly cover the dish, place that dish in a larger one that has been half-filled with water, and cover the larger dish as well. Place the two dishes in the oven and bake-steam for about 20 minutes at 400 degrees F. The key to bake-steaming is to protect the food against direct access to the steam; if you keep the meatballs well covered, they are less likely to fall apart in the steaming process.

You can also form the meatball mixture into a long sausage-like roll and cook it as described above. If you steam it in a steamer, you should wrap it first in plastic wrap before you cook it. The roll should take 1 to 1½ hours to cook, whether you are steaming it or bake-steaming it.

VARIATION 1: *Spaghetti and "Meatballs"*

Add ¼ cup dark miso to the raw mixture. This will give the meatballs a richer flavor. Form the mixture into small balls and cook them according to the recipe above. (You may prefer to sauté the meatballs.) Prepare a tomato sauce (see page 159); then add the cooked meatballs to heat through. Prepare spaghetti or other pasta. Spoon the sauce and meatballs over the spaghetti.

VARIATION 2: *Italian Soysage*
(for the Berner Platte, page 155)

4 teaspoons *Pâté Seasoning (page 35)*
4 teaspoons *fennel seed*
2 tablespoons *smoked yeast*
1 teaspoon *salt*

Add these ingredients to the basic "meatball" mixture. Mix well. Form the "meatball" mixture into a long, sausage-shaped roll and steam (or bake-steam) the roll for 1 to 1½ hours.

VARIATION 3: *Königsberger Klopse*
with Sardaline Sauce

4 tablespoons *chopped savory*
4 tablespoons *Vogue Vegy Base*
3 cloves *garlic, minced*
4 teaspoons *black pepper*
2 teaspoons *salt*
1 pound *chopped tofu*
1 cup *uncooked whole wheat couscous*
½ cup *gluten flour*
prepared pasta of your choice
Sardaline Sauce (page 163)

Add these ingredients to the basic "meatball" mixture. Combine ingredients thoroughly. Taste, and add more salt if the mixture seems bland. Form the mixture into 1¼-inch-diameter balls and steam-bake them on a rack. Prepare about 1 cup of pasta for each person. Serve the Königsberger Klopse over pasta, topped with Sardaline sauce.

Bulgur Walnut Loaf

YIELD: *1 loaf; 8 servings*
TIME: *20 to 30 minutes preparation; 1 hour baking*

3 cups water
1½ cups bulgur
1½ cups finely diced onions
3 cloves garlic, minced
1½ cups peeled and finely diced carrots
1 tablespoon sesame oil
6 tablespoons barley miso
1¼ teaspoons powdered thyme
*1 cup roasted and finely ground walnuts**
¼ cup roasted sunflower seeds (optional)
½ cup gluten flour
½ cup whole wheat flour

*Roast the walnuts at 425 degrees F for 10 minutes, stirring occasionally. Put them through a food processor until they are mealy. Be careful not to overprocess them; you do not want to end up with a paste.

*S*erve slices of this loaf with a vegetable side dish and perhaps a leafy salad. You may wish to serve the loaf with a sauce, such as Espagñol, Carrot, Tahini Lemon, or Velouté Sauces (see pages 160–165).

Bring the water to boil in a medium saucepan. Add the bulgur and let it simmer for 5 minutes, or just long enough to absorb the water in the pot. The bulgur must be cooked but dry.

Sauté the onions, garlic, and carrots in the oil. Then add the miso and thyme. (You may have to mash the miso into the vegetable mixture.) Cook the mixture over medium heat, stirring constantly, until the vegetables are soft. Then add the ground walnuts and sunflower seeds (if you wish) and mix well.

Mix the two flours together. Then add them to the bulgur. (If the flours aren't thoroughly mixed, the gluten flour may create lumps in the loaf.) Finally, stir the sautéed vegetables into the bulgur mixture.

Oil a 1-quart loaf pan and press the mixture into the pan. Bake, covered, in a preheated oven at 350 degree F for 50 to 60 minutes. Cool the loaf in the pan for about 5 minutes. Then take the loaf out of the pan and cool for 30 minutes.

Millet Loaf

YIELD: *1 loaf; 8 servings*
TIME: *30 minutes
preparation; 1 hour cooking*

1½ cups millet
3¾ cups water
2 teaspoons sea salt
1½ cups peeled and finely
    diced carrots
1 cup finely diced celery
1 cup finely diced onions
1 clove garlic, minced
2 tablespoons sesame oil
1½ teaspoons dill weed
1 teaspoon dried thyme
1 cup pistachio nuts or
    roasted sunflower seeds
    (optional)
3 tablespoons unbleached
    flour
3 tablespoons gluten flour

*Y*ou can also serve this versatile loaf for lunch or as an appetizer. Place slices on a bed of Bibb lettuce with vegetable garnishes and a light, creamy salad dressing.

Rinse the millet and put it in a medium saucepan with the water and ½ teaspoon sea salt. Cook the millet, covered, over medium heat for about 30 minutes or until soft; the millet should absorb all of the water. (If the grains are too moist, the loaf will not bind properly.)

Sauté the carrots, celery, onions, and garlic in oil for 6 minutes, or until the onions are translucent. Add the seasonings, including the remaining 1½ teaspoons of salt. Mix the cooked millet and the vegetables together, along with the nuts or seeds, if you wish. Mix the two flours together and add them to the millet mixture, blending it well so the loaf will hold together.

Lightly oil and flour a large loaf pan. Press the millet mixture into the pan and bake in a preheated oven at 400 degrees F for about one hour. (If the millet mixture is warm when you put it in the pan, reduce the baking time to about 45 minutes.) Allow the loaf to cool for 10 minutes; then carefully remove it from the pan. To avoid breaking the loaf, you may wish to slice it while it is still in the pan.

Polenta

YIELD: *One 7-cup mold;*
about 8 servings
TIME: *10 to 15 minutes*
preparation; 30 minutes
cooking; allow several hours
to soak the kidney beans and
2 hours to cook them

1 tablespoon olive oil (or corn
    oil)
1 cup peeled and finely diced
    carrots
1 cup finely diced onions
1 cup finely diced celery
1 tablespoon minced garlic
2 teaspoons sea salt
½ teaspoon finely ground
    black pepper
1 teaspoon chopped basil
4 cups water
½ cup drained stewed
    tomatoes
2 cups yellow corn grits (or
    2¼ cups cornmeal)
1 cup cooked, drained kidney
    beans*

*If you are cooking the kidney
beans yourself, soak ½ cup dried
beans in water for several hours.
Then cook them in about 2 cups of
fresh water for about 2 hours. You
can also use canned kidney beans.

*P*olenta is a popular northern Italian dish made from corn grits or cornmeal. You can spoon out the warm polenta and eat it directly, almost as a porridge. Or you can put it into a mold, allow it to set, and then slice it. With plain polenta, the slices may be grilled, but you can also enjoy the cold sliced polenta without further cooking.

Heat the oil in a large saucepan. Sauté the carrots, onions, celery, and garlic, along with the salt, pepper, and basil, for about 8 minutes. Cut the stewed tomatoes into small pieces and add them to the vegetables, along with the 4 cups of water. Bring to a simmer. Then add the corn grits and kidney beans and mix well. Cook for about 20 minutes, stirring occasionally to prevent burning. (The polenta may take longer than 20 minutes to cook. Check by tasting. It should have a soft, gritty texture.)

Lightly oil a 2 quart mold and press the polenta into it, working out any air pockets. Smooth out the surface and allow it to cool to room temperature. Refrigerate the mold un-

til it is cold. Then unmold the polenta onto a tray, garnish it, and serve it in slices.

Note: If you are using cornmeal instead of corn grits, it is best to soak the cornmeal separately, in 2 cups of cold water; add the remaining 2 cups of water to the vegetables and then combine the two mixtures.

VARIATION: *Millet Polenta*
Use 2 cups of millet and 5 cups of water in place of the corn grits and the 4 cups of water.

American Loaf

YIELD: *1 loaf; 8 servings*
TIME: *30 minutes preparation; 1½ hours cooking*

1¼ cups Job's tears
2¾ cups water
1¼ teaspoons sea salt
2 tablespoons corn oil, or olive oil
1 cup whole-kernel corn
¾ cup diced onions
2 teaspoons minced garlic
¾ cup peeled, julienned carrots
4 packed teaspoons chopped cilantro
1 teaspoon chopped basil (or ½ teaspoon dried basil)
1¼ teaspoons sea salt
¼ teaspoon black pepper

*J*ob's tears are a type of grain similar to pearl barley. You could use barley in place of the Job's tears, but the flavor of this special grain is much better than that of barley.

Because this loaf is time-consuming to make, it isn't an everyday meal. Save it for a special occasion. The cilantro gives this loaf a wonderful flavor.

Combine the Job's tears, 2¾ cups of water, and ¼ teaspoon salt. Cook in a covered pot over medium heat until done (about 30 minutes); they should be soft.

Heat the oil in a saucepan. Sauté the corn, onions, garlic, and carrots, along with the seasonings and the remaining 1 teaspoon of salt, for about 6 minutes. Remove from heat and allow the vegetables to cool slightly. Add the cooked Job's tears to the vegetable mixture and let stand.

Put the tofu, arrowroot, agar flakes, and ¼ cup of water in a food processor and process until the mixture is smooth. Add this tofu mixture to the vegetables and Job's tears.

Make the Spinach Tofu Pâté according to the directions on page 242. However, omit the nutritional yeast and add 2 tablespoons of arrowroot.

¾ *pound firm or extra firm silken tofu*
¼ *cup arrowroot*
3 *tablespoons agar flakes*
¼ *cup water*
Spinach Tofu Pâté (page 242; see directions below for recipe alterations)

Line a large loaf pan with a baking sheet liner and oil the liner. Press a ½-inch layer of the pâté onto all sides of the pan. Lightly press the center full with the vegetable and Job's tears mixture. Top the loaf with the remaining pâté. Cover with an oiled sheet of baking liner. Bake the loaf in a water bath at 425 degrees F for about 75 minutes. Allow the loaf to cool slightly; then remove it from the pan, unwrap it, and cut it into 1-inch slices. Serve with a sauce of your choice.

Quinoa Loaf

YIELD: *1 loaf; 6 servings*
TIME: *30 minutes preparation; 45 minutes baking*

1½ *cups quinoa*
3 *cups water*
½ *teaspoon sea salt*
2 *tablespoons olive oil*
2 *cups finely diced celery*
½ *cup finely diced fennel*
1 *cup finely diced onions*
4 *teaspoons minced garlic*
½ *cup finely diced red bell pepper*
1 *teaspoon sea salt*
2 *teaspoons dried marjoram*
½ *teaspoon cardamom*
4 *tablespoons sesame seeds*
1½ *cups cooked pinto beans*
4 *tablespoons tahini*
4 *tablespoons stone-ground whole wheat flour*
4 *tablespoons gluten flour*

S erve slices of this loaf with a vegetable side dish and perhaps a leafy green salad. You may also wish to serve it with a sauce, such as Tahini Lemon, Carrot, or Tomato Sauces (see pages 159–160).

Place the quinoa in a medium saucepan along with the water and ½ teaspoon salt. Bring to a simmer and cook, covered, until all the water has evaporated (about 15 minutes). Set aside.

Heat the oil in a medium saucepan. Sauté the celery, fennel, onions, garlic, and bell pepper, along with the salt, marjoram, and cardamom, for about 5 minutes. Stir occasionally to prevent burning. Add the cooked quinoa and the sesame seeds, pinto beans, and tahini to the sautéed vegetables. Blend the ingredients.

Mix the two flours together and blend into the vegetable and quinoa mixture. Line a large loaf pan with a baking sheet liner and lightly oil the liner. (In lieu of the baking sheet liner, you could just oil and flour the pan.) Press the mixture into the pan. Bake at 400 degrees F for about 45 minutes. (The loaf should reach an internal temperature of 180–200 degrees F.) Let the loaf cool, inverted, for 10 minutes before removing it from the pan. Serve the loaf in slices.

Polish Pierogi

YIELD: *8 servings*
TIME: *70 minutes preparation; 20 minutes cooking*

1 tablespoon warm liquid lecithin
2 cups stone-ground whole wheat flour
1 cup unbleached flour
1 teaspoon sea salt
1 teaspoon cider vinegar
10½ ounces firm silken tofu
½ cup water
pierogi filling (see recipes below)
Vegan Sour Cream (page 90)

I was raised in a Polish household and have eaten pierogi all my life. I decided that this national dish of Poland needed to go through a nutritional metamorphosis. My family members, who are my best food critics, love this recipe. I would like to dedicate this recipe to the memory of my beloved mother, Sophie.

Warm the lecithin by placing the bottle in simmering water on the stove until the lecithin is runny. Stir the lecithin into the flours and the salt, and set aside.

Blend the vinegar, tofu, and water until smooth. Combine this with the flour mixture, stirring or handling until the dough has a medium-stiff consistency.

Roll out the dough on a floured board, forming a 12″×6″ rectangle, about ³⁄₁₆-inch thick. Cut into 8 equal pieces, about 3″×3″ each. (Rolling the dough a little thinner will yield an additional 3 pieces.) Place about 1½ tablespoons of filling on one half of each piece. Wet the edges of the dough. Stretch one corner of the piece to meet the opposite corner, forming a triangle, and press the edges together, sealing the pierogi completely.

Bring water to a simmer in a large pot. Drop the pierogi carefully in the water. Cook the pierogi in the simmering water until they rise to the surface. Remove and drain. At this point, you can wrap the pierogi in plastic wrap, sealing them well, and refrigerate them for later use. They also can be frozen at this point.

To serve the pierogi, sauté them in oil until lightly browned. Serve with Vegan Sour Cream.

Potato Onion Filling

6 medium potatoes, peeled
    and quartered
2 tablespoons smoked yeast
    (optional)
1 teaspoon sea salt
½ teaspoon black pepper
1 tablespoon unrefined corn
    oil (or margarine)
1 cup finely diced onions
5 ounces firm silken tofu

Place the potatoes in a pot of water with a pinch of salt, cover, and cook until tender (about 30 minutes). Drain the cooked potatoes and mash them immediately until they are smooth, using a processor or potato ricer. You should have 4 packed cups of mashed potatoes. Add the yeast, salt, and pepper to the potatoes.

Sauté the onions in the oil until they are translucent. Blend the tofu until smooth, or put it through the potato ricer. Stir the onions and tofu into the mashed potatoes. This filling should keep in the refrigerator for about a week.

Cabbage Garbanzo Filling

2 tablespoons canola oil (or
    corn oil or margarine)
2 cups finely diced cabbage
1 cup finely diced red onions
1 teaspoon caraway seeds
½ teaspoon black pepper
2 teaspoons minced garlic
1 teaspoon sea salt
2 teaspoons smoked yeast
1 cup hot water
½ cup garbanzo flour

Heat the oil in a large skillet. Add the cabbage, onions, and all seasonings. Cook for about 5 minutes, stirring constantly. Add the water and flour to the mixture and cook until thickened. If necessary, add more garbanzo flour, a tablespoon at a time. This filling should keep in the refrigerator for about a week.

Pasta Primavera

YIELD: *6 servings*
TIME: *40 to 45 minutes*

6 tablespoons olive oil
1 cup diced onions
1½ tablespoons minced garlic
½ cup diced red bell peppers
½ cup chopped scallions
3 tablespoons chopped basil,
*   packed (or 1 tablespoon*
*   dried basil)*
6 tablespoons unbleached
*   flour*
1 quart soy milk
¾ cup puréed butternut or
*   other squash (optional)*
3 tablespoons nutritional
*   yeast*
1 tablespoon salt
½ teaspoon black pepper
½ to 1 teaspoon ground
*   fennel seeds (optional)*
1 cup sliced mushrooms
1 cup thinly sliced celery, cut
*   on the diagonal*
1 cup sliced carrots, steamed
6 cups cooked pasta
chives and tomatoes, for
*   garnish*

This dish is rich enough to make you believe you are eating the original buttery, creamy pasta dish. The vegetable sauce is also superb over baked potatoes instead of pasta.

Heat the oil in a medium saucepan. Sauté the onions, garlic, bell peppers, scallions, and basil for 5 minutes, stirring constantly. Add the flour. Then gradually add the soy milk, continuing to stir, to create a smooth cream sauce. Also add the squash, if you wish. Cook for 5 minutes longer on a low heat.

Add the yeast, salt, pepper, and ground fennel (if you wish) and mix well. Then stir the mushrooms, celery, and steamed carrots into the sauce. Cook for 3 to 5 minutes over low heat. Spoon the vegetable sauce over prepared pasta and garnish with chopped chives and a tomato-peel rose on each plate.

VARIATION
Substitute cooked couscous for the pasta.

Herb Cream on Soba Pasta

YIELD: *4 to 6 servings*
TIME: *25 to 30 minutes*

4 tablespoons olive oil
1 cup peeled and julienned
  carrots
½ cup chopped cilantro
1 cup sliced scallions
4 cups chopped cauliflower
4 cups chopped broccoli
4½ cups soy milk
1 teaspoon salt
½ teaspoon black pepper
½ cup cornstarch
½ cup chopped watercress
6 cups cooked soba pasta

While visiting my family in Petosky, Michigan, I received some fresh watercress and cilantro. I wanted to create a special pasta dish for my family; this recipe is the result. It is a unique and delightful pasta entrée with a superb flavor.

Heat the oil in a large saucepan. Sauté the carrots, cilantro, and scallions for 2 minutes. Add the cauliflower and broccoli and sauté for 4 to 5 minutes, stirring constantly. To the vegetables, add 4 cups of soy milk and the salt and pepper. Bring to a simmer.

Mix the remaining ½ cup soy milk and the cornstarch together until smooth. Add it to the vegetables to create a smooth sauce.

Stir the chopped watercress into the sauce and set aside for 2 minutes. Spoon the sauce over the pasta and serve immediately.

Fettuccine with Creamy Squash Sauce

YIELD: *6 servings*
TIME: *25 to 35 minutes*

*1 medium butternut squash,
  peeled, diced, and steamed
  (3 cups)*
2 cups soy milk
*2 tablespoons arrowroot (or
  cornstarch)*
3 tablespoons olive oil
*1 cup thinly sliced celery, cut
  on the diagonal*
*½ cup peeled and thinly sliced
  carrots, cut on the diagonal*
2 cups diced onions
2 teaspoons dried rosemary
1 tablespoon dried savory
1 tablespoon minced garlic
1½ teaspoons sea salt
*2 tablespoons chopped basil
  (or 2 teaspoons dried basil)*
*6 cups cooked pasta (whole
  wheat fettuccine is
  especially good)*

*T*he squash in the sauce adds richness without any fat. It also adds a sweetness that can be balanced with a little salt.

Blend the steamed squash with the soy milk and the arrowroot or cornstarch until smooth. Set aside.

Heat the oil in a saucepan. Sauté the celery, carrots, onions, and seasonings for about 5 minutes. Add the squash mixture and continue cooking, stirring constantly until the sauce has thickened. Spoon the sauce over the cooked pasta.

VARIATION

Substitute 1½ cups broccoli florets for the celery and 1 cup quartered mushrooms for the carrots. Or you may wish to use these vegetables in addition to the celery and carrots.

Alsatian Onion Pie

YIELD: *One 10-inch pie; 6 servings*
TIME: *30 minutes preparation; 30 minutes baking*

2 tablespoons oil (preferably corn oil)
3 large onions, finely diced
1 cup soy milk
⅓ cup firm tofu, crushed by hand
1½ teaspoons sea salt
¼ teaspoon black pepper
⅛ teaspoon ground nutmeg
2 tablespoons unbleached flour
1 tablespoon couscous
1 whole wheat pie shell in a 10-inch tart pan

Jean-Marie Martz was raised in Alsace, in the northeast of France, and it was Jean-Marie who brought the dairy version of this recipe to my attention. This nondairy version is splendid, too. Because it is so delicate, it actually resembles a dairy vegetable pie. It has been a success in every place I have served it, and it is very easy to prepare.

Sauté the onions in oil until translucent, stirring occasionally. Blend the soy milk, tofu, salt, pepper, nutmeg, and flour until smooth. Then combine the onions, the soy milk mixture, and the couscous. Pour into the prepared 10-inch pie shell. Bake in a preheated oven at 350 degrees F for about 30 minutes.

Onions were grown by farmers in the Middle East as much as 5,000 years ago. Because the layers of the onion form a sphere within a sphere, the Egyptians revered the onion as a symbol of eternity. Our word onion *actually comes from the Latin word* unis, *meaning "unity of many things in one."*

Tofu Spinach Pie

YIELD: *One 10-inch pie; 6 servings*

TIME: *30 minutes preparation; 35 to 45 minutes baking*

whole wheat pie dough for one double-crusted pie (see page 225)

6 cups chopped fresh spinach (or one 10-ounce package frozen spinach—thawed, squeezed dry, and chopped)

2 to 4 tablespoons sesame oil (or olive oil)

3 cups diced onions

1 tablespoon minced garlic

1 cup sliced mushrooms

2 tablespoons chopped parsley (or 1 tablespoon dried parsley)

2½ teaspoons dill weed

2 tablespoons chopped basil (or 1 tablespoon dried basil)

2 teaspoons sea salt

4 cups (2 pounds) firm tofu or extra firm silken tofu

2 tablespoons arrowroot dissolved in 1 tablespoon water

¼ cup barley malt syrup (optional)

Roll out half of the pie dough and prepare the bottom crust in a 10-inch pie pan. Then roll out the top crust. Set aside.

If you are using fresh spinach, steam or sauté the spinach for about 5 minutes.

Heat the oil in a large saucepan. Sauté the onions, garlic, mushrooms, and seasonings until the onions are semi-transparent. Then add the spinach and allow it to cook down for 3 to 5 minutes.

Rinse the tofu and mash it. Add it to the vegetables and continue cooking until the tofu is heated through. Then add the dissolved arrowroot.

Pour the filling into the pie shell. Place the top crust over the filling and seal the edges. Bake in a preheated oven at 350 degrees F for 35 minutes. (When the pie has baked for about 20 minutes, you can glaze the top crust with a mixture of ¼ cup barley malt syrup and 2 tablespoons water. Just lightly glaze the crust and return the pie to the oven. The glaze will make the crust shiny and brown.) Serve the pie hot.

VARIATION

You can also prepare this pie open-faced, with only a single crust. In this case, brush the top with a little oil immediately after baking; this will give the top a fresh glossy look.

Auberge Hanfield Pie

YIELD: *Two small (8- or 9-inch) pies or one large (11- or 12-inch) pie*
TIME: *70 minutes (if the Soysage is made already)*

2 tablespoons olive oil
3 cups peeled and finely diced potatoes
2 cups peeled and finely diced onions
1 cup peeled and finely chopped broccoli stems
1 teaspoon minced garlic
½ teaspoon cinnamon
1 teaspoon allspice
½ teaspoon black pepper
½ teaspoon sea salt
2 cups Soysage (page 105)
2 cups firm tofu or extra firm silken tofu, crushed by hand
whole wheat pie dough for two double-crusted pies
¼ cup barley malt syrup or honey (optional)

*T*his pie has a delicious soybean "sausage" and potato filling. Because it is time-consuming to prepare, you may want to save it for special occasions such as holidays. As a main course, this savory pie is typical of French country cuisine.

The word *auberge* implies more than its literal translation of "country inn." Unlike most rural inns, which can be rustic, the French auberge brings the sophistication of city life to a country setting. The auberges of France are run by some of the world's top chefs.

This recipe can be used in making smaller pies for individual servings and also appetizers. The recipe will yield sixteen 6-inch pies or 56 tiny appetizer pies of 3½ inches.

Heat the oil in a large frying pan. Sauté the potatoes, onions, broccoli, and garlic for a few minutes. Add the seasonings and continue cooking for a few minutes, stirring constantly. Finally, add the Soysage and tofu and cook until the mixture is hot, stirring constantly.

Roll out half of the dough and prepare the bottom crust for each of two small pies (or one large pie). Put 3 cups of filling in each pie pan (about 6 cups for a large pie). Roll out the top crusts and place them over the pies. Seal the edges of the top and bottom crusts, wetting the edges first with water. Bake in a preheated oven at 400 degrees F for 40 minutes or until the top crusts are browned. (When the pie has baked for about 30 minutes, you can glaze the top crust with a mixture of ¼ cup barley malt syrup or honey and 2 tablespoons water. Just lightly glaze the crust and return the pie to the oven. The glaze will make the crust shiny and brown.)

VARIATION
You may prefer to add a bread crumb topping to the pie instead of a top crust. Prepare the topping by lightly mixing ½ cup whole wheat bread crumbs and ¼ cup oil. Sprinkle it over the pie filling and bake the pie according to the recipe.

Russian Vegetable Pie

YIELD: *One 9-inch pie; 6 servings*
TIME: *40 minutes preparation; 30 to 40 minutes baking*

whole wheat pie dough for
    one single-crusted pie
¼ pound fresh mushrooms
3 tablespoons canola oil
1 cup chopped onions
1 cup shredded green cabbage
1 cup peeled and thinly sliced
    broccoli stems
1 cup peeled and thinly sliced
    carrots
1 teaspoon ground caraway
    seeds
2 teaspoons chopped basil
½ teaspoon sea salt
¼ teaspoon black pepper
¼ cup white wine
¼ cup whole wheat flour
1 finely chopped scallion
1 cup Tofu "Cottage Cheese"
    (page 89), or tofu ricotta
    cheese
¾ cup (10.5-ounce package)
    soft silken tofu, puréed
paprika, preferably
    Hungarian

Roll out the pie dough and line the bottom of a 9-inch pie pan. Set aside.

Remove the mushroom caps from the stems and set aside the caps. Chop the stems into fine pieces.

Heat 2 tablespoons of oil in a large saucepan. Sauté the onions, cabbage, broccoli, and carrots until tender. Add the caraway seeds, basil, salt, pepper, wine, and flour. Combine the ingredients well and remove from heat. Add the chopped scallion.

Spread the Tofu "Cottage Cheese" or ricotta cheese in the bottom of the pie shell. Spoon the vegetable filling over this layer. Spread the puréed silken tofu on top.

Sauté the mushroom caps in the remaining 1 tablespoon of oil for a few minutes. Arrange these mushroom caps evenly on top of the pie. Dust with paprika. Bake at 350 degrees F for 30 to 40 minutes. Allow the pie to stand for 10 minutes before cutting, but serve while still hot.

Focaccia

YIELD: *One 12-inch round; 6 servings*
TIME: *70 minutes preparation; 20 minutes baking*

¼ ounce (1 package) dry yeast
1¼ cups warm water
1 teaspoon brown rice syrup (or ½ teaspoon honey)
1½ cups stone-ground whole wheat flour
1¼ cups unbleached flour
¾ teaspoon sea salt
about ⅓ cup olive oil
cornmeal
4 cloves garlic
salt and pepper
1½ cups sliced mushrooms
1 cup sliced red onions
1 tablespoon chopped thyme (or 1 teaspoon dried thyme)

*F*ocaccia is the mother of pizza and generally has a few herbs and perhaps vegetables. Actually, pizza as we know it today could not have existed in Europe before the sixteenth century, when the tomato was introduced from South America. Even then, the tomato was held in low esteem by most Europeans.

Dissolve the yeast in the warm water, along with the rice syrup or honey. Let stand until the yeast starts to foam (10 to 15 minutes).

Combine the flours and salt in a bowl. Add 2 tablespoons of olive oil and knead together on a lightly floured surface until the dough is smooth and elastic (7 to 10 minutes). Put the dough into an oiled bowl and cover loosely with a towel (or lightly oil the surface of the dough). Let the dough rise in a warm, draft-free place until it has doubled in volume and an indentation remains when you press it gently (about 1½ hours). While you are waiting for the dough to rise, you can roast the garlic.

Toss the garlic cloves with a little olive oil, salt, and pepper. Spread them on a baking sheet and roast them in a preheated oven at 350 degrees F until they are soft (about 45 minutes). Cool. Remove the skins and slice the cloves.

When the dough has risen, roll it out to form a 12-inch round. Sprinkle cornmeal into a pizza tin or on a baking sheet. Carefully slide the pizza tin or baking sheet under the dough. Pinch up the edges and brush the surface with 2 to 3 tablespoons of olive oil.

Sauté the mushrooms and onions in 1 tablespoon of olive oil for 3 to 5 minutes. The vegetables should still be crisp. Sprinkle the vegetables, garlic, and thyme evenly over the dough and bake in a preheated oven at 375 degrees F for 15 to 20 minutes or until golden brown. (If you are using a roasting oven, use the bottom rack.)

Renaissance Pizza

YIELD: *2 pizzas, each about 16" × 10"*
TIME: *90 minutes*

Sauce

2 cups peeled and grated carrots
1 cup finely diced onions
2 tablespoons minced garlic
½ cup finely diced celery
2 tablespoons olive oil
1½ teaspoons sea salt
¼ teaspoon white pepper
1 tablespoon chopped basil
1 tablespoon oregano (or 1 teaspoon dried oregano)
1 tablespoon parsley (or 1 teaspoon dried parsley)
pinch of black pepper
1½ teaspoons honey or other sweetener
6 cups tomato purée

Dough

3 packages (¾ ounce) dry yeast
2½ cups warm water
1 tablespoon brown rice syrup (or Sucanat or other sweetener)

*I*n all, Americans eat about 75 acres of pizza a day! By fast-food standards, it is one of the most healthful fast foods available. The key to an even more healthful pizza is to eliminate the cheese and other high-fat, high-cholesterol toppings. I developed this recipe while I was executive chef of a restaurant in Milwaukee.

Sauce

Sauté the carrots, onions, garlic, and celery in the oil for about 5 minutes. Add the seasonings and continue to sauté for another 5 minutes. Then add the honey. Add the tomato purée and simmer for 1 to 2 hours. (This recipe should yield about 7 cups of sauce.)

Dough

Dissolve the yeast in ½ cup of warm water, along with the rice syrup. Let stand until the yeast starts to foam (10 to 15 minutes).

Mix the two flours together. Then combine the yeast mixture and the flours. Add the oil, salt, and remaining 2 cups of warm water. Knead by hand or use the dough hook on a food processor to make a medium-stiff dough. (If the dough is too stiff, add more water.)

Divide the dough into two even pieces. Lightly oil two large, rectangular pans and sprinkle them with cornmeal. Roll out each piece of dough to an even, rectangular shape to fit the pan. Let the dough rise. Prebake the pizzas for 5 minutes at 350 degrees F or until the gluten sets (that is, until the dough springs back). Remove from oven.

2¾ cups pastry flour
2¾ cups unbleached flour
2 tablespoons olive oil
1 teaspoon sea salt
cornmeal

Spice Mix

2 tablespoons dried basil
2 tablespoons dried oregano
2 tablespoons dried parsley
½ teaspoon garlic powder
½ teaspoon black pepper

Vegetable Topping

3 cups halved and sliced
    onions
2 cups thickly sliced
    mushrooms
2 cups broccoli stems and
    florets
2 cups cauliflower pieces
4 tablespoons olive oil

½ recipe pizza dough
1 cup pizza sauce
1 cup shredded soy cheese
1 cup cooked Italian Soysage
    (page 108)

Spice Mix

Mix the spices together until well blended.

Vegetable Topping

Mix the vegetables together. Sauté them for 4 to 5 minutes in the oil. (The broccoli should be bright green in color.) Remove from heat and transfer to a second pan if you are not using them immediately. This recipe should yield about 6 cups of vegetable topping.

Assembling the Pizza

On each pizza, spread about 1½ cups of pizza sauce, add about 3 cups of vegetable topping, sprinkle 2 teaspoons of pizza spice mix over the sauce, and spread about 1 cup of shredded soy cheese if you wish. Bake at 375 degrees F for about 10 minutes, until the pizza is hot and the cheese is melted. (If the ingredients are cold when you assemble the pizza, it will take longer to bake.)

Note: Keep in mind that soy cheese is high in fat, although not a saturated fat. Therefore, it should be used with prudence.

VARIATION: *Mini Sicilian Pizzas*
Prepare the pizza dough. Pat it into 6-inch rounds, about 1 inch thick. Pinch the edges up so they are a little higher than the middle. Place the pizzas on a baking sheet. (You should have 3 mini pizzas.) Spread the sauce over each pizza and sprinkle on the soy cheese. Then crumble the Soysage over the pizzas. Bake as directed in the recipe above.

Calzones

YIELD: *Eighteen 6-inch calzones*
TIME: *75 minutes preparation; 20 minutes baking*

3½ cups stone-ground whole wheat flour
¼ cup oil
1½ teaspoons salt
1 tablespoon honey
1 cup water
calzone filling

Filling

¼ cup olive oil
½ cup finely chopped parsley
2 cups finely chopped onions
1 cup peeled and grated carrots
1 cup sliced mushrooms
1 cup diced celery
1 quart chopped fresh spinach (optional)
2 teaspoons sea salt
4 teaspoons minced garlic
1 teaspoon dried oregano
1 teaspoon dried basil
1 teaspoon ground fennel seeds
1 teaspoon ground rosemary
¼ cup nutritional yeast
1 teaspoon black pepper
4 cups mashed tofu
1 cup okara (or couscous)
½ cup water
2 tablespoons whole wheat flour

*T*hese vegan calzones are delicious and also freeze well. Smaller calzones—perhaps 3 inches in diameter—make wonderful appetizers, too.

Mix the flour and oil until crumbly. Dissolve the salt and honey in the water. Then combine the flour mixture and the sweetened water and mix to form a dough. Roll out the dough on a floured board and cut out 6-inch rounds. Then roll out the dough scraps and cut out an equal number of 5-inch rounds. Place ⅓ cup filling on each 6-inch piece, wet the edges, place a 5-inch round on top, and crimp the edges together with a fork. Bake at 350 degrees F for 15 to 20 minutes, or until light brown. Serve while hot. You may wish to serve them with a light tomato sauce, one that is not too spicy.

Filling

Heat the oil in a large saucepan. Sauté the parsley, onions, carrots, mushrooms, celery, and spinach (if you wish), along with the seasonings, for about 7 minutes. Add the tofu, okara or couscous, water, and flour, and continue to cook 4 to 5 minutes longer. Remove from heat and cool.

Lebanese Lemon Bake

YIELD: *6 servings*

TIME: *20 minutes preparation (allow several hours to soak the garbanzo beans and 3 hours to cook them); 20 minutes baking*

1⅓ *cups dried garbanzo beans*
5 *cups water*
2 *tablespoons olive oil*
2 *cups diced onions*
2 *cups peeled and diced carrots*
4 *teaspoons minced garlic*
1 *teaspoon salt*
½ *teaspoon black pepper*
1 *tablespoon Vogue Vegy Base*
1 *tablespoon whole rosemary*
4 *teaspoons dried oregano*
2 *cups peeled and diced eggplant*
4 *cups chopped fresh spinach*
2 *tablespoons fresh lemon juice*
2 *tablespoons arrowroot dissolved in 2 tablespoons water*

*T*o make this dish in a hurry, use canned garbanzo beans. This casserole is excellent served with the Tahini Lemon Sauce (page 165).

Soak the garbanzo beans in water for several hours. Discard the water and cook in about 5 cups of fresh water for 3 hours.

Heat the oil in a large saucepan. Sauté the onions, carrots, and garlic, along with the seasonings, for a few minutes. When the onions become translucent, add the eggplant. Then add the spinach and lemon juice, and continue to cook for 3 to 5 minutes. Stir in the dissolved arrowroot. Then add the cooked garbanzo beans.

Oil a shallow 8″×10″ baking dish. Pour the garbanzo bean mixture into the baking dish and bake at 325 degrees F for 20 minutes. Serve hot over a brown rice pilaf.

Greek Moussaka

YIELD: *6 servings*
TIME: *1½ hours preparation (allow several hours to soak the beans); 40 minutes baking*

¾ cup dried aduki beans
2 teaspoons brown rice vinegar
1 piece of kombu, 2 inches long
about 1 tablespoon sea salt
1 cup long-grain brown rice
1 large eggplant
4 tablespoons gluten flour
¾ cup whole wheat flour
2 tablespoons dried oregano
4 teaspoons dried basil
2 teaspoons garlic powder
½ teaspoon white pepper
1 cup whole wheat bread crumbs
½ cup olive oil (or sesame oil)
1 cup tomato sauce
2 teaspoons dried marjoram
Moussaka Topping (recipe follows)

Wash the beans and soak them for several hours. Discard the water. Cook the beans in 2 cups of fresh water, along with the brown rice vinegar and kombu. After the beans have cooked for 40 minutes, add ½ teaspoon salt and continue cooking 20 minutes longer. If the water evaporates before the beans are cooked, add more water sparingly. Meanwhile, cook the rice.

Wash the rice. Cook it in a covered pot with 2 cups water and a pinch of salt for about 45 minutes.

Cut the eggplant into about 12 slices, each ⅜-inch thick. Prepare the eggplant breading mixture by combining the flours, 4 teaspoons oregano, 2 teaspoons salt, as well as the basil, garlic, and pepper. Pour about 3 cups of water in a bowl. Put the bread crumbs into a third bowl. Dip the eggplant into the water, drain for a few seconds, and dip it into the breading mixture. Dip it back into the water very quickly again; then dip it into the bread crumbs. (You probably will use only one fourth of the breading mixture.)

Heat the oil in a skillet and fry the eggplant slices on both sides until golden brown. Set aside.

Combine 2 cups of the cooked rice and 2 cups of the cooked beans with the tomato sauce, marjoram, 2 teaspoons of oregano, and ½ teaspoon salt.

Assemble the moussaka as follows: Lightly oil an 8″ × 11″ baking dish; place half of the rice and bean mixture in the bottom of the dish; layer six eggplant slices on top. Repeat the layers of rice and bean mixture and eggplant slices. Spread the topping over the eggplant slices. Bake, covered, at 400 degrees F for 40 minutes. You may wish to brown the top under a broiler for about 20 seconds.

Moussaka Topping

½ cup tofu, crushed by hand
½ cup nutritional yeast
½ cup water
¼ cup oil
½ teaspoon sea salt
½ teaspoon garlic powder
⅛ teaspoon white pepper
1 tablespoon arrowroot
   (optional)

Blend all of the ingredients together until smooth.

Mushroom Moussaka

YIELD: *8 to 10 servings*
TIME: *90 minutes*

½ cup garbanzo flour
1 teaspoon garlic powder
4 teaspoons dried oregano
1 tablespoon sea salt
1¼ cups unbleached flour
1 tablespoon gluten flour
1 medium or large eggplant
cooking oil for sautéing or
   broiling the eggplant
2 cups cashew nuts
1 tablespoon dried basil
1¾ teaspoons black pepper
2 tablespoons minced garlic
1 tablespoon olive oil (or
   sesame oil)
1 quart sliced fresh
   mushrooms
2 cups sliced onions
1 cup bulgur

*B*ecause this dish is time-consuming to make, you may want to save it for a special occasion. The Lemon Cream Dressing (page 92) complements this moussaka quite well.

Mix the garbanzo flour, garlic powder, 1 teaspoon oregano, and ½ teaspoon salt. Set aside.

Mix ¼ cup unbleached flour with the gluten flour and ½ teaspoon salt. Set aside.

Slice the eggplant into ¼-inch slices; you should get about 24 slices. Pour 1½ cups of water into a bowl. Dip the eggplant into the gluten flour mixture, then into the water, and finally into the garbanzo flour mixture. Broil or sauté the eggplant slices on both sides. (If you are broiling them, lightly oil a baking sheet to prevent the eggplant from sticking; if you are sautéing them, use only a small amount of oil and a fairly high heat.) Set aside.

Blend the cashews and 1 cup of water into a smooth cream. Add 2 cups more water, the basil, 1 teaspoon pepper, 1 teaspoon salt, and 1 tablespoon each of oregano and minced garlic. Then bring these ingredients to a simmer, stirring constantly.

Mix the remaining cup of flour with 1 cup of water. Add this to the cashew mixture and cook until the sauce thickens. Set aside.

Heat 1 tablespoon of olive oil in a saucepan. Sauté the mushrooms, onions, and remaining tablespoon of garlic, teaspoon of salt, and ¾ teaspoon of pepper. Cook until the vegetables are soft. Add the vegetables to the cashew sauce and set aside.

Bring 2 cups of water to a simmer and add the bulgur. Cook, covered, for 5 minutes. Uncover and let stand. (The bulgur should be cooked and dry; there should be no excess moisture in the pan.)

Lightly oil a baking dish. Spread the bulgur evenly on the bottom of the dish. Pour 2 cups of sauce over the bulgur. Layer half of the eggplant on the sauce. Add 1½ cups of sauce and layer the remaining eggplant slices. Finally, add another 1½ cups of sauce. (You should have plenty of sauce left over.) Bake the moussaka at 350 degrees F for about 1 hour. Serve with a rice pilaf.

Hungarian Cabbage Rolls

YIELD: *8 rolls; 8 servings*
TIME: *15 to 20 minutes preparation; 30 minutes baking*

8 large cabbage leaves, with no holes in them
pinch of salt
1 cup bulgar
1 cup sunflower seeds or walnut pieces
1 tablespoon unrefined corn oil
1 cup diced onions
1 cup peeled and diced carrots
1 tablespoon minced garlic
¾ teaspoon ground thyme
1 tablespoon dried basil
2 teaspoons paprika
2 tablespoons white miso, dissolved in 2 tablespoons water
3 tablespoons tamari

Cabbage rolls are a common Slovak dish. Usually they are filled with meat, vegetables, and grains. My "friendly foods" approach uses nuts, seeds, and beans in place of meat. A vegetable side dish of carrots with dill makes an excellent ethnic complement to these cabbage rolls.

Blanch the cabbage leaves in boiling water for 3 to 5 minutes or until they are soft but not cooked completely. (As an option, you could freeze the cabbage leaves overnight and let them thaw the next morning; the result is the same as blanching.) Set aside.

Bring to a boil 2 cups of water with a pinch of salt. Stir in the bulgar, cover, and simmer 4 to 5 minutes. Remove from heat and let stand about 15 minutes.

Roast the sunflower seeds or walnut pieces at 350 degrees F for about 10 minutes, or until they are lightly browned.

Heat the oil in a saucepan. Sauté the onions, carrots, garlic, and spices for 5 minutes, stirring constantly. Add the miso and tamari. Stir in the roasted seeds or nuts and the bulgar.

Roll each cabbage leaf as follows: Place ½ cup filling at the top of the leaf and make one roll down the leaf while pressing firmly; roll the sides into the center and continue rolling the leaf downward at least one more time.

Oil an 8-inch square baking dish and place the cabbage rolls in the pan, seam down. Pour 1 cup of water over the cabbage rolls and cover the dish with foil. Bake at 350 degrees F for 30 minutes. Serve hot with a sauce of your choice. The Dill Sauce (page 163) complements cabbage rolls nicely.

Chinese Spring Rolls

YIELD: *10 rolls; 5 servings*
TIME: *45 minutes*

*2 tablespoons roasted sesame
oil*
1 cup finely diced onions
*1 cup chopped fresh bean
sprouts*
*1 cup finely chopped
mushrooms*
*1 cup sliced water chestnuts
(15-ounce can)*
*1½ teaspoons Chinese Five
Spices powder*
1 tablespoon minced garlic
1 cup chopped seitan (or tofu)
3 tablespoons tamari
*3 tablespoons arrowroot,
dissolved in 3 tablespoons
water*
*10 spring roll skins (or egg
roll skins)*
*2 tablespoons barley malt
syrup*
*2 to 3 cups cooking oil for
frying (not roasted sesame
oil)*

You can buy the spring roll skins or egg roll skins at any Asian market and at most gourmet specialty food stores. Choose the type of skins that do not contain eggs.

Heat the oil in a large saucepan. Sauté the vegetables and spices. When the vegetables are half-cooked, add the seitan or tofu and tamari, and continue cooking for 4 to 5 minutes. Add the dissolved arrowroot to the vegetables, stirring constantly. When the sauce has thickened, remove from heat.

Brush the edges of each spring roll skin with barley malt syrup. Put some filling in the middle of a skin and roll as shown in the diagram below. Keep the seam facedown.

Heat the cooking oil in a deep skillet or fryer to about 350 degrees F. Dip a metal spoon into the oil; then lift it out and place a spring roll on the spoon, gently settling it in the oil. Repeat until the skillet or fryer is filled with spring rolls. Fry the rolls until they are lightly browned. Drain on paper towels. Serve immediately with a Sweet and Sour Sauce (page 166). Serve with a brown rice pilaf and steamed vegetables.

Sweet and Sour Tempeh

YIELD: *5 servings*
TIME: *20 minutes*
preparation; 20 to 30 minutes
cooking

1 quart apple juice
¼ cup barley malt syrup
¼ cup brown rice syrup (or 3 tablespoons apple juice concentrate)
6 tablespoons cider vinegar
1 tablespoon minced garlic
2 teaspoons grated ginger
1 cup halved and sliced onions
¼ cup arrowroot, dissolved in ¼ cup water
1 cup julienned carrots
1 cup julienned parsnips
1 cup julienned onions
1 cup thinly sliced celery, cut on the diagonal
½ cup sliced red bell pepper
3 tablespoons sesame oil
2 cups tempeh (one 8-ounce piece)
4 tablespoons tamari
½ teaspoon coriander

Combine the apple juice, syrups, vinegar, garlic, ginger, and sliced onions in a saucepan. Cook for 10 minutes over medium heat. Remove from heat and add the dissolved arrowroot, stirring constantly. Return to heat and continue to cook until the sauce has thickened. Set aside.

Sauté the julienned vegetables, celery, and bell pepper in 1 tablespoon of oil for 4 to 5 minutes. Add these to the sauce.

Mix the tempeh, tamari, and coriander gently but thoroughly. Heat the remaining 2 tablespoons of oil in a pan and lightly brown the tempeh. Add it to the sauce. Serve hot, with udon noodles or any pasta of your choice.

Southern Fried Tofu

YIELD: *4 servings*
TIME: *30 to 45 minutes*

1 pound firm tofu
3 tablespoons Vogue Vegy Base
1¼ cups unbleached flour
2 tablespoons gluten flour
1 teaspoon salt
4 tablespoons Spice Blend (see recipe below)
1 tablespoon canola oil (or other oil)
1 cup water
2 cups sesame oil, canola oil (or other oil) for frying
Southern Country Gravy (see recipe next page)

Spice Blend

2 teaspoons whole thyme
2 teaspoons curry powder
2 teaspoons onion powder
2 tablespoons Vogue Vegy Base
4 teaspoons dried parsley
2 teaspoons whole savory
2 teaspoons salt
2 teaspoons garlic powder
2 teaspoons dried basil

Drain and rinse the tofu. Slice it horizontally into two even pieces. Then cut each of these pieces into 8 cubes. Place all 16 cubes in a bowl and add 1 tablespoon soup base. Gently mix well and set aside.

Stir together ½ cup of the unbleached flour and the remaining 2 tablespoons of soup base. Set aside this breading mixture.

Mix the remaining ¾ cup of unbleached flour, gluten flour, salt, and Spice Blend. Blend well so the gluten flour does not create lumps. Stir in the water and 1 tablespoon of canola oil. (If the gluten flour creates lumps, blend the batter in a blender.)

Heat the oil in a deep skillet. Dip a piece of tofu into the breading mixture and coat it completely. Then dip it into the batter, using prongs. Remove and hold it above the batter for about 10 seconds, tapping it gently against the side of the bowl to release excess batter. Then hold about one third of the piece of tofu in the hot oil for about 15 seconds to sear the bottom so it won't stick to the pan. Release the tofu and let it completely submerge. Repeat for the other pieces. Deep-fry the tofu to a light brown. Remove with a slotted spoon and drain on paper towels for 30 seconds. You can place the tofu in the oven at 250 degrees F for up to 15 minutes to retain crispness.

To serve, pour equal portions of the Southern Country Gravy into each plate and set the hot fried tofu into the gravy.

Spice Blend

Mix the spices and herbs together and set aside.

Southern Country Gravy

1 cup diced onions
¾ teaspoon minced garlic
3 tablespoons oil (use the oil
     from frying the tofu)
¼ cup leftover breading
     mixture (from the main
     recipe) or unbleached flour
1½ teaspoons smoked yeast
5 teaspoons Vogue Vegy Base
½ teaspoon salt
⅛ teaspoon black pepper
1 cup water

Sauté the onions and garlic in the oil for 4 to 5 minutes. Stir in the breading mixture, yeast, soup base, salt, and pepper and cook 3 to 4 minutes longer. Add half of the water, whisking it into the onion and flour mixture. When it thickens, add the remaining water, whisking to a light consistency.

Tofu Swiss Steak

YIELD: *4 servings*
TIME: *15 minutes
preparation; 30 minutes
cooking*

2 tablespoons sesame oil (or
     canola oil)
1½ cups sliced fresh
     mushrooms
1 cup halved and sliced onions
1 cup diced green bell peppers
2 tablespoons minced garlic
1 tablespoon chopped basil
¼ cup dark barley miso,
     dissolved in ¼ cup water
2 cups tomato purée

*T*his is one of my favorite everyday foods.

Heat 2 tablespoons of oil in a medium saucepan. Sauté the mushrooms, onions, bell peppers, and garlic with the basil for 5 to 8 minutes. Stir in the dissolved miso. Then add the tomato purée, water, pepper, and fresh tomatoes, if you wish. Simmer for 5 minutes.

Pour the tamari over the tofu pieces, distributing it evenly. Heat the ¼ cup of sesame oil in a skillet. Sauté the tofu on both sides until golden brown.

Place a little sauce in an 8-inch square baking dish, place the tofu on the sauce, and cover with the remaining sauce. Cover the dish and bake at 350 degrees F for 20 to 25 min-

1 cup water
½ teaspoon black pepper
4 tomatoes, blanched, peeled,
    seeded, and chopped
    (optional)
4 to 6 teaspoons tamari
4 pieces of firm tofu, 2 ounces
    each
¼ cup sesame oil

utes. (If the tofu is baked too long, the sauce will evaporate and may not look appetizing; adding more water should solve the problem.)

Serve hot with mashed potatoes and a green vegetable.

VARIATION
Use seitan cut into steak size pieces in place of tofu. Follow the directions in the same manner.

Tempeh Stew

YIELD: *8 servings*
TIME: *35 minutes*

two 10-ounce packages of
    tempeh
½ cup tamari
4 tablespoons sesame oil
2 cups diced onions
¾ cup diced green bell
    peppers and ¾ cup diced
    yellow bell peppers (or 1½
    cups of diced bell pepper of
    either color)
2 tablespoons minced garlic
1 tablespoon ground
    coriander
½ teaspoon black pepper
1 tablespoon tamari
2 cups water
3 cups broccoli florets
3 tablespoons arrowroot,
    dissolved in 3 tablespoons
    water

Cut each piece of tempeh into eight smaller pieces. Pour the ½ cup of tamari into a dipping bowl and marinate the tempeh for 10 minutes. Drain. Heat the oil in a skillet and sauté the tempeh until browned. Remove the tempeh and set aside. In the same skillet, sauté the onions and bell peppers, along with the garlic, coriander, pepper, and remaining tablespoon of tamari, for 4 minutes, stirring constantly.

Bring the water to a simmer. Add the water and broccoli to the other vegetables. Finally, add the dissolved arrowroot, stirring to create a smooth, thick sauce, and add the tempeh. Serve hot with brown rice or any pasta of your choice.

Thanksgiving Day Tofu

YIELD: *1 medium loaf; 4 servings*
TIME: *90 minutes*

1½ pounds tofu
2 tablespoons arrowroot
3 tablespoons Vogue Vegy Base
¾ teaspoon sea salt
¼ teaspoon white pepper
1½ teaspoons agar flakes (or 1 teaspoon agar powder)
Sage Dressing (see recipe below)
2 tablespoons barley malt syrup, dissolved, with 2 tablespoons water

Sage Dressing

½ cup finely diced onions
½ cup finely diced celery
½ cup finely diced carrots
2 cloves garlic, minced
2 tablespoons unrefined corn oil
½ teaspoon ground sage
¼ teaspoon dried basil
3 tablespoons Vogue Vegy Base
1 teaspoon sea salt
⅛ teaspoon black pepper
1 cup water
2 cups cubed dry whole wheat bread

*T*his is a superb substitute for the traditional Thanksgiving turkey. It's also good for other times of the year! It's really the dressing that carries the dish. The corn oil gives it that wonderful buttery taste that poultry dressing usually has.

Wash the tofu, pat it dry, and cut it into small pieces. Put the tofu, arrowroot, soup base, salt, pepper, and agar flakes in a food processor and blend to a smooth paste. Oil and flour the loaf pan (or line it with baking liner paper after oiling). Spread a layer of tofu paste inside the pan, lining the bottom and all four sides. (Spread only a thin layer on the ends.) Use all but about 1 cup of the paste.

Firmly but gently press the dressing into the pan, on top of the tofu paste "liner." Try to avoid displacing the tofu. Cover the dressing with the remaining tofu, carefully sealing the edges. Cover the pan with foil, making certain the foil doesn't come in contact with the tofu. (The tofu will eat into the foil.)

Bake in a preheated oven at 350 degrees F for 30 to 40 minutes. Then remove the foil cover, glaze the top of the loaf with the dissolved barley malt syrup, turn the oven up to 450 degrees F, and continue baking for 10 minutes. Remove from oven and allow the loaf to cool for about 10 minutes. Unmold, slice, and serve hot with a sauce of your choice. The Mushroom Cream Sauce (page 163) would be an excellent choice.

Sage Dressing

Sauté the onions, celery, carrots, and garlic in oil for 5 minutes. Add the sage, basil, soup base, salt, and pepper, and continue cooking 5 minutes longer.

Add the water and bring to a simmer. Stir in the bread crumbs and cook for a few minutes. Then remove from heat.

Tofu Jamaican Run Down Stew

YIELD: *4 servings*
TIME: *25 to 30 minutes; allow
1½ hours to make the sauce*

1 cup diced onions
2 cups (¾ pound) diced firm
   tofu
½ cup water
½ cup diced red bell pepper
½ cup peeled and grated
   carrots
2 teaspoons minced garlic
½ teaspoon sea salt
¼ teaspoon black pepper
1½ cups Run Down Sauce
1 cup diced chayote squash

Run Down Sauce

3 cups unsweetened
   "macaroon" coconut (sold
   in Chinese stores)
3 cups water
1 can (14 ounces) coconut
   milk
2 tablespoons cooking oil,
   preferably sesame oil
2 cups finely diced onions
½ cup diced bell peppers, red
   or green
4 teaspoons minced garlic
½ teaspoon coarsely ground
   black pepper
1½ teaspoons sea salt
1½ teaspoons chopped thyme
half of a small hot pepper,
   seeded and finely chopped

*T*his recipe is dedicated to Anne, Josanne, and Sharain, three lovely women who enlightened me about Jamaican food.

Put all of the ingredients, including the sauce but except the squash, in a saucepan. Simmer for about 15 minutes. Then add the squash and continue cooking until the vegetables are tender-crisp. Serve over rice. You could also serve it over pasta if you wish, although in Jamaica rice would be preferred.

Blend the coconut, water, and coconut milk together until smooth (3 to 5 minutes). Set aside.

Heat the oil in a saucepan. Sauté the vegetables and seasonings over medium heat for 5 minutes, stirring constantly. Add the coconut mixture and cook for 45 minutes to 1 hour.

1 diced chayote squash
1 cup peeled and thickly sliced
    parsnips
¾ cup peeled and thickly
    sliced carrots
1 cup broccoli florets and
    stems, peeled and sliced
2 cups Run Down Sauce

Here is a different version of the Run Down Stew.

Put all of the ingredients except the broccoli in a saucepan. Simmer for 15 minutes, or until the vegetables are almost cooked. Add the broccoli and continue cooking for 5 minutes longer. Serve with rice.

Tofu Paneer

YIELD: *6 servings*
TIME: *20 to 30 minutes; allow
30 minutes to make the
garam masala*

¼ cup unrefined corn oil
1 cup diced onions
2 tablespoons minced garlic
4 teaspoons minced ginger
1½ teaspoons salt
1 teaspoon turmeric
⅛ teaspoon cayenne pepper
2 teaspoons ground coriander
4 teaspoons cilantro
2 tablespoons garam masala
    (see recipe below, or use
    commercially prepared
    spice blend)
one 35-ounce can Italian
    peeled tomatoes
½ pound firm tofu or extra
    firm silken tofu
1½ cups green peas (fresh if
    possible, but frozen will
    suffice)

*M*acrobiotic cooking doesn't subscribe much to the use of spices or herbs, since these ingredients are considered too yin. It also may have something to do with the macrobiotic roots being in Japan. If macrobiotics were founded in Italy instead of Japan, the diet probably would include garlic!

Indian cuisine balances spices in the same way that macrobiotics balances yin and yang foods. Cumin, turmeric, and coriander are the principal spices that are perfectly balanced in Indian food.

Heat the oil in a saucepan. Sauté the onions, garlic, ginger, salt, turmeric, cayenne, coriander, cilantro, and garam masala for about 5 minutes.

Drain the juice from the tomatoes into the sautéed vegetables. Then crush the tomatoes by hand and add them to the vegetables. Dice the tofu into ½-inch cubes and add to the vegetables. Continue to cook for 10 to 15 minutes over low heat. Then add the peas and cook another 4 minutes. Serve hot over brown rice. A coriander coconut chutney (or other chutney) is an excellent accompaniment.

Garam Masala

five 3-inch pieces cinnamon
  stick
1 cup whole cardamom pods
½ cup whole cloves
½ cup whole cumin seeds
½ cup whole black
  peppercorns
¼ cup coriander seeds

Preheat the oven to 200 degrees F. Place the ingredients on a baking sheet and roast for 30 minutes, or until the spices give off an aroma. (Some chefs suggest roasting each ingredient separately, since each gives its characteristic aroma at a different time.)

Separate the cardamom pods from the seeds. Discard the pods. Crush the cinnamon. Combine the cinnamon, cardamom seeds, and other spices until the mixture is powdery. Store in a sealed jar.

Seitan —Method I

YIELD: *14 ounces uncooked;
16 ounces cooked*
TIME: *1 hour preparation; 2
hours cooking*

6 cups stone-ground whole
  wheat bread flour or high-
  gluten unbleached white
  flour
3 cups water (or more,
  depending on the amount
  of gluten in the flour)
½ cup tamari
12 slices fresh ginger, each ⅛
  inch thick
1 piece kombu, about 3 inches
  long

*T*his is the most basic, straightforward method for making seitan. The recipe may seem long, but that is only because the steps are carefully explained. Once you understand the procedure and the practice, the production of seitan will seem less formidable.

To take the work out of making seitan, Brother Ron has developed an instant seitan mix that condenses all the following preparation into about 10 minutes and costs much less than buying prepared seitan. Arrowhead Mills sells this seitan mix at natural food stores across the United States and Canada.

1 Mix the flour and water by hand or in a machine to make a medium-stiff but not sticky dough. 2 Knead the dough by hand on a breadboard or tabletop, until it has the consistency of an earlobe, or by machine until the dough forms a ball that follows the path of the hook around the bowl. You may need to add a little extra water or flour to achieve the desired consistency. Kneading will take about 10 to 12 minutes by hand or about 6 to 8 minutes by machine. 3 Allow the dough to rest in a bowl of cold water for about 10 minutes.

While the dough is resting, prepare the stock. In a large pot, bring to boil 3 quarts of water. Add the tamari, ginger, and kombu, and cook for 15 minutes. Remove from heat and allow to cool. This stock must be cold before it is used. (The cold liquid causes the gluten to contract and prevents the seitan from acquiring a bready texture.) You will be using this stock to cook the seitan later.

4 To wash out the starch, use warm water to begin with. Warm water loosens the dough and makes the task easier. Knead the dough, immersed in water, in the bowl. **5** When the water turns milky, drain it off and refill the bowl with fresh water. In the final rinses, use cold water to tighten the gluten. If you wish, save the bran by straining the water through a fine sieve; the bran will be left behind. Save the starch by allowing the milky water to settle in the bottom of the bowl; slowly pour off the water and collect the starch, which you can use for thickening soups, sauces, and stews.

6 When kneading, remember to work toward the center of the dough so that it does not break into pieces. **7** After about eight changes of water, you will begin to feel the dough become firmer and more elastic. The water will no longer become cloudy as you knead it. **8** To make sure you have kneaded and rinsed it enough, lift the dough out of the water and squeeze it. The liquid oozing out should be clear, not milky.

To shape the seitan, lightly oil a 1-pound loaf pan. Place the rinsed seitan in the pan and let it rest until the dough relaxes. (After the dough has been rinsed for the last time in cold water, the gluten will have tightened and the dough will be tense, tough, and resistant to taking on any other shape.) After it has rested for 10 minutes, it will be much more flexible.

Seitan is cooked in two steps. In the first step, the dough is put into a large pot with about 3 quarts of plain, boiling water. Boil the seitan for about 30 to 45 minutes, or until it floats to the surface. Drain the seitan and cut it into usable pieces (steaks, cutlets, 1-inch chunks, or whatever) or leave whole. Return the seitan to the cold tamari stock. Bring the stock to a boil, lower the temperature, and simmer in the

MAKING
SEITAN
STEP BY STEP

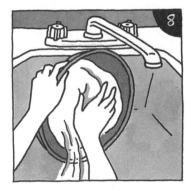

stock for 1½ to 2 hours (45 minutes if the seitan is cut into small pieces). This second cooking step may also be done in a pressure cooker, in which case it would take between 30 and 45 minutes.

To store seitan, keep it refrigerated, immersed in the tamari stock. Seitan will keep indefinitely if it is brought to a boil in the tamari stock and boiled for 10 minutes twice a week. Otherwise, use it within eight or nine days.

VARIATIONS
Instead of boiling the seitan in plain water and then stock, let the seitan drain for a while after it has been rinsed. Slice it and either deep-fry or sauté the slices until both sides are brown. Then cook it in the tamari stock according to the recipe.

Seitan also may be cooked (at the second step) in a broth flavored with carrots, onion, celery, garlic, tamari, and black pepper, which will give it a flavor similar to that of pot roast. Shiitake mushrooms may also be added to the stock.

Seitan —Method II

YIELD: *1¾ pounds uncooked; 2½ pounds cooked*
TIME: *40 to 50 minutes preparation; 3 to 4 hours cooking*

16 cups (5 pounds) white bread flour
6 to 8 cups water, or more
¾ cup tamari
1 onion, peeled and sliced
1 piece kombu, about 4 inches long
¼ cup ginger, sliced (or 2 teaspoons ginger powder)

*T*his recipe yields considerably more seitan, and the flavor of the stock is slightly different. This recipe is enough for about three different seitan dishes.

Mix the flour and water together to make a medium-stiff dough. Knead it until it is elastic when pulled (about 8 to 10 minutes). Allow the dough to rest for about 5 minutes in a bowl of cold water.

Wash out the starch by filling a large bowl (1½ to 2 gallons) with warm water and kneading the dough in it, underwater. When the water turns white (after 1 to 2 minutes), drain it through a strainer, adding the floury residue back to the ball of dough. Keep kneading, washing, and changing the water, until no more starch is given off. This may take as many as eight rinses, about 20 to 25 minutes.

Pour 6 pints of water into a large pot. Add the tamari, onion, kombu, ginger, and dough, and simmer for about 3 hours. (To speed up the cooking, you could cut the dough into small pieces, each about 1½ inches; the pieces would cook in about one hour.) The seitan is properly cooked when it is firm to the touch and when it is firm in the center. You can check by cutting into the seitan. If it is not done, it will feel like raw dough in the center.

Seitan à la Normandie

YIELD: *4 servings*
TIME: *30 minutes preparation; 2 hours baking*

4 cups sliced onions
2 tablespoons minced garlic
2 tablespoons sesame oil (or other cooking oil)
4 pieces seitan, 2 ounces each; fried and simmered (see special note above)
6 tablespoons tamari
4 tablespoons apple juice concentrate
1 cup water
½ cup ground, roasted pecan nuts (optional; the dish is more delicate without it)
3 medium apples, peeled (optional), cored, and thinly sliced
2 tablespoons mirin (or calvados or sherry)

*A*pples add taste and texture to seitan as they do to meat. Apples are also a good source of pectin, a soft, water-soluble fiber. Pectin is found close to the skin, so the apples should not be peeled. For this dish, which is suitable for lunch or dinner, use golden or yellow apples. Red apples may be used, but they are not as decorative.

Special note: This recipe needs uncooked seitan. Cut the seitan into four thin pieces (⅛ to ¼ inch thick), each about 2 ounces. The thinner the better. Fry the seitan in a hot oil until lightly browned and then simmer it in a little water for about 30 minutes before using. If you don't simmer it first, you may need need to add more liquid to the recipe.

Sauté the onions and garlic in the oil until the onions are soft and translucent but not fully cooked.

Place the seitan in an ovenproof baking dish and cover it with tamari, apple juice concentrate, and water. Cover with the sautéed onion mixture and sprinkle the ground pecans over it, if you wish. Fan the apples over the onions and pour the mirin on top. Cover the dish with a tight-fitting lid or aluminum foil, and bake at 300 degrees F for 2 hours. Serve hot.

New England Boiled Dinner

YIELD: *4 servings*
TIME: *1 hour (if seitan is already made)*

1 cup peeled and coarsely grated carrots
2 cups thickly sliced onions
2 potatoes, halved (peeled or unpeeled)
2 cups sliced parsnips (optional)
8 thick slices of seitan (or 1 pound tofu)
8 cups water (or 4 cups seitan water and 4 cups plain water)
¼ cup minced basil (or 4 teaspoons dried basil)
½ teaspoon black pepper
2 tablespoons (or more) minced garlic
1 cup butternut squash, peeled, halved, and cut into ½-inch-thick slices
1½ cups thinly sliced celery, cut on the diagonal
4 wedges of cabbage, each 2 inches wide
2 to 6 tablespoons barley miso
½ cup arrowroot, dissolved in ½ cup water
cucumber slices, fresh parsley, or tomato-peel roses, for garnish

*A*n example of country-style cooking, this dish is called *pot au feu*, or "pot on the fire" in France. The key to this recipe is proper timing in cooking the vegetables. A practical way is to start by cooking those that take the longest time and add the other vegetables in order. As each vegetable is cooked, remove it from the pot and keep it warm until needed.

Cook the carrots, onions, potatoes, parsnips (if you wish), and seitan in the water with the basil, pepper, and garlic. When they are almost cooked, add the squash, celery, and cabbage and cook until these three vegetables are tender-crisp. (As an alternative, stir the squash into the stew and place the cabbage and celery on top of the other ingredients. Cover the pot and let the vegetables steam briefly.) Check the vegetables frequently and remove them promptly when done.

Dissolve the miso into some of the stock, return to the pot, and let simmer for about 5 minutes. To thicken the stock, drain the vegetables and seitan from the stock and set aside. Put the stock over a low heat and add the dissolved arrowroot, stirring constantly to make a smooth sauce.

Divide the seitan and vegetables evenly onto four dinner plates. Pour the sauce evenly over each serving. Garnish with cucumber slices, a sprig of fresh parsley, or a tomato-peel rose.

German Sauerbraten

YIELD: *4 or 5 servings*

TIME: *1 to 2 days marinating;
45 minutes preparation and
cooking*

1 cup chopped carrots
1 cup chopped onions
1 cup chopped celery
4 teaspoons minced garlic
*2 tablespoons unroasted
    sesame oil*
⅛ teaspoon white pepper
2 tablespoons pickling spices
2 cups dry red wine
2 cups water
*¼ cup red wine vinegar or
    cider vinegar*
2 tablespoons tomato paste
2 tablespoons molasses
*1 tablespoon barley malt
    syrup*
3 tablespoons tamari
*1 pound sliced seitan,
    preferably in 2-ounce
    pieces*
*½ cup Vegan Sour Cream
    (page 90)*
roux (see recipe next page)

*I*n this recipe, the flavorings in the marinade need time to fuse together, but the recipe itself is not difficult to put together. In Germany, beef used to come from cows that were too old for milking. The meat was tough and the marinating process made it tender and gave it some added flavor. In this recipe, seitan replaces beef.

Sauté the carrots, onions, celery, and garlic in oil, together with the pepper and pickling spices for about 5 minutes over medium heat. (You *must* use unroasted sesame oil in this recipe.) Add the remaining ingredients (except for the Vegan Sour Cream and roux). Bring to a simmer and cook for about 5 minutes. Let the mixture cool to room temperature, cover, and refrigerate for at least one day.

To assemble the sauerbraten, remove the marinade from the refrigerator, heat it just to warm the seitan (not even to a simmer), and strain the liquid into a saucepan. Make sure that all of the juice is strained from the vegetables, and press the seitan a little to ensure that it is as dry as possible. Set the seitan aside in a warm place in a covered pan, with ¼ cup water to keep it from drying out.

Heat the strained marinade over medium heat. Whip in the Vegan Sour Cream and add the roux gradually (a couple tablespoons at a time), stirring constantly to create a smooth sauce. (You will need about half of the roux to make this sauce.) Keep adding the roux in increments of about 2 tablespoons, whipping while cooking, until the sauce reaches the desired consistency; it should thinly coat the back of a spoon. Do not boil the sauce.

Serve the sauerbraten with a delicate potato side dish, arranging the sauce partially over the seitan and potatoes. Braised red cabbage is another good accompaniment.

Roux

1 cup whole wheat pastry flour
½ cup unroasted sesame oil (or soy oil)

To prepare the roux, heat the oil and add the flour, stirring constantly to ensure that it cooks evenly. Cook over medium heat for about 5 minutes, remove from heat, and set aside until needed. You will need about half this recipe for the sauerbraten; it is not practical to make less than a full recipe of roux, however.

Seitan Parmesan

YIELD: *6 servings*
TIME: *20 minutes (if seitan is already made)*

6 slices seitan, each about ¼-inch thick
3 tablespoons gluten flour
½ cup whole wheat pastry flour (or bread flour)
1 teaspoon sea salt
1 tablespoon chopped basil
1 tablespoon chopped oregano
¼ teaspoon white pepper
½ cup olive oil (or ¼ cup unroasted sesame oil and ¼ cup peanut oil)
2 cups Tomato Sauce (see recipe on page 159)
Vegan Cheese (see recipe next page)

In this recipe, the thickness of the seitan "cutlets" is important. If your seitan loaf is too small to yield six slices of about 4 ounces each, you may have to divide the slices into smaller pieces; just make sure that each slice is about ¼ inch thick. Drain the seitan but leave it slightly moist.

Put the gluten flour in a large bowl so it can be used to dredge the seitan. In another large bowl, mix the pastry flour, salt, basil, oregano, and pepper. In a third bowl, have a little water available, if needed.

Dredge the pieces of seitan in the gluten flour and, if the seitan is sticky-moist, dip it directly into the seasoned flour mixture and coat thoroughly. If the seitan is too dry after being dipped into the gluten, give it a quick flash dip into the bowl of water and then into the seasoned flour. Lay the dredged seitan on a piece of floured plastic wrap. Set aside until you are ready to fry the seitan.

To fry the seitan, heat the oil in a large skillet over medium heat. When the oil is hot (but not smoking), add the seitan and sauté both sides until brown. Remove and drain on paper towels for a few minutes. Then place the cutlets on a baking sheet and top with ½ cup of tomato sauce and 2 tablespoons cheese. If all of the ingredients are warm, the baking time will be substantially shorter. Bake at 375 degrees F for about 10 to 20 minutes. Serve hot, straight from the oven, with a pasta of your choice and vegetables.

Vegan Cheese

8 ounces firm tofu
⅓ cup tahini
2 teaspoons umeboshi paste
⅛ teaspoon garlic powder
⅛ teaspoon dried oregano
½ cup water

Blend all of the ingredients until smooth, creamy, but thick. For a creamier cheese, use up to a full cup of water. The creamier cheese will be a little runny.

1 cup whole wheat pastry
 flour
¼ cup gluten flour
½ teaspoon salt
½ cup water
½ cup beer

VARIATION

You can also make this recipe using batter-dipped seitan.

Mix the flours and salt together. Add the water and the beer, and mix until the batter is smooth. If necessary, add more beer to thin out the batter to the consistency of heavy cream. Follow the directions for making Seitan Parmesan up to and including dredging the seitan with gluten flour. Dip the floured seitan cutlets into the batter and then immediately into the hot oil. Brown on both sides and serve as suggested above.

Hearty Seitan

YIELD: *6 to 8 servings*
TIME: *30 minutes (if seitan and sauce are made already); you may need to allow 2 to 3 hours to make the sauce*

3 cups sliced mushrooms
2 cups diced onions
2 cloves garlic, minced
¼ cup sesame oil
1½ teaspoons sea salt
4 cups flaked seitan
1 cup diced red or yellow bell peppers
½ cup dry red wine
3 cups Espagñol Sauce (page 160) or other basic brown sauce
1 cup tomato purée
1 cup diced green bell peppers
1 cup thinly sliced celery, cut on a diagonal

*T*his is a favorite recipe of mine. It brings back fond memories of my apprenticeship at Washburne's Culinary School in Chicago. Upon becoming a vegetarian, I looked for the ideal food to replace meat. Seitan was the answer. To make this recipe at its best, use the basic brown sauce (Espagñol Sauce) included in this chapter. A quick basic brown sauce will work, but I recommend taking the time to make the slow-cooking sauce.

Over a medium heat in a skillet or saucepan that holds at least 2½ quarts, sauté the mushrooms, onions, and garlic in the oil. Add the salt, seitan, red bell peppers, and wine. Reduce the wine to almost nothing. Add the Espagñol Sauce and tomato purée. Simmer for 30 minutes, being careful not to burn the mixture. Add the green bell peppers and celery at the very end to prevent their overcooking. Cook these vegetables for just 5 minutes. Their color will bloom and make the entrée very attractive. Serve this hearty seitan dish over rice, noodles, or mashed potatoes and a mixed vegetable side dish.

Seitan Pepper Steak

YIELD: *6 to 8 servings*

TIME: *1 to 1½ hours (if the seitan is already made)*

1.4 ounces (1 package) dried, sliced shiitake mushrooms (or 1 to 1½ cups regular, sliced mushrooms)

2 cups water*

3 tablespoons tamari*

2 cups flaked (angle-cut) seitan

1 cup diced onions

½ cup diced red bell peppers

2 tablespoons sesame oil

2 tablespoons minced garlic

2 tablespoons chopped basil

½ cup diced green bell peppers

¼ cup sherry

2 cups water

3 tablespoons barley miso or other dark miso

2 tablespoons tomato paste (optional)

1 tablespoon tamari (optional)

¼ cup arrowroot, dissolved in ¼ cup water

*You will need these ingredients only if using the shiitake mushrooms.

*T*his recipe is a modified version of the classic recipe for beef pepper steak and is a "friendly foods" version in terms of nutrition, time, and expense. It is especially delicious served over jerusalem artichoke pasta, flat spinach noodles, or quinoa noodles.

If you are using the shiitake mushrooms, place them in a bowl and cover them with hot water. Soak until soft (about 30 minutes). Then place the soaked mushrooms in a pot with 2 cups of water (use the soaking liquid) and 3 tablespoons tamari. Simmer, uncovered, for 30 minutes, and set aside.

Sauté the seitan, mushrooms, onions, and red bell peppers in the oil, along with the garlic and basil. When the vegetables are tender (half-cooked), add the green bell peppers, sherry, and 1¾ cups water.

Mix the miso and ¼ cup water, along with the tomato paste and the tablespoon of tamari, if you wish. Add to the sautéed vegetables. Add the dissolved arrowroot and continue to simmer, while stirring constantly, until the sauce has thickened. Serve the seitan pepper steak with noodles, rice, or mashed potatoes.

VARIATION: *Tofu Pepper Steak*

For this recipe, take a 1-pound block of tofu and cut it into ½-inch-thick slices. Cut those slices into quarters. You will need 2 cups of tofu squares. Following the recipe above, using tofu in place of seitan.

San Francisco Stir-Fry

YIELD: *4 servings*

TIME: *20 to 25 minutes (if the seitan is already made)*

¼ *cup arrowroot*

2 teaspoons ginger powder

4 teaspoons minced garlic

2 tablespoons tamari

2 tablespoons barley malt syrup

3 cups water

¼ *cup roasted sesame oil*

1 cup coarsely diced red bell pepper

1 cup coarsely diced onions

1½ cups flaked seitan (or 2 cups diced firm tofu)

4 to 8 mushrooms, quartered

1 cup coarsely diced green bell pepper

1 cup thinly sliced celery, cut on a diagonal

14 snow pea pods, stemmed and cut in half diagonally

3 cups cooked brown rice

scallions and tomato-peel roses, for garnish (optional)

*T*his entrée, like all stir-fry dishes, is easy to make. The Chinese style of cooking is one of the best in the world, because it uses minimal cooking with maximum heat. However, you must take the time to prepare and set out all of your ingredients before you start. Unless you do that, whatever is in the pan will overcook while you are preparing the next ingredient, and the finished dish will not have the tender-crisp quality that is the mark of a good stir-fry.

Combine the ingredients for the sauce (the first six ingredients on the list) and set aside.

Preheat your wok or sauté pan before adding the oil. (If the oil is put in first, it will burn before the vegetables go in.) When the oil is hot, sauté the red bell pepper, onions, seitan, and mushrooms for a minute. Continue stir-frying until the vegetables are half-cooked (about 2 minutes). Add the green bell pepper, celery, and snow peas, and continue stir-frying for another 3 minutes, still over high heat.

Give the sauce a quick stir to dissolve the arrowroot. Then pour it in the wok and blend all the ingredients. Stir vigorously to prevent the sauce from lumping. (The sauce will not thicken unless the ingredients are thoroughly mixed. If necessary, dissolve about 3 tablespoons of arrowroot in water and add immediately.) Serve over brown rice, using ¾ cup rice per portion. Garnish with a scallion "flower" and/or a tomato-peel rose, if you wish.

Seitan Stroganoff

YIELD: *4 servings*

TIME: *15 minutes prepara-tion; 20 minutes cooking (if the seitan is made already)*

1 tablespoon sesame oil
1½ cups diced onions
1½ teaspoons minced garlic
1½ teaspoons finely chopped
    parsley
1½ cups fresh sliced
    mushrooms
2 tablespoons barley miso
1½ cups water
1 teaspoon stone-ground
    prepared mustard
2 tablespoons tamari
½ cup dry sherry (optional)
2 cups seitan, thinly sliced,
    then cut into small pieces
3 tablespoons arrowroot (or
    kuzu or cornstarch),
    dissolved in 3 tablespoons
    water
½ cup cashew nuts or
    blanched almonds
4½ teaspoons umeboshi paste
2 to 3 cups cooked whole-
    wheat noodles or fettuccini

I always enjoy transforming rich, heavy, traditional dishes into lighter, satisfying "friendly foods." This dish has less cholesterol and fat than the original meat-based stroganoff and may be served for lunch or dinner.

Heat the oil and sauté the onions until translucent. Add the garlic, parsley, and mushrooms. Sauté for 6 to 10 minutes, or until soft.

Dissolve the miso into ¼ cup of water. Add the miso, another ¾ cup of water, the mustard, tamari, and sherry (if you wish) to the sautéed vegetables. Bring the mixture to a simmer. Add the seitan and simmer for another 5 minutes. Then add the dissolved arrowroot, stirring vigorously to create a smooth consistency.

Blend the cashews or almonds with the remaining ½ cup of water and the umeboshi paste until smooth. Add this mixture to the vegetables and stir well. Heat gently and serve with noodles.

VARIATION

Instead of the cashew and umeboshi paste mixture, substitute one cup of Cauliflower "Sour Cream" (recipe on next page) or dairy sour cream, if you wish.

Cauliflower "Sour Cream"

1 cup chopped, cooked
    cauliflower
1 tablespoon tahini
1 tablespoon umeboshi paste
1 tablespoon brown rice
    vinegar
1 tablespoon water

Blend all of the ingredients until smooth.

Swiss-Style Shredded Seitan

YIELD: *8 servings*
TIME: *15 minutes prepara-*
tion; 20 minutes cooking

1 tablespoon barley miso
1 tablespoon barley malt
    syrup
1 tablespoon water
¼ cup sesame oil
1 cup sliced scallions
2 cups sliced mushrooms
4 cups thin strips seitan
½ cup sherry or dry white
    wine
4 teaspoons tamari
½ teaspoon black pepper
½ teaspoon minced garlic
¼ cup arrowroot
3 cups soy milk
8 cups cooked jerusalum
    artichoke spaghetti or udon
    noodles

*T*his recipe is based on a traditional Swiss dish that features veal and cream. This vegan version features seitan and soy milk instead.

Make a "demiglace" by dissolving the miso and syrup in the water. Set aside.

Heat the oil in a skillet and sauté the scallions for 1 minute. Add the mushrooms and seitan and sauté briefly. Add the "demiglace," sherry, tamari, pepper, and garlic and bring the mixture to a simmer.

Dissolve the arrowroot in the soy milk and add to the seitan mixture. Stir constantly until thickened. Pour the mixture over cooked noodles and serve while hot.

Szekely Goulash

YIELD: *4 servings*
TIME: *20 to 30 minutes*

1 cup diced onions
1½ cups flaked seitan
1 tablespoon oil
1 tablespoon Vogue Vegy Base
1 teaspoon salt
1 tablespoon paprika,
* preferably Hungarian,*
* because it is sweeter*
1 cup sauerkraut, measured
* after being rinsed and*
* pressed relatively dry*
¼ cup Vegan Sour Cream
* (page 90) or Cauliflower*
* "Sour Cream" (page 153)*
2 cups Béchamel Sauce (page
* 163) or Soy Milk Sauce*
* (recipe follows)*

*T*his is the Hungarian version of the Russian stroganoff. It has a superb taste and a delicate texture. It contains no cholesterol while maintaining the flavor of rich Hungarian cuisine.

Sauté the onions and seitan in the oil, along with the soup base, salt, and paprika, over medium heat, stirring for about 5 minutes. Add the sauerkraut, Vegan Sour Cream, and Béchamel Sauce, and mix in well. Continue to stir the mixture over medium heat. If the mixture becomes too thick, add just enough water to thin it to a sauce consistency (one that will coat the back of a spoon to $\frac{1}{16}$ of an inch or so). Serve this dish hot, over noodles, and with a vegetable side dish.

Soy Milk Sauce

3 tablespoons canola oil (or
* other cooking oil)*
¼ cup unbleached flour
2 cups soy milk

This recipe yields exactly 2 cups, the amount needed for the Sezekle Gulos recipe.

Heat the oil until it is hot but not smoking. Add the flour and stir constantly to prevent it from burning. Cook this roux for 3 to 5 minutes.

In a separate pan, heat the soy milk. Add all of the roux to the hot milk and whip it in vigorously to make a smooth sauce. When the sauce thickens, cook it for a few more minutes.

Berner Platte

YIELD: *4 servings*
TIME: *25 minutes (if the protein accompaniments are made already)*

2 whole medium potatoes
2 cups diced onions
1 cup peeled and shredded carrots
2 tablespoons oil
1 tablespoon caraway seeds
1 teaspoon salt
½ teaspoon black pepper
1 tablespoon smoked yeast
½ cup white wine
3 cups water
1 cup rinsed and drained sauerkraut
1 cup peeled and shredded potatoes
Protein Accompaniments (see items next page)
4 tomato-peel roses, for garnish
chopped fresh parsley, for garnish

*I*n Switzerland, this dish centers around various sausages, with accompanying vegetables. This version highlights vegetables, which are accompanied by a variety of meat substitutes, including slices of tofu, seitan, Soysage, and nut or grain loaves. Sauerbraten (page 146) without the sauce, and filling from Vegetable Rolls (pages 247–249), with a little added binder, are also acceptable. Generally, you should use only three varieties of proteins.

Peel the 2 whole potatoes, cut them in half horizontally, and lightly boil or steam them until tender. Do this first so that the potatoes can cook while you are preparing the vegetables.

Sauté the onions and carrots in the oil, with the caraway seeds, salt, pepper, and yeast, until the onions are semi-translucent. Add the wine, water, sauerkraut, and shredded potatoes. Cook until the potatoes are soft and the mixture has the consistency of a sauce (about 15 minutes). While the vegetables are simmering, prepare the Protein Accompaniments.

To serve, make sure that all of the ingredients are warm. Spoon about ¾ cup of sauerkraut mixture in the center of each dinner plate. Fan the Protein Accompaniments on one side, place a half potato on the other side, and garnish with a tomato-peel rose and chopped parsley.

Protein Accompaniments

8 slices firm tofu, each
    weighing 1 ounce
8 slices seitan, each weighing
    1 ounce
4 teaspoons tamari
8 teaspoons smoked yeast
cooking oil
4 slices cooked Soysage, 2
    ounces each (page 105)

Lightly brush ¼ teaspoon tamari on each slice of tofu and seitan and coat each slice evenly with about ½ teaspoon smoked yeast. Lightly sauté the slices on both sides in a minimum of oil (about ¼ cup). Do not sauté the Soysage.

Broccoli Seitan Delmonico

YIELD: *5 to 6 servings*
TIME: *25 to 30 minutes*

3 tablespoons corn oil (or
    margarine)
1 cup finely chopped onions
½ cup sliced mushrooms
¼ teaspoon sea salt
¼ teaspoon nutmeg
6 tablespoons unbleached
    flour
2 teaspoons nutritional yeast
½ cup chopped green olives,
    pimiento-stuffed
¼ cup cashew nuts
2 cups soy milk
2½ cups broccoli florets
1½ cups cooked and diced
    seitan
6 cups cooked pasta
    (spaghetti, linguine, soba,
    or other pasta)

Heat the oil in a medium saucepan. Sauté the onions and mushrooms with the salt and nutmeg until the onions are translucent. Stir in the flour and yeast and cook 3 to 5 minutes longer. Then add the chopped olives. Set aside.

Blend the cashews with 1 cup of soy milk until it makes a smooth paste. (You should be able to feel only a slight gritty texture if you rub the mixture between your fingers.) Add the remaining 1 cup of soy milk and blend for a few seconds.

Pour the cashew milk over the sautéed onion mixture and stir until well blended. Cook over medium heat, stirring occasionally, until the sauce thickens. (This would be a good time to begin cooking the pasta.)

Steam the broccoli for about 5 minutes, or until tender but crisp. Add it to the sauce mixture. Finally, stir in the diced seitan. Spoon the broccoli seitan sauce over pasta and serve hot.

Hot Seitan Sandwich

YIELD: *1 serving*
TIME: *15 minutes*

*4 slices seitan, cut ⅛ inch
thick*
2 slices whole-grain bread
*½ cup Espagñol Sauce (page
160; or any other brown
sauce)*
¾ cup mashed potatoes
*¼ cup cooked peas and
carrots (or other vegetable
of your choice)*
*peeled, sliced tomato and a
scallion, for garnish*

*T*his sandwich is a "friendly foods" version of the hot roast-beef sandwich, which was a very popular item in my parents' restaurant in the 1960s.

Heat the seitan in some of the cooking broth, or steam it. Remove from heat, drain the seitan slices, and pat them dry. Place the seitan on top of one slice of bread. (Make sure the seitan is dry or it will cause the sandwich to become soggy.) Place ¼ cup of sauce over the seitan. Then place the other slice of bread on top. Cut the sandwich in two and place on a dinner plate. Mound the potatoes next to the sandwich and the cooked vegetables beside the potatoes. Make a hollow in the center of the potatoes and pour the remaining ¼ cup of sauce over the potatoes and over the vegetables, if you wish. Garnish with tomato slices and a scallion. Serve warm. (This sandwich is meant to be eaten with knife and fork!)

Seitan, Lettuce, and Tomato Sandwich

YIELD: *1 serving*
TIME: *15 minutes*

2 teaspoons smoked yeast
2 tablespoons tamari
2 tablespoons water
1 tablespoon minced garlic
4 slices seitan (about 1 ounce
   each)
2 tablespoons sesame oil
2 slices whole wheat bread
2 slices tomato
2 pieces leaf lettuce
2 tablespoons soy
   mayonnaise

Mix the smoked yeast, tamari, water, and garlic together. Marinate the seitan in this mixture for a few minutes.

Heat the oil in a small skillet. Sauté the seitan until golden brown. Drain.

Toast the bread and spread the soy mayonnaise on both pieces. Place the seitan on one piece of bread. Add the tomato slices and lettuce leaves, and top with the other slice of bread.

VARIATION: *Tofu, Lettuce, and Tomato Sandwich*
Substitute an equal amount of sliced firm tofu for the sliced seitan. Prepare the sandwich according the recipe above.

SAUCES

Tomato Sauce

YIELD: *5 cups of sauce*
TIME: *25 minutes preparation; 1½ hours cooking*

2 tablespoons olive oil
1 cup finely diced onions
1 tablespoon minced garlic
*½ cup peeled and finely diced
    carrots*
½ cup finely diced celery
*2 tablespoons chopped basil
    (or 2 teaspoons dried basil)*
*2 teaspoons whole rosemary
    leaves*
*1 tablespoon fresh oregano
    (or 1 teaspoon dried
    oregano)*
1 teaspoon salt
*¼ teaspoon finely ground
    black pepper*
*¼ teaspoon ground fennel
    seeds (optional)*
*one 14-ounce can whole
    tomatoes, hand-crushed,
    with juice*
1¼ cups tomato paste
2 cups water

Heat the oil in a large saucepan. Sauté the onions, garlic, carrots, and celery, along with the seasonings, for about 15
minutes.

Add the tomatoes and continue cooking for about 10
minutes. Stir together the tomato paste and water. Add this
mixture to the sauce and continue cooking for 1½ hours.

Espagñol Sauce

YIELD: *5 cups of sauce*
TIME: *20 minutes prepara-*
tion; 1¼ hours cooking

¼ *cup cooking oil*
½ *cup grated onions*
½ *cup grated carrots*
½ *cup finely chopped*
   mushrooms
½ *cup grated celery*
1 *tablespoon shallots*
1 *teaspoon minced garlic*
1 *cup finely ground whole*
   wheat pastry flour
¼ *cup dark miso*
2 *tablespoons Vogue Vegy*
   Base
2 *bay leaves*
6 *sprigs of thyme, 2 inches*
   each (or ¼ teaspoon dried
   thyme)
¼ *teaspoon rosemary*
2 *cloves (or ⅛ teaspoon*
   ground cloves)
several parsley stems, minced
   (or 1 tablespoon dried
   parsley)
⅛ *teaspoon black pepper*
¼ *cup tamari*
6 *tablespoons dry red wine*
5 *cups water*
¼ *cup tomato paste*

Heat the oil in a saucepan. Sauté the onions, carrots, mushrooms, celery, shallots, and garlic over high heat, stirring occasionally to ensure even cooking. When the vegetables are lightly browned, add the flour. Continue to cook for another 5 minutes, until the flour is cooked and slightly browned. Add the miso, soup base, and seasonings.

In a separate bowl, stir together the tamari, wine, water, and tomato paste. Add this to the vegetable mixture, stirring vigorously to blend well. Cover and simmer for 1 hour. Strain the sauce through a fine-meshed strainer or cheesecloth.

1 cup dry red wine
½ cup minced shallots or
  scallions
1 teaspoon minced thyme (or
  ¼ teaspoon dried thyme)
½ teaspoon black pepper
½ cup finely diced firm tofu

VARIATION: *Bordelaise Sauce*

For this recipe, you will need 1 quart of Espagñol Sauce and the ingredients listed here.

In a medium-sized saucepan, simmer all ingredients except the Espagñol Sauce until reduced to half the original volume. Add the Espagñol Sauce and simmer briefly.

Vegan Béarnaise Sauce

YIELD: *1 quart sauce*
TIME: *30 to 45 minutes*

2 cups white wine
1 cup red wine vinegar
5 tablespoons minced shallots
4 tablespoons minced parsley
4 teaspoons chopped tarragon
  leaves
2 bay leaves
zests from 2 medium-sized
  lemons, finely minced
1 tablespoon black pepper
½ teaspoon turmeric
2 packages firm silken tofu,
  10½ ounces each
2 tablespoons corn oil
½ teaspoon salt
2 tablespoons lemon juice
2 to 4 tablespoons softened
  soy margarine

Place the wine, vinegar, shallots, parsley, tarragon, bay leaves, lemon zests, pepper, and turmeric in a saucepan. Bring to a boil, and then simmer until reduced to about ¾ to ½ cup of liquid. Remove the bay leaves.

Blend the tofu and corn oil until smooth. Set aside. When the wine mixture is ready, add it to the blended tofu, along with the salt, lemon juice, and margarine and blend to a smooth sauce. This sauce will keep, refrigerated, for 7 to 10 days.

Velouté Sauce

YIELD: *1 quart of sauce*
TIME: *35 minutes; allow an additional 2½ hours to make the stock*

1 quart vegetable stock (recipe follows)
2 tablespoons Vogue Vegy Base
½ teaspoon salt
¼ teaspoon white pepper
⅓ cup canola oil
¾ cup unbleached flour

In a large saucepan, heat the vegetable stock, soup base, salt, and pepper to a simmer.

Meanwhile, heat the oil in a small saucepan and add the flour. (The oil should be hot enough to cause the flour to sizzle.) Mix well to ensure even cooking. Cook the roux until it is smooth. Then add a small amount (about 2 cups) of stock to the roux. Add more stock, a little at a time to prevent lumping. Finally, stir the roux into the remaining stock to create a smooth sauce.

Vegetable Stock

3 tablespoons safflower oil (or canola oil)
5 unpeeled carrots, coarsely chopped
4 stalks celery, coarsely chopped
3 onions, coarsely chopped
4 cloves garlic, quartered
3 bay leaves
20 parsley stems
6 sprigs of thyme
½ teaspoon cracked black pepper
1 teaspoon salt
1½ gallons water

Sauté the vegetables in the oil, in a large stockpot. Add the herbs and seasonings and the water, and bring to a boil. Reduce heat and simmer for about 2 hours. Cool and strain the stock.

Vegan Béchamel Sauce

YIELD: *4½ cups of sauce*
TIME: *30 minutes*

2 cups soy milk
1½ cups water
¼ cup cashew nuts
1 teaspoon sea salt
⅛ teaspoon white pepper
dash of nutmeg
¼ cup cooking oil (preferably sesame oil or corn oil)
½ cup unbleached flour

¼ cup Vogue Vegy Base
1 teaspoon salt
2 tablespoons drained capers

2 tablespoons cooking oil
1 cup finely diced onions
1 cup sliced mushrooms
1 tablespoon smoked yeast
1 tablespoon white miso

1 tablespoon paprika, preferably Hungarian
2 tablespoons dill weed
1 cup soy milk

Blend the soy milk, water, cashews, and seasonings in a blender until smooth. Pour into a double boiler and heat.

Meanwhile, heat the oil in a small saucepan. Add the flour to make a roux. Then whisk it into the heated soy milk mixture to make a light, creamy sauce. For a thicker sauce, use more roux.

VARIATION: *Sardaline Sauce*
For this recipe, you will need 6 cups of the Vegan Béchamel Sauce and these ingredients. Mix all the ingredients well.

VARIATION: *Mushroom Cream Sauce*
For this recipe, you will need 3½ cups of the Vegan Béchamel Sauce and these ingredients.

Heat the oil in a saucepan and sauté the onions and mushrooms over a medium heat until the onions are translucent.

In a large bowl, whisk the yeast and miso into the béchamel sauce. Then add this mixture to the sautéed vegetables. Bring to a simmer, stirring constantly.

VARIATION: *Dill Sauce*
To 4½ cups of the Vegan Béchamel Sauce, add the following ingredients and mix well:

Carrot Sauce

YIELD: *3¾ cups of sauce*
TIME: *25 minutes*

4 cups peeled and thinly sliced
    carrots
2 cups water
½ teaspoon salt
5 ounces firm silken tofu
¼ cup white miso
⅛ teaspoon white pepper
2 teaspoons Vogue Vegy Base
1 tablespoon minced orange
    zests and ⅛ teaspoon
    nutmeg (optional)
2 teaspoons curry powder
    (optional)

*T*his is a delicately flavored sauce with a sweet dill flavor. It is delicious with bulgar dishes, grain loaves, steamed vegetables, and pastas.

Cook the carrots in 1 cup of water with the salt in a covered pan until the water has evaporated. Transfer the carrots to a blender and add the tofu, miso, pepper, soup base, and remaining cup of water. Return to the saucepan and cook over low heat for 3 to 5 minutes. Add either set of optional seasonings, if you wish.

Miso Sauce

YIELD: *1 quart of sauce*
TIME: *15 minutes*

2 cups peanut oil
1 cup water
2 tablespoons apple cider
    vinegar
2 tablespoons tamari
1 tablespoon honey
1 cup white miso
¼ cup chopped onions
8 ounces (or more) firm tofu

Place all of the ingredients in a blender and blend until smooth. If the sauce seems to separate, add more tofu. Pour the sauce into a saucepan, bring to a simmer, and cook gently for a few minutes.

1 tablespoon sesame oil
2 cups sliced mushrooms
½ cup red onions
1 tablespoon minced garlic
1 teaspoon minced ginger

VARIATION: *Oriental Miso Sauce*
Heat the oil and sauté the vegetables with the seasonings until the onions are translucent. Add these ingredients to the Miso Sauce (recipe previous page).

Tahini Lemon Sauce

YIELD: *2½ cups of sauce*
TIME: *20 minutes*

¾ cup tahini
4 ounces firm silken tofu
½ teaspoon minced garlic
½ cup lemon juice
¾ cup water
¼ cup minced scallions or
    minced onions
¼ cup minced parsley, loosely
    packed (or ¼ cup dried
    parsley)
⅛ teaspoon sea salt
¼ teaspoon cumin
dash of cayenne pepper

*L*ike all blender sauces, this sauce is easy to make but must be heated delicately to avoid separating or solidifying.

Put all ingredients in a blender and blend until smooth. Transfer to a saucepan and bring to a simmer, stirring occasionally (10 minutes).

Sweet and Sour Sauce

YIELD: *2 cups of sauce*
TIME: *20 minutes*

½ cup peeled and julienned
   carrots
¼ cup julienned red bell
   peppers
½ cup onions, quartered and
   thinly sliced
1 tablespoon cooking oil
1½ cups apple juice
2 tablespoons barley malt
   syrup
1 tablespoon tamari
1 tablespoon cider vinegar (or
   2 tablespoons brown rice
   vinegar)
1½ teaspoons minced ginger
   (or ½ teaspoon ginger
   powder)
1½ teaspoons minced garlic
   (or ½ teaspoon garlic
   powder)
1 tablespoon arrowroot
   dissolved in 1 tablespoon
   water

Simmer the vegetables, oil, apple juice, syrup, tamari, vinegar, ginger, and garlic over medium heat for 5 minutes. Remove from heat and add the dissolved arrowroot, stirring constantly. Return to heat and cook for about 2 minutes, or until the sauce is thickened.

Broccoli Sauce

YIELD: *5½ cups of sauce*
TIME: *35 to 45 minutes*

2 cups peeled and diced
  potatoes
2 cups broccoli stems and
  florets
¼ cup soy oil
½ cup chopped onions
2 teaspoons minced garlic
1 teaspoon sea salt
1 cup soy milk
1 cup water
¼ teaspoon white pepper
1 teaspoon smoked yeast
2 teaspoons Vogue Vegy Base
1 teaspoon dill weed
1 teaspoon ground fennel
  seeds (optional)

Cook the potatoes in water to cover, until the potatoes are soft. Meanwhile, steam the broccoli in a small amount of water. Drain.

Heat the oil in a saucepan. Sauté the broccoli, onions, and garlic, with the salt, for 5 to 7 minutes. You may need to add up to ¼ cup of water to prevent burning.

Blend the sautéed vegetables and potatoes with the soy milk and water until smooth. Strain the liquid and return to the blender. Blend the sauce with the remaining ingredients. Transfer to a saucepan and heat through.

Yellow Pepper Beurre Blanc

YIELD: *1 cup of sauce*
TIME: *30 to 40 minutes*

2 medium yellow bell peppers
1 small potato, peeled and diced
2 tablespoons white wine (or mirin)
3 tablespoons lemon juice
¼ teaspoon salt
⅛ teaspoon white pepper
½ cup soy margarine
¼ teaspoon saffron (optional)

Roast the peppers over an open flame (under a broiler or over a stove flame) until the skin blisters. Then peel off the skin. Seed the peppers, chop them into small pieces, and purée them in a blender until smooth. (This should yield ½ cup purée.) Set aside.

Place the diced potato in a saucepan with water to cover. Cook until soft. Drain the cooked potato and transfer to a blender. Add the pepper purée, wine, lemon juice, salt, and pepper. Blend until smooth. Pour this mixture into a small saucepan and whip the margarine vigorously into the sauce, along with the saffron, if you wish. Heat through and serve warm.

Vegetable Side Dishes

*T*here is an old adage, "When you are green inside, you are clean inside." This is one of my favorite sayings, and I believe there is a great deal of merit in what it tells. Vegetables are indeed "friendly foods." They are loaded with vitamins, minerals, fiber, and carbohydrates. In my opinion, every meal should include some form of fresh vegetables.

The recipes in this chapter focus on vegetables. Many of these dishes are hearty enough to serve as main courses, especially with the addition of some protein such as tofu, tempeh, or seitan. Alone, or with pasta or grains, these vegetable dishes are fine as light supper entrées or lunches.

Vegetables of all kinds are represented in these recipes, including root vegetables, leafy green vegetables, squashes, tomatoes, beans, sea vegetables, and so on. Most recipes call for fresh vegetables, with the exception of sea vegetables, which are packaged in a dried form. (Some mushrooms are also packaged dried.) When fresh vegetables are unavailable, some frozen vegetables are fine. I almost never cook with canned vegetables, except for sauerkraut, beets, and beans (such as garbanzo beans and kidney beans).

When shopping for fresh produce, choose vegetables that are firm, with no soft spots. The produce should have a bright color, with no dark spots, blemishes, or other signs of deterioration. When buying bulb or root vegetables such as onions or potatoes, avoid produce that is already sprouting new growth. It's a good idea to ask the produce manager at your local supermarket which days of the week he or she usually restocks. Obviously, you will find a wider selection of produce, and probably fresher produce, on those days. If your local supermarket does not carry organic produce, ask the manager to look into the possibility.

Pesticide Contamination

My earlier chapter on food quality (pages 9–28) discusses pesticides and organic produce. You may be wondering how common it is to find pesticide contamination in the produce you consume. Here are some startling figures from the Natural Resources Defense Council.

PRODUCE	PERCENT OF DOMESTIC SAMPLES WITH RESIDUES	PERCENT OF IMPORTED SAMPLES WITH RESIDUES
Bell peppers	30%	82%
Broccoli	14%	33%
Cabbage	20%	53%
Carrots	47%	58%
Cauliflower	2%	22%
Celery	72%	75%
Corn	1%	5%
Cucumbers	29%	80%
Green beans	28%	46%
Lettuce	52%	58%
Onions	28%	19%
Potatoes	39%	24%
Spinach	46%	23%
Sweet potatoes	30%	11%
Tomatoes	23%	70%

As this chart shows, not all domestic produce is lower in chemicals. Sweet potatoes, onions, and bell peppers are a few examples.

Vegetable Nutrition

Vegetables grown underground (such as carrots) tend to have more minerals and less chlorophyll than those vegetables grown above ground (such as broccoli). Of course, this is just a general guideline, not an absolute rule. Because vegetables differ in the nutrients they offer, it's a good idea to eat a wide variety of vegetables.

Some vegetables purportedly have special health benefits. Cruciferous vegetables, such as broccoli, cauliflower, and cabbage, are considered to be anticarcinogenic. Of course, eating them cannot guarantee you will not get cancer. But studies have shown that the chances of getting colorectal cancer are greatly reduced by a diet that includes cruciferous vegetables on a daily basis.

Garlic is another "magic" food. Laboratory research shows that raw garlic actually kills cancer cells. The implication is that raw garlic, eaten in large quantities, may control cancer. No one knows for certain what is the anticarcinogenic element in this plant. Researchers do know that cooking garlic or heat-treating it (for capsules) causes the garlic to lose its anticarcinogenic properties.

The chief glory of the carrot is its carotene content, which is a bright-colored compound of carbon and hydrogen. Carotene is found in many plant foods but especially in carrots. A healthy liver changes carotene into vitamin A, which is essential for life, growth, and health. Vitamin A helps keep skin healthy, produces a substance called visual purple (which helps us see dim lights), maintains color and peripheral vision, helps the body resist infections, and helps the adrenal glands.

Carrots have been cultivated in almost every part of the world from the earliest times. They were known as "honey underground" in early Celtic literature. They did not become a popular vegetable in England until the time of Elizabeth I, but they were eaten almost daily in stews, soups, and puddings in Scotland, Wales, and Ireland.

Folic acid is another special nutrient that contributes to good health. Medical researchers have linked diets deficient in folic acid with increased risks of lung and cervical cancer. Some good sources of folic acid in the vegetable kingdom are asparagus, broccoli, brussels sprouts, cabbage, corn, dried beans and peas, romaine lettuce, and raw spinach. Folic acid is easily destroyed by cooking, so it is best to cook these foods using a minimum of heat.

There are several ways to prepare vegetables so they will retain maximum nutritional value. You can sauté them, bake them, grill them, steam them, or blanch them. If you boil vegetables, you will lose water-soluble vitamins; of course, you could use the water for soups or sauces instead of discarding it. If you are deep-frying vegetables, you may lose oil-soluble vitamins; this will not necessarily happen if you are sautéing the vegetables. It's best to use as little oil or water as possible in the cooking. And it's best to cook the vegetables until they are barely done. Overcooking vegetables destroys the nutrients.

Sea Vegetables

Sea vegetables are classified into eight major groups. Three of these groups contain plants used as food. Red seaweed, or *Rhodophyta*, includes dulse, purple nori, ogo, agar, and Irish moss. Brown seaweed, or *Phaeophyta*, includes kelp, kombu, wakame, arame, hijiki, and rockweed. Sea lettuce belongs to the *Chlorophyta*, or green sea vegetables.

Sea vegetables have excellent nutritional value. They are low in fat and rich in complex carbohydrates. Sea vegetables are good in soups, sauces, stews, salads, sandwiches, omelets, and many other dishes. Most sea vegetables are high in vitamins C, B_1, B_2, E, K, and niacin, and many are rich in protein, fiber, and minerals.

It is uncertain whether sea vegetables are a source of vitamin B_{12}. In separate studies in 1987, researchers found that what seems to be vitamin B_{12} actually just resembles this vitamin. The following chart shows the levels of various nutrients in several commonly consumed sea vegetables, per 100 grams of vegetable.

VEGETABLE	CALCIUM (IN MG)	IRON (IN MG)	VITAMIN A (IN MG)	NIACIN (IN MG)	PROTEIN (IN G)
Agar (kanten)	400	5.0	0	0	2.3
Arame	1,170	12.0	0	2.6	7.5
Dulse	567	6.3	0	0	0
Hijiki	1,400	29.0	0	4.0	5.6
Kombu	800	0	11	1.8	7.3
Nori	260	12.0	20	10.0	35.6
Wakame	1,300	13.0	15	10.0	12.7

Sea vegetables have one setback, and that is their high sodium content. Sodium levels vary from trace amounts to more than 4,000 milligrams per 100 grams of vegetable. Rinsing the vegetable can remove much of the salt, and some nutritionists believe that the sodium is offset by the plant's high level of potassium, which maintains the body's fluid balance. The sodium-to-potassium ratio in a typical sea vegetable is 3 to 1, which is close to the 5-to-1 ratio in our bodies. Table salt has a 10,000-to-1 ratio of sodium to potassium.

Because sea vegetables contain little cellulose, they discolor and spoil quickly. Thus, they usually are sold dried. You can find sea vegetables in health food stores and in Asian and West Indian markets. Japanese grocery stores sometimes stock sea vegetables preserved in brine. Soaking in cold water returns most dried seaweed to its fresh state. One third of an ounce of dry sea vegetable equals about one cup when rehydrated.

Sunburst Zucchini

YIELD: *3 servings*
TIME: *25 to 30 minutes*

*1 cup peeled and diced
   butternut squash (or
   carrots)*
1 tablespoon olive oil
1 cup diced zucchini
*1 cup diced yellow squash
   (such as crookneck squash)*
1 tablespoon minced garlic
*1 tablespoon minced ginger
   (or 1½ teaspoons ground
   ginger)*
½ teaspoon sea salt
¼ teaspoon white pepper
*¼ cup finely diced red bell
   peppers, for garnish*

Steam the butternut squash until tender. Heat the oil in a skillet. Sauté the zucchini, yellow squash, garlic, and ginger, along with the salt and pepper, until the vegetables are tender. Stir together these vegetables and the butternut squash. Serve hot, garnished with the diced red bell peppers.

Carrots, Pecans, and Fennel

YIELD: *4 servings*
TIME: *15 minutes preparation; 20 minutes cooking*

2 cups peeled and julienned carrots
½ cup thinly sliced fennel (or 1 teaspoon ground fennel seeds)
1 tablespoon olive oil (or canola oil)
¼ cup maple syrup
¼ cup roasted pecan nuts
2 teaspoons cornstarch
1 tablespoon water
1 tablespoon chopped parsley

Steam the carrots in a small amount of water, just until tender-crisp. Be sure not to overcook them.

In a skillet, sauté the fennel in oil for 2 minutes. Add the syrup, pecans, and carrots, and simmer.

In a small bowl, mix the cornstarch and water together. Add this mixture to the carrot mixture. Finally, stir in the chopped parsley and serve hot.

Kale and Parsnips

YIELD: *4 servings*
TIME: *25 minutes*

1 cup halved and sliced onions
1 cup halved and sliced parsnips
1 tablespoon corn oil
1 cup water
2 tablespoons minced ginger (or ½ teaspoon ground ginger)
1 quart kale, with veins removed and cut into bite-sized pieces

Sauté the onions and parsnips in oil for about 5 minutes, stirring occasionally to prevent burning. Add the water and ginger. Cover and simmer for 4 to 5 minutes. Add the kale and continue cooking 4 to 5 minutes longer. Stir occasionally but keep the saucepan covered otherwise. Serve hot.

VARIATION: *Kale and Carrots*
Substitute an equal amount of sliced carrots for the parsnips, and follow the directions for the recipe above.

Steamed Kale with Lemon Miso Sauce

YIELD: *6 servings*
TIME: *15 to 20 minutes*

2 cups water
½ lemon, cut into three pieces
1½ teaspoons peeled and finely chopped ginger
¼ cup white miso
1 cup diced daikon
1 cup diced carrots
2 cups fresh chopped kale, packed

*M*ost of us were told as children that we had to eat our vegetables before we could eat dessert. I would prefer to reverse the expression and serve this vegetable for dessert; a jaded palate would not know the difference if the vegetables were young and sweet. Then, too, white miso itself is quite sweet.

Put the water, lemon, ginger, and miso in a saucepan and bring to a simmer, stirring to dissolve the miso. Add the daikon and carrots and cook until the vegetables are tender. Then add the kale and mix well. Simmer 3 to 5 minutes. Remove the lemon pieces. Serve hot.

Hijiki with Green Beans

YIELD: *4 servings*
TIME: *30 minutes; allow 1 hour to soak the hijiki beforehand*

½ cup dried hijiki
1 tablespoon tamari
½ cup halved and sliced onions
1 tablespoon finely chopped garlic
2 tablespoons canola oil
½ teaspoon salt
2 cups fresh green beans
2 tablespoons grated ginger (or 1 tablespoon ginger juice or 1½ teaspoons ginger powder)

Soak the hijiki in 3 cups of water for about 1 hour. Then wash it carefully to remove any sand, and place it in a saucepan with the tamari and a few cups of water. Cook at medium heat until the water has nearly evaporated.

Meanwhile, sauté the onions and garlic in oil, along with the salt, for about 4 minutes. Cut the tips from the green beans and add them to the sautéed onions. Cook until the beans are tender-crisp. Then add the hijiki and ginger and mix well. Continue cooking for another minute or so, and serve immediately.

Savory Autumn Squash Bounty

YIELD: *6 servings*
TIME: *25 minutes*

1 tablespoon corn oil
2 cups sliced onions
2 cups peeled and diced winter
  squash
2 cups thinly sliced parsnips,
  cut on the diagonal (or 2
  cups sliced carrots)
¼ cup water
4 teaspoons chopped savory
  (or 2 teaspoons dried
  savory)
¼ teaspoon salt
½ cup sliced scallion greens
4 teaspoons grated ginger (or
  2 teaspoons ginger juice, or
  ¾ teaspoon ginger powder)

Heat the oil in a large saucepan. Sauté the onions, winter squash, and parsnips for about 5 minutes, stirring occasionally. Add the water, savory, and salt. Then cover and cook on low heat for 10 minutes. Add the scallion greens and ginger, stir gently, and let stand, covered, for 5 minutes. Serve hot.

Luscious Nectared Butternut Squash

YIELD: *8 servings*
TIME: *20 to 25 minutes*

*2 cups peeled and coarsely
   diced butternut squash*
1 cup thinly sliced carrots
1 cup coarsely chopped onions
1 cup water
*juice from 1 orange (about
   ⅓ cup)*
3 tablespoons white miso

Place the vegetables and water in a saucepan and simmer for 15 minutes or until the squash is tender. Dissolve the miso in the orange juice. Add this mixture to the vegetables. Simmer for a few more minutes and serve hot.

VARIATION 1

Add 2 cups of broccoli florets after the other vegetables have cooked about 5 minutes.

VARIATION 2

Add 1½ cups of stemmed and coarsely chopped kale to the main recipe. You should add the kale after the other vegetables have cooked for 3 to 4 minutes.

Lemon Garlic Cauliflower-Broccoli Sauté

YIELD: *6 servings*
TIME: *25 to 30 minutes*

2 tablespoons canola oil
1 cup diced onions
1 tablespoon minced garlic
*1 tablespoon peeled and
   minced ginger*
1 teaspoon salt
1 cup water
*3 cups cauliflower (cut into
   bite-sized pieces)*
*3 cups broccoli (cut into bite-
   sized pieces)*
1 tablespoon lemon juice
*1 tablespoon lemon zest
   (optional)*

*T*his vegetable dish has a delicately balanced flavor. A word of caution, however: When an acid is used with a green vegetable, the vegetable will lose its appealing bright green color. To avoid this, you might add the lemon juice just before you serve the vegetables.

Heat the oil in a large skillet. Add the onions, garlic, ginger, and salt. Sauté for 5 to 6 minutes. Add the water and cauliflower, cover the pan, and steam the vegetables for 3 minutes. Then add the broccoli, cover again, and steam for 4 minutes longer. (The broccoli should be bright green and tender.) Add the lemon juice to the vegetables just before serving. If you wish, sprinkle lemon zest over the vegetables as a garnish.

Cauliflower "au Gratin"

YIELD: *6 servings*
TIME: *10 minutes preparation; 45 to 55 minutes cooking; allow an additional 25 to 30 minutes to make the sauce*

*1 large head cauliflower
  (about 6 cups)*
1 cup diced onions
*2 cups Vegan Béchamel Sauce
  (page 163)*
½ teaspoon salt
½ teaspoon black pepper
½ teaspoon garlic powder
1 teaspoon nutritional yeast
*2 tablespoons whole wheat
  bread crumbs*
*½ teaspoon paprika,
  preferably Hungarian*

Cut the cauliflower into medium pieces and place in a bowl with the onions. Set aside.

Heat the sauce in a small saucepan. Add the salt, pepper, garlic powder, and yeast to the sauce. Pour the sauce over the vegetables and stir gently.

Oil a loaf pan. Pour the vegetables and sauce into the pan and press lightly. Sprinkle the bread crumbs and paprika over the vegetables. Cover and bake in a preheated oven at 350 degrees F for 45 to 55 minutes.

Most fresh produce in the United States travels an average of 1,300 miles before it is eaten. These lengthy journeys result in lost nutritional value, especially for the more volatile vitamins such as vitamins C and A. Refrigerated broccoli, for example, loses nearly 20 percent of its vitamin C in one day and nearly 35 percent in two days.

American-Style Brussels Sprouts

YIELD: *5 servings*
TIME: *15 to 20 minutes*

3 tablespoons dried arame
½ cup warm water
1 tablespoon sesame oil
1 cup diced onions
1½ teaspoons minced garlic
½ cup julienned carrots
½ cup whole-kernel corn
1 teaspoon chopped thyme (or
    ½ teaspoon dried thyme)
¼ teaspoon sea salt
1 cup stemmed and halved
    brussels sprouts

A rame is probably the mildest of the sea vegetables, which makes it appropriate to use in a transitional diet. Because arame grows close to the surface of the ocean, it is quite clean and does not need the thorough rinsing that other sea vegetables require. Arame is rich in iron and calcium.

Soak the arame in the warm water for 5 minutes. Drain and chop the arame into small pieces. (You should have about ¼ cup of soaked arame.) Heat the oil in a saucepan. Sauté the onions, garlic, carrots, and corn, along with the seasonings, for 5 minutes, or until the onions are translucent. Add the arame and brussels sprouts and continue to cook 8 to 10 minutes longer. (The brussels sprouts should still be bright green and firm.) Serve hot.

VARIATION
Omit the corn and sea salt and add 5 teaspoons of umeboshi vinegar to the cooked vegetables.

Arame with Onions and Carrots

YIELD: *8 servings*
TIME: *25 to 30 minutes*

2 tablespoons roasted sesame
    oil
2 cups halved and sliced
    onions
½ cup peeled and grated
    carrots

Heat the oil in a large skillet. Sauté the onions and carrots with the tamari for 5 minutes, stirring constantly. Add the remaining ingredients and stir well. Cover the skillet and cook until the vegetables have absorbed all of the water (about 20 minutes). Serve hot.

VARIATION: *Sautéed Arame in Onion Baskets*
Cut each of 4 onions in half crosswise. Cut a thin slice from the bottom of each onion half so it will sit level. Hollow out

1 tablespoon tamari
2 cups dried arame
2 cups water
*1 tablespoon barley malt
    syrup*
2 tablespoons gomasio*
2 tablespoons tahini

*Gomasio is a condiment available in most health food stores. You can also make your own; see page 36.

the center, leaving about three layers of onion. Steam the onion halves for 3 to 4 minutes. Set aside.

Prepare the recipe for Arame with Onions and Carrots. Fill the onion halves with the arame mixture while it is still hot. Garnish with thinly sliced scallions and serve immediately.

Collard Greens with Arame and Carrots

YIELD: *6 servings*
TIME: *25 minutes*

5 tablespoons dried arame
½ cup warm water
4 teaspoons olive oil
1 cup sliced onions
1 cup julienned carrots
½ teaspoon minced ginger
½ cup water
*1 cup summer squash, cut
    into ¼-inch slices and
    halved*
*2 cups stemmed and chopped
    collard greens, packed*
2½ tablespoons white miso
2 tablespoons lemon juice

Soak the arame in warm water for 5 to 10 minutes. Drain and chop the arame into small pieces. (You should have about ⅔ cup of chopped arame.)

Heat the oil in a saucepan. Sauté the onions, carrots, and ginger for about 5 minutes, or until the onions are translucent. Add the ½ cup of water. Then stir in the summer squash and collard greens and cook about 4 minutes.

Mix the miso and lemon juice together and add to the vegetables. Cook the vegetables about 3 minutes longer. (The greens should be cooked thoroughly.) Serve hot.

Sautéed Fiddleheads with Fresh Herbs

YIELD: *6 servings*
TIME: *20 minutes*

2 tablespoons olive oil
¾ cup chopped onions
2 teaspoons minced garlic
½ cup julienned carrots
½ teaspoon salt
1 tablespoon chopped
    cilantro, packed
1 tablespoon chopped basil
2 cups fresh fiddleheads,
    trimmed of their black tips

*F*iddleheads are available only in the springtime, so this recipe will be one to look forward to during the rest of the year. The fresh herbs are a superb complement to the recipe. In Canada, the fiddlehead ''harvesters'' travel northward, following the warm weather and picking the fiddleheads that blossom with the change in season.

Heat the oil in a saucepan. Sauté the onions, garlic, carrots, salt, and fresh herbs for about 3 minutes. Add the fresh fiddleheads and sauté 5 minutes longer, stirring occasionally to ensure even cooking. (The fiddleheads should be a rich green and semi-soft.) Serve hot.

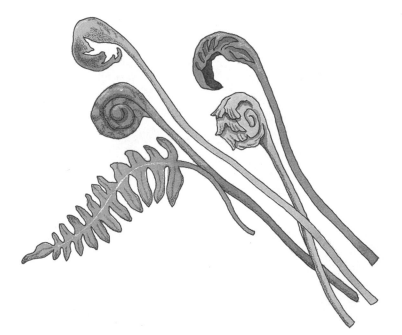

Bouquetière of Vegetables

YIELD: *4 servings*
TIME: *15 minutes preparation; 30 minutes cooking*

2 large, firm tomatoes (about 3½ inches in diameter)
1 carrot
12 broccoli florets
12 cauliflower florets
ice water
8 medium-size mushrooms herb olive oil (see recipe below)
¼ cup whole wheat bread crumbs (optional)

Cut each tomato in half crosswise and scoop out a third of the flesh from the center of the tomato. Peel the carrot and cut 8 carrot curls, using a peeler, and roll the curls fairly tightly. Steam the carrot curls and the broccoli and cauliflower florets about 1 to 2 minutes. (They should be tender-crisp; the carrots may need to cook longer than the other vegetables.) Douse the vegetables in ice water, drain, and set aside.

Sauté the mushrooms or use them raw. Distribute the vegetables evenly among the tomato halves. Lightly brush the vegetables with herb olive oil. Sprinkle bread crumbs on top, if you wish. Bake in a preheated oven at 350 degrees F for 10 to 15 minutes. Serve immediately.

Herb Olive Oil

½ cup olive oil
1 teaspoon garlic powder
1 teaspoon salt
1 teaspoon dried basil
1 teaspoon dried tarragon

Mix all of the ingredients together.

Peas Bonne Femme

YIELD: *6 servings*
TIME: *20 to 30 minutes*

2 tablespoons corn oil
1 cup chopped onions
1 teaspoon minced garlic (or
    ½ teaspoon garlic powder)
1 teaspoon salt
¼ teaspoon white pepper
¼ cup unbleached flour
1 tablespoon smoked yeast
1 cup soy milk
2 cups green peas
¼ cup smoked tempeh
    (optional)
1 cup shredded lettuce

Heat the oil in a medium saucepan. Sauté the onions and garlic with the salt and pepper until the onions are semi-translucent. Add the flour and smoked yeast, stirring constantly for 3 minutes, or until the flour is cooked. Add the soy milk, pouring only half at a time and blending well with each addition.

Add the peas and the smoked tempeh, if you wish, and cook for about 5 minutes. (The peas should become bright green and barely soft.) Add the shredded lettuce, mixing into the sauce; the lettuce need not be cooked. Serve hot.

VARIATION 1: *Italian Green Beans Bonne Femme*
Substitute 2 cups of green beans for the peas. You may need to cook the beans for more than 5 minutes, unless you use precooked beans.

VARIATION 2: *Carrots Bonne Femme*
Substitute 2 cups of carrots for the peas. First, peel and slice the carrots into ¼-inch slices. Steam them *al dente* and add them to the sauce as you would add the peas. (If you wish to have both carrots and peas in the dish, use 1 cup of each.)

VARIATION 3: *Butternut Squash Bonne Femme*
Peel and dice a butternut squash to substitute for the peas. Measure out 2 cups of prepared squash and steam it until soft. Add the squash to the sauce as you would add the peas.

Side Dish Grains, Potatoes, and Pasta

*P*rotein is often the focus of a meal and is often looked upon as the core of a diet. In my opinion, complex carbohydrates are the heart and soul of good nutrition. This chapter focuses on grains, potatoes, and pastas, which are excellent sources of complex carbohydrates, besides supplying essential vitamins and minerals to the diet. Grains are also an excellent source of fiber.

In macrobiotics, grains are considered an ascending energy—also called a heavens energy or a vertical energy. (Meat, on the other hand, is considered an earth energy, or horizontal energy.) In general, people on a whole-grains diet tend to exude more energy, since grains are easy to digest and are packed with complex carbohydrates. Although grains, potatoes, and pasta are included in many of the entrée recipes in this book, the dishes in this chapter are intended to accompany other entrées that are more protein-based, such as tofu, seitan, or tempeh dishes.

Cooking Grains

The following table gives yields and cooking times for various grains. Each quantity begins with one cup of the dried grain.

GRAIN	WATER	COOKING TIME	YIELD
Medium-grain brown rice	2 cups	45 minutes	3 cups
Millet	3 cups	45 minutes	3½ cups
Bulgar wheat	2 cups	20 minutes	2½ cups
Whole barley	3 cups	75 minutes	3½ cups
Buckwheat (kasha)	2 cups	15 minutes	2½ cups
Cracked wheat	2 cups	25 minutes	2⅓ cups
Coarse corn meal	4 cups	25 minutes	3 cups

GRAIN	WATER	COOKING TIME	YIELD
Wild rice	3 cups	60 minutes	4 cups
Quinoa	2 cups	15 minutes	2½ cups
Whole wheat berries	3 cups	2 hours	2⅔ cups
Wehani rice	2¼ cups	60 minutes	3 cups

Always cook grains in a pan with a fairly tight-fitting lid. Note that as the quantity of rice increases, the amount of cooking water decreases proportionately. This is because water evaporation lessens with the greater mass of rice.

Some Facts About Grains

There are four main parts of a grain—the husk, bran, endosperm, and germ. The husk is a protective covering that has little or no nutritional value. The bran consists primarily of cellulose, an insoluble fiber, and contains small amounts of the B-complex vitamins, minerals (especially iron), and protein. The endosperm is the largest part of the grain and contains the starch that is converted into glucose for energy. This part contains protein, amino acids, and trace amounts of other nutrients. The germ is the center of the grain and is especially high in B vitamins, vitamin E, protein, unsaturated fat, minerals, and carbohydrates.

RICE   Rice has been the staple food in much of Asia since 3000 B.C.; currently, it is the staple food for more than half the world's population. About 200 billion pounds of rice are produced each year. The United States grows one percent of the world's rice; Americans consume a small percentage of that amount. The average Asian eats about 400 pounds of rice a year, whereas the average American eats about 10 pounds a year.

Rice supplies a very small amount of protein as well as calcium, iron, zinc, and most of the B vitamins. There are many different types of rice, including short grain, medium grain, long grain, and sweet rice. When it comes to rice dishes, some of the most creative combinations come in the form of pilafs, in which rice is cooked with various seasonings and other ingredients (such as nuts and seeds, vegetables and fruit, and so on). When buying rice, check the grains, if you can. Avoid buying packages in which there are a lot of green-tipped grains. These indicate that the rice was harvested a little too soon. Fully mature rice will be of higher quality.

To prepare rice in a pressure cooker, first wash the rice thoroughly and place it in the pressure cooker; do not add salt. Add water and cook over a low heat for about 15 minutes. Then add the salt, fasten the cooker lid, and increase to high heat. When the pressure is up, place a flame deflector under the pressure cooker, reduce the heat to low, and cook for 50 minutes. Bring the pressure down by placing a chopstick (or similar long, thin utensil) under the pressure gauge. This allows the pressure to release more quickly and makes a lighter, fluffier rice.

To prepare a rice pilaf, sauté the raw rice first in preheated oil, over medium heat, until the rice is golden brown and begins to let off a toasty scent. Add vegetables and seasonings and sauté for about three to five minutes, being careful not to burn the rice. Then add water, cover, and cook until the water is absorbed and the rice is tender.

WHEAT   This grain is common throughout the world; it is particularly popular in the United States. Wheat was first brought to Mexico by the Spaniards in 1530. It was brought to New England and planted there by colonists in 1602. Around the same time, in 1611, early colonists planted wheat in Virginia.

Like most grains, wheat is an acid food and is therefore somewhat mucoid. When soaked, however, the wheat berries become alkaline. In this form, the alkaline wheat inhibits mineral absorption. Whole wheat is a good source of B-complex vitamins. It is also a modest source of calcium, iron, and protein.

MILLET   Millet takes its name from the Latin word meaning "a thousand"— perhaps because of the plant's prolific seeds. Millet is believed to be the one grain that could support life in the absence of all other grains. It also has played an important part in the history of food.

Millet has been found in the pyramids and tombs of ancient Egyptians. The ancient Greek philosopher Pythagoras encouraged his followers to eat millet to improve their health and vitality. In the Bible (Ezekiel 4), God tells Ezekiel to make bread from millet and other grains. This grain even plays a part in the history of art: millet was the favorite grain of Leonardo da Vinci!

Today, millet is still popular in Africa, where it feeds both people and animals. It is native to eastern Asia and is today the staple food of northern China. Finally, millet is the staple food of the Hunzas, who are renowned for their longevity.

Millet is the only alkaline grain; as such, it can be enjoyed by people who are sensitive to high-acid foods—for example, those suffering from ulcers, diabetes, or arthritis. It has all of the essential amino acids, in percentages comparable to meat or dairy products. It is rich in calcium, magnesium, potassium, iron, vitamins B_1, B_2, A, and C, and choline, which helps control cholesterol levels.

BARLEY   Barley is one of the oldest cultivated grains and probably originated in Africa or Asia. As long ago as 5000 B.C., the Egyptians used barley as food for both people and animals. It was used in China about 3000 B.C. Barley was the chief grain for bread for the ancient Greeks, Hebrews, and Romans. This grain contains all nine essential amino acids, as well as natural sugars and starches. It is a good source of calcium, iron, B_1, B_2, and B_3. Barley has the same type of beneficial soluble fiber as oats.

JOB'S TEARS   Hato mugi, or Job's tears, is a highly esteemed grain that has been considered since ancient times to be both delicious and nutritious. The ancient Greeks called it Hera's tears (Hera being the wife of Zeus). The Romans called it *lacryma*, the Latin word for "tears." The Bible refers to this grain by its current name of Job's tears.

This giant grain has been cultivated in China for more than 4,000 years. It was introduced recently into the natural foods industry in the United States by Japanese suppliers of macrobiotic foods. Job's tears is known in natural foods circles as pearl barley and sometimes is labeled as such. This name is easily confused with the common small grain, pearled barley. It is also known by its Japanese name, hato mugi.

Job's tears has excellent nutritional composition and is a good source of dietary fiber. A two-ounce serving supplies 38 grams of carbohydrates and contains just 216 calories. The grain is high in potassium, magnesium, phosphorus, protein, thiamine, iron, and zinc. It is extremely low in fat, cholesterol, and sodium. Job's tears are delicious cooked by themselves or combined with other grains—in pilafs, grain salads, soups, or stews.

CORN   Corn is actually a vegetable and not a grain, although the kernels are dried and ground into flour much as kernels of wheat are ground. According to archaeologists, corn grew wild in southern Mexico 9,000 years ago. The Mayans, Incas, and Aztecs worshipped corn. Later, other Native Americans incorporated corn into their religion, calling it the "seed of seed," "sacred mother," or "blessed daughter." It is still a main source of food for many indigenous peoples of the Americas.

Corn is more economical as a crop because its yield per acre is about three times that of wheat. Corn is rich in unsaturated fats. Ground, it is excellent in polenta and bread. The whole kernels are a wonderful addition to any pilaf.

Pastas

There was a time in the United States when pasta simply meant spaghetti. With a growing interest in nutrition, pasta has become a very popular food. There is now a wide range of pastas available, both dried and fresh. In addition, some whole foods companies are marketing a variety of pastas made from organically grown grains.

Pasta is formed from a paste of high-gluten flour (durum wheat semolina flour) moistened with water (and sometimes with egg). The paste is squeezed between rollers until it is a densely compacted sheet; pasta makers call this process laminating. The harder the dough is rolled, the better "bite" the pasta will have when it is cooked. Shaped pastas, such as shells, rotini, and wagon wheels, are extruded and don't have the same bite as rolled pastas.

There are several advantages to fresh pasta over dried pasta: fresh pasta is more colorful and flavorful, cooks in less time, and absorbs the flavor of sauce more fully. On the other hand, it is more expensive than dried pasta, requires refrigeration (and must be used within a few days), and is less available than dried pasta. Dried pastas are now becoming available in an interesting assortment of exciting flavors.

Generally speaking, most whole wheat pastas are heavy and fall apart easily. I recommend experimenting with different brands; some are much lighter than others. Whole wheat pasta offers more beneficial fiber. However, if you are planning to serve pasta with a fresh vegetable dish, your meal may not need the additional fiber of whole wheat pasta; a lighter pasta actually may be more appropriate.

One type of pasta I recommend highly is lupini, made from durum semolina flour, whole triticale (a cross between wheat and rye), and whole sweet lupine seed flour. The lupine is a pea-like plant that has been cultivated by every civilization since ancient Babylon. Botanists have developed the sweet lupine plant through 50 years of selective breeding. The sweet lupine seed tastes fresh and sweet. When ground and combined with high quality cereal flour, the result is a complete-protein pasta. A four-ounce serving of lupini pasta contains more protein than three eggs, more fiber than five slices of whole wheat bread, and more calcium than four ounces of milk. In addition, it contains no cholesterol or salt, and this same serving offers 15 percent fewer calories than most other pastas! Another unique element of this pasta is that it does not stick after cooking.

The proper cooking of pasta is essential to a beautiful end product. The first stage is to bring the water to a boil with a little sea salt and some oil (about a tablespoon per quart of water). Then lower the heat to a simmer and add the pasta. Keep the quantity of pasta in proper proportion to the water so the pasta cooks evenly. Stir the pasta frequently for the first few minutes to prevent it from sticking. Then stir it occasionally until it is done. Use a wooden spoon to stir pasta, because the sharp edge of a steel spoon may cut into it. After cooking the pasta, rinse it in cold water to prevent further cooking and drain. If you are not planning to serve the pasta immediately, it is best to add a little oil to it and toss it every once in a while; this will help prevent the pasta from sticking.

Savory Vegetable Rice Pilaf

YIELD: *6 servings*
TIME: *15 minutes preparation (allow 1 hour to cook the rice); 1 hour baking*

2½ cups water
1⅓ cups short-grain brown
   rice
½ teaspoon sea salt
2 tablespoons olive oil
1½ cups julienned carrots
1½ cups julienned onions
1 tablespoon minced garlic
4 teaspoons chopped savory
   (or 2 teaspoons dried
   savory)
4 teaspoons chopped basil (or
   2 teaspoons dried basil)
1 teaspoon cumin
¼ teaspoon black pepper
1½ cups thinly sliced celery

Bring the water to a boil in a medium saucepan. Add the rice and ½ teaspoon salt. Cook, covered, for about 1 hour.

Heat the oil in a large skillet. Sauté the carrots, onions, and garlic, along with the savory, basil, cumin, and pepper, for 5 minutes. Add the celery and continue cooking 3 to 4 minutes. Stir in the cooked rice and pour the mixture into a baking dish. Cover and bake at 350 degrees F for 1 hour.

Aduki Bean Brown Rice Pilaf

YIELD: *7 servings*
TIME: *90 minutes*

1 cup aduki beans
one 2-inch piece kombu
1 cup brown rice
pinch of sea salt
1 tablespoon sesame or
 safflower oil
1 cup finely diced carrots
1 cup peeled and finely diced
 onions
2 tablespoons minced garlic
 (or 1 tablespoon garlic
 powder)
3 tablespoons tamari
½ cup water
1 scallion, finely sliced, for
 garnish
¼ cup finely diced red bell
 pepper, for garnish

Wash the beans and put them in a medium saucepan with the kombu and 6 cups of water. Cover and cook until the beans are soft but not mushy (about 1½ hours). Meanwhile, you can cook the rice.

Wash the rice and place it in a small saucepan with 2 cups of water and the salt. Cover, simmer, and cook for 35 to 45 minutes, or until the rice is soft. Set aside.

Heat the oil in a large skillet. Sauté the carrots, onions, and garlic, along with the tamari, for a few minutes. Add about ½ cup water when the vegetables begin to brown. Cook until the vegetables are soft (about 10 minutes). Combine the rice, beans, and vegetables. Serve hot, garnished with the scallion and red bell pepper.

The best way to lighten a pilaf is to add shredded or finely cut raw vegetables to the pilaf shortly before serving.

Bulgur Rice Pilaf

YIELD: *4 servings*
TIME: *45 to 50 minutes*

½ cup brown rice
1 cup bulgur
¾ teaspoon sea salt
1 tablespoon olive oil
¾ cup finely diced onions
¾ cup finely diced carrots
4 teaspoons minced garlic (or
  2 teaspoons garlic powder)
2 tablespoons dill weed
⅛ teaspoon black pepper
¾ cup green peas (fresh or
  frozen)
1 tablespoon dark miso

Wash the rice and place it in a saucepan with 1 cup of water. Bring to a simmer, cover, and cook until soft (about 40 minutes).

Meanwhile, place the bulgur in a separate pan with 2 cups of water and ¼ teaspoon of the salt. Bring to a simmer, cover, and cook until soft (about 20 minutes).

Heat the oil in a skillet. Add the onions, carrots, garlic, dill weed, pepper, and remaining ½ teaspoon salt. Sauté for 5 to 8 minutes, or until the vegetables are barely tender. (If necessary, add just enough water to keep the vegetables from sticking to the pan.) Add the peas and miso to the vegetables. Continue cooking for 5 minutes. Then add the cooked rice and bulgur and cook 5 minutes longer. Serve hot.

German Rice Pilaf

YIELD: *7 servings*
TIME: *15 minutes; allow 45 minutes to cook the rice beforehand*

2 tablespoons sesame oil
2 cups diced red onions
1 cup unpeeled potatoes, diced

*T*his recipe calls for cooked rice. If necessary, refer to the chart on page 186 for directions on cooking rice.

Heat the oil in a large skillet and add the onions, potatoes, celery, caraway seeds, and pepper. When the vegetables begin to brown, add the water. Continue cooking until the water evaporates completely (10 to 15 minutes). Then add

1 cup diced celery
1 tablespoon caraway seeds
¼ teaspoon black pepper
    (optional)
¾ cup water
2 to 4 tablespoons white miso,
    dissolved in ¼ cup water
4 cups cooked brown rice

the dissolved miso and mix thoroughly. (Use the larger quantity of miso if you want a stronger flavor.) Stir in the cooked rice, heat through, and serve hot.

Indian Rice Pilaf

YIELD: *6 servings*
TIME: *15 minutes; allow 45 minutes to cook the rice beforehand*

2 tablespoons sesame oil
2 cups diced onions
¾ cup sliced carrots
1 cup finely diced potatoes
4 teaspoons minced garlic (or
    2 teaspoons garlic powder)
1 tablespoon curry powder
1 teaspoon salt
1 cup water
1 cup green peas (fresh or
    frozen)
½ cup dark raisins
3 cups cooked brown rice
½ cup toasted coconut or ½
    cup toasted almonds or ¼
    cup each (optional)

*T*his recipe calls for cooked rice. If necessary, refer to the chart on page 186 for directions on cooking rice.

Heat the oil in a saucepan. Add the onions, carrots, potatoes, garlic, curry powder, and salt. Sauté until the onions are translucent. Then add the water and continue cooking for about 5 minutes. Add the peas and raisins, and cook until the peas become bright green. (The peas should still be firm.) Stir in the cooked rice, mixing well. Add the toasted coconut and/or the toasted almonds, if you wish. Serve hot.

Special Baked Potatoes

YIELD: *4 servings*

TIME: *20 minutes preparation; 50 minutes baking*

*3 medium-sized baking
    potatoes*
*2 to 3 tablespoons unrefined
    corn oil*
½ cup finely diced onions
*¼ cup finely diced red bell
    peppers*
¼ cup finely diced scallions
*1 teaspoon minced garlic (or
    ½ teaspoon garlic powder)*
½ to 1 teaspoon salt
¼ teaspoon black pepper
*1 tablespoon smoked yeast or
    nutritional yeast*

Wash the potatoes and wrap them in foil. Bake them in a preheated oven at 375 degrees F for 40 minutes. (They should be soft in the center.) Remove from oven and unwrap. Cut each potato in half lengthwise and scoop out the potato pulp, leaving a thin layer next to the skin. (For this recipe, you will need only four good potato skin shells, but the pulp from all three potatoes.) Run the pulp through a ricer or food processor to make a smooth paste.

Heat 2 tablespoons of oil in a skillet. Add the onions, bell peppers, scallions, garlic, salt, and pepper. Sauté until the onions are translucent. Add the sautéed vegetables and the yeast to the potato pulp. Blend well. For a moister, richer taste, add another tablespoon of oil to the potato mixture if you wish. Spoon the mixture into a pastry bag and pipe it into the four potato skin shells. (You may spoon the mixture directly into the shells if you prefer.) Bake the stuffed potatoes in a preheated oven at 350 degrees F for 5 to 10 minutes. Serve hot.

Florentine Potatoes

YIELD: *8 servings*
TIME: *45 minutes*

*8 cups peeled and diced
  potatoes*
4 cups water
1¼ teaspoons sea salt
*1½ tablespoons olive oil (or
  unrefined corn oil)*
1¼ cups finely diced onions
½ teaspoon minced garlic
*2 packed cups chopped
  spinach, with stems
  removed*
¼ teaspoon black pepper
1 cup soy milk

Place the potatoes in a large saucepan with the water and ¼ teaspoon of salt. Cover and simmer for about 25 minutes, or until the potatoes are soft. Set aside.

Heat the oil in a skillet. Add the onions, garlic, and spinach, with the pepper and the remaining teaspoon of salt. Sauté for 5 minutes.

Drain the potatoes and mash them until they are smooth. Add the spinach mixture and the soy milk. Mix well and serve hot.

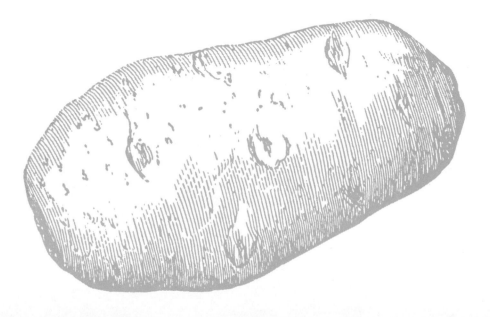

Millet "Mashed Potatoes"

YIELD: *10 to 12 servings*
TIME: *10 minutes preparation; 45 minutes cooking*

2 cups millet
6 cups water
4 cups cauliflower pieces
¼ teaspoon black pepper
2 tablespoons soy margarine
  (or unrefined corn oil)
1½ teaspoons sea salt
  (optional)
⅛ teaspoon nutmeg (or ¼
  teaspoon dill weed;
  optional)

Wash and drain the millet. Place all ingredients (except the optional spice) in a large pot and bring to a simmer over high heat. Lower heat, cover, and continue cooking until the millet mixture is soft (about 45 minutes). Check periodically to make sure the mixture does not burn. Mash the mixture using a potato masher, or blend it for about 30 seconds in a food processor. Add one of the optional spices, if you wish, and serve hot.

Hungarian Noodles and Cabbage

YIELD: *4 to 6 servings*
TIME: *15 to 20 minutes*

2 cups sliced green cabbage
2 tablespoons unrefined corn
  oil
1 cup halved and sliced onions
2 teaspoons minced garlic
¾ teaspoon sea salt
¾ teaspoon black pepper
1½ tablespoons paprika,
  preferably Hungarian

*T*he combination of cabbage and noodles pleases the palate. In preparing this dish, I recommend sautéing the cabbage and onions separately. This method brings out the flavor of each food.

This side dish is a wonderful accompaniment to German Sauerbraten (page 146), Sezekle Gulos (page 154), and Swiss-Style Shredded Seitan (page 153).

Sauté the cabbage in 1 tablespoon of corn oil for about 15 minutes. Set aside.

In a separate pan, sauté the onions and garlic, along with

2 cups cooked noodles of your
choice (whole wheat, udon,
jerusalem artichoke, or
other type of noodles)*
chopped fresh parsley for
garnish

*The noodles should be cooked *al
dente* and rinsed in cold water.

the salt, pepper, and paprika in the remaining corn oil. Cook until the onions are translucent. Stir the onions and cabbage together. Add the cooked noodles and reheat. Serve hot, garnished with parsley.

Soba Noodles and Vegetables

YIELD: *4 to 6 servings*
TIME: *25 minutes*

2 tablespoons olive oil
1 cup julienned carrots
1 cup diagonally sliced
   scallions
1 tablespoon minced garlic
1 tablespoon chopped basil (or
   2 teaspoons dried basil)
½ teaspoon sea salt
4 cups cooked soba noodles
¼ cup white miso, dissolved
   in ¼ cup plus 2 tablespoons
   water

Heat the oil in a saucepan. Add the carrots, scallions, garlic, basil, and salt. Sauté for 5 minutes. Stir the cooked noodles into the vegetables and heat thoroughly. Add the dissolved miso and continue to cook for 2 minutes. Serve hot.

Job's Tears and Corn

YIELD: *5 servings*

TIME: *40 to 50 minutes*

1¼ cups Job's tears (or
   pearled barley)
4 cups water
1 to 2 teaspoons sea salt
½ teaspoon black pepper
2 tablespoons olive oil
1 cup whole-kernel corn
1 cup diced onions
4 teaspoons minced garlic (or
   2 teaspoons garlic powder)
2½ tablespoons chopped
   savory (or 1½ tablespoons
   dried savory)

Place the Job's tears, water, salt, and pepper in a saucepan. Cover and cook until the grain is soft (30 to 40 minutes). Set aside.

Heat the oil in a skillet. Add the corn, onions, garlic, and savory. Sauté until the onions are translucent. Add the vegetables to the cooked Job's tears and mix well. Serve hot.

Breads

*B*read is considered the staple of life. I don't know of any culture that doesn't have some sort of bread in its diet. This food has always been a part of my diet, and some of my favorite bread recipes are included in this section.

Flour is the primary ingredient in bread. There are many types of flours on the market, including wheat, rye, rice, millet, soy, barley, and oat flours. The chemistry of these flours is different, due to the nature of each grain and the form of processing. Oat flour, for example, is high in fat and has good binding qualities. Rye flour has virtually no gluten. Rye bread benefits from the addition of a higher gluten flour such as wheat flour.

There are also different types of wheat flour, including bread flour, cake or pastry flour, and all-purpose flour. (You should use bread flour for the recipes in this book unless otherwise indicated.) Bread flour has a high gluten content. All-purpose flour and pastry flour are low in gluten. Gluten acts as a binder, giving structure to the final product. In fact, it's the gluten in flour that gives bread dough its elasticity. In making bread using low-gluten flour, you can add binders, such as eggs, or you can add gluten flour.

Gluten flour is wheat flour that has had all of the bran and starch removed; as such, it is pure gluten. Any bread can be made lighter by the addition of gluten flour. I normally use a 25/75 mixture of gluten and whole wheat flour (or other flour or starch). Because gluten flour is highly osmotic, it will lump up if added directly to water without an extender. If you are using this flour in a bread recipe, you should mix it with the extender before adding wet ingredients.

Yeast needs food, moisture, and warmth to grow. A dough that is too dry and stiff will not rise properly. The moisture necessary for yeast growth will depend on the gluten content of the flour. Because gluten content varies from one wheat harvest to another, it will vary in the flour formula. In making yeast breads, you may wish to use a smaller quantity of water than that indicated in a recipe. You can always add more water if the dough seems dry or stiff.

Yeast will grow in cool water, but the growth is very slow. Warm water of about 80 to 85 degrees F is ideal. If the water is too warm (110 degrees or more), it will kill the yeast. At 85 degrees, the yeast will activate quickly.

Preparation time for yeast breads depends to some extent on the temperature of the environment and the dough. If the room or the dough is cold, it will take significantly longer for the dough to rise. It's a good idea to keep all ingredients slightly warm in order to maintain yeast growth. You should also let the rising dough rest in a warm place—not to exceed 120 degrees F.

Active yeast should be used within a few weeks, because the yeast will die over a period of time. Dry yeast can be kept in the refrigerator if the room temperature is very high. In recipes calling for yeast, you can use cakes of yeast (compressed yeast) or dry packaged yeast. As a rule of thumb, 1 ounce of compressed yeast equals ½ ounce, or 1½ tablespoons, of dry yeast.

Following are some helpful hints for making bread:

- In recipes calling for baking powder, you can substitute baking soda, following these guidelines: For 1 tablespoon of baking powder, use 1½ teaspoons of baking soda and 1 tablespoon of cider vinegar.
- To form loaves for yeast bread, first flatten out the dough into a round. Then fold the sides in toward the center and press down. Next, fold in the upper edges to a point (like an envelope). Then roll this point downward in a tight roll, pulling it as you roll it, and seal the dough at the end. Gently rock the rolled loaf back and forth until it is long enough to fit into the bread pan.
- Liquid lecithin is a good glazing medium. Simply warm it and brush or gently wipe it onto the bread immediately after baking it. The baked bread will absorb the lecithin, which will give the crust a shine, as if it were egg-washed.

In general, 16 ounces of raw dough will yield 15 ounces of baked bread.

Whole Wheat Onion Herb Bread

YIELD: *3 loaves*

TIME: *30 minutes preparation; 1 to 1½ hours for rising and baking*

2 cups unbleached flour

3 cups stone-ground whole wheat flour

1½ cups finely diced onions

2 teaspoons minced garlic (or 1 teaspoon garlic powder)

1 teaspoon dried basil

1 teaspoon dried thyme

1 teaspoon dried whole rosemary

1 teaspoon salt

4 teaspoons dry yeast

2 tablespoons Sucanat

2 cups warm water

2 tablespoons soy margarine, melted

In a large bowl, mix together the two flours and add the onions, garlic, herbs, and salt.

In a separate bowl, dissolve the yeast and Sucanat in water, and let stand until it begins to foam. Pour this yeast mixture into the flour and herb mixture. Add the melted margarine and mix to form a medium-stiff dough. (Add a little more flour if the dough is too wet or sticky.)

Oil the bread pans. Divide the dough into three equal parts and put the dough in the pans. Lightly oil the top of the dough and place the loaves in a warm area. Allow the dough to rise until nearly doubled in size (30 to 40 minutes). The dough should retain an imprint when you touch it with your finger. When the dough has risen sufficiently, bake the loaves in a preheated oven at 350 degrees F for about 30 minutes, or until golden brown.

Pecan Maple Whole Wheat Bread

YIELD: *1 loaf*
TIME: *25 minutes
preparation; 70 minutes for
rising and baking*

*½ cup roasted, finely ground
    pecans**
*½ ounce (2 packages) dry
    yeast*
½ cup maple syrup
1 cup warm water
*1¾ cups finely ground whole
    wheat flour*
1 cup unbleached flour
¾ teaspoon salt
*about 2 tablespoons unrefined
    corn oil*

*Roast the pecans first at 375
degrees F for 10 to 15 minutes.
Set aside to cool. Then grind the
pecans in a food processor. Be
careful not to overprocess them,
or you will end up with pecan
butter.

*T*his is a superb breakfast bread.

Dissolve the yeast and 2 tablespoons of maple syrup in the water. Set aside until the yeast begins to foam (about 5 minutes).

Combine the two flours, salt, and pecan meal in a large bowl. Add the yeast mixture and the remaining 6 tablespoons of maple syrup to the dry ingredients. Mix to form a medium-stiff dough, and continue mixing (or kneading) for 4 to 5 minutes. Roll out the dough on a lightly floured surface, form into a loaf, and place it in a lightly oiled loaf pan. Brush the top of the bread with a little oil, and put the pan in a warm place for the dough to rise. (The risen dough should hold a dent when gently touched.) Bake in a preheated oven at 375 degrees F for about 40 minutes. Immediately on removing the bread from the oven, lightly brush a little unrefined corn oil on the top crust.

Oat Bran Russian Black Bread

YIELD: *1 large loaf*
TIME: *15 minutes
preparation; 65 to 70 minutes
for rising and baking*

*1 ounce (3 tablespoons) dry
    yeast
1 teaspoon Sucanat
1 cup warm water
¾ cup rye flour
2 cups stone-ground whole
    wheat flour
1 teaspoon salt
1 cup oat bran
1 tablespoon carob or cocoa
    powder
1 teaspoon caraway seeds
1 teaspoon fennel seeds
2 tablespoons cider vinegar
2 tablespoons dark molasses
2 tablespoons corn oil
1 tablespoon minced onion*

Dissolve the yeast and Sucanat in about ½ cup warm water and set aside until the yeast is foamy (about 5 minutes).

Combine the rye flour, whole wheat flour, salt, oat bran, carob or cocoa powder, caraway seeds, and fennel seeds.

In a separate bowl, combine the vinegar, molasses, corn oil, and onion. Add the wet ingredients to the dry ingredients and blend well. Add the yeast mixture and the remaining ½ cup water and mix thoroughly. If the dough is stiff or dry, add another ¼ cup warm water; if the dough is sticky, add up to ½ cup more whole wheat flour. Turn the dough out onto a floured surface; flatten it out; and shape it into a round, shallow loaf. Place the loaf on a lightly oiled baking sheet, brush the surface of the dough with oil, and let it rise in a warm spot until the dough holds an imprint when gently touched (about 30 minutes). Bake the loaf in a preheated oven at 375 degrees F for 35 to 40 minutes. Remove the bread from the oven, place it on a rack to cool, and lightly brush the top with oil.

Arame Sea Vegetable Bread

YIELD: *2 loaves*
TIME: *20 minutes
preparation; 55 to 65 minutes
for rising and baking*

*¼ cup dried arame
2 tablespoons Sucanat (or
    other natural sweetener)*

*Y*ou might want to experiment with this bread, adding different herbs and spices to give it a really exciting flavor.

Mix the arame, Sucanat, and yeast in 1 cup of warm water for 5 minutes.

Combine the flours, salt, and seasonings, and mix well. Add the oil and the yeast mixture to the flour mixture. Then

2 tablespoons dry yeast
2 ½ cups warm water
2 ¼ cups whole wheat flour
2 ¾ cups unbleached flour
1 teaspoon sea salt
1 tablespoon ginger powder
2 tablespoons cooking oil
1 teaspoon garlic powder

add the remaining 1 ½ cups of warm water and mix to form a medium-stiff, elastic dough.

Oil two loaf pans or two 9-inch pie pans. Turn the dough out onto a floured board and roll out the dough to release air pockets. Divide the dough in half, place in the pans, and lightly oil the tops of the loaves. Let stand until the dough has doubled in size and holds a dent when lightly pressed. Bake in a preheated oven at 375 degrees F for 30 to 40 minutes, or until the crusts are medium brown. Remove from the pans and place on a wire rack to cool for at least 10 minutes.

Carrot Corn Bread

YIELD: *1 loaf*
TIME: *15 minutes preparation; 20 to 30 minutes baking*

1 cup corn flour
1 cup unbleached flour
¼ cup Egg Replacer
2 teaspoons baking powder
1 teaspoon salt
½ cup peeled and finely shredded carrots
¼ cup maple syrup (or any liquid sweetener)
2 tablespoons corn oil
¾ cup soy milk

*L*ong ago, corn bread was called corn cakes and was considered a poor man's food. Marie Antoinette loved to dress up as a peasant, venture out into the countryside, and make corn cakes. History claims that this famous queen said of the peasants, "Let them eat cake." She probably was speaking of corn cakes, which were a staple of the peasants' diet.

Mix together the dry ingredients. Then add the carrots, maple syrup, corn oil, and soy milk. Mix just to combine the ingredients. If you overmix, the bread will be tough.

Oil and flour the loaf pan. Pour the batter into the pan, spreading it evenly. Bake the bread in a preheated oven at 375 degrees F for 15 to 20 minutes, or until lightly browned. Carefully remove the baked bread from the pan and cool for five minutes. Serve the bread warm.

Millet Oatmeal Bread

YIELD: *2 loaves*
TIME: *30 minutes preparation; 1 to 1½ hours for rising and baking*

⅓ cup millet
1 cup water
pinch of salt
4 teaspoons dry yeast
½ cup Sucanat
2½ cups warm water
3¾ cups whole wheat flour
1¼ cups gluten flour
1¾ cups rolled oats
2 teaspoons salt
6 tablespoons sunflower seeds
2 tablespoons oil

Wash the millet and put it in a saucepan with 1 cup of water and a pinch of salt. Cover and cook over medium heat until the water is absorbed and the millet is soft. (If the millet isn't cooked completely, add more water, a little at a time, to prevent it from burning.)

Dissolve the yeast and Sucanat in about 1¼ cups warm water. Let stand for about 5 minutes, or until the mixture begins to foam.

In a large bowl, mix together the whole wheat flour, gluten flour, oats, salt, and sunflower seeds. Add the oil, warm millet, yeast mixture, and the remaining 1¼ cups of warm water. Mix into a medium-stiff dough. If the dough is too stiff, add more water, a little at a time. The dough should be light and spongy but not too sticky. Mix on a medium-speed mixer for about 5 minutes, or knead by hand vigorously for about 10 minutes.

Divide the dough into two equal pieces. Lightly oil the loaf pans. Roll out the dough and put it in the pans. Lightly oil the tops of the loaves, and leave the pans in a warm but airy location for about 30 minutes. (The dough will have risen sufficiently when it retains an imprint of your finger when lightly touched.) Bake the loaves in a preheated oven at 375 degrees F for about 30 minutes, or until lightly browned. Immediately on removing from the oven, lightly oil the top of the bread to tenderize the crust.

Quick Rye Beer Bread

YIELD: *One 8-inch round loaf*
TIME: *20 minutes*
preparation; 70 to 75 minutes
for rising and baking

1¼ cups whole wheat flour
1¼ cups unbleached flour
1¼ cups rye flour
¾ cup beer
2 tablespoons honey
1 tablespoon corn oil
½ ounce (2 packages) dry
    yeast
1 tablespoon honey (optional)
1 cup warm water
1 teaspoon caraway seeds
2 teaspoons sea salt
½ teaspoon garlic powder
glaze (optional; see recipe
    below)

Stir the flours together in a large bowl. In a small saucepan, heat the beer, 2 tablespoons of honey, and oil until warm. Meanwhile, dissolve the yeast (and an additional tablespoon of honey, if you wish) in warm water in a large, warm bowl. (The additional honey will help activate the yeast.)

To the yeast mixture, add the warmed beer mixture, caraway seeds, salt, garlic powder, and 1½ cups of the combined flours. Beat until smooth. Stir in the remaining flours. If necessary, add more unbleached flour to make a soft dough. Turn the dough out onto a floured board and knead it until smooth (about 4 minutes). Shape the dough into a ball. Place it in an oiled 8-inch round pan, then flip it upside-down so the top is oiled. Flatten the dough to fit the pan. Cover the pan with a clean cloth and let the dough rise in a warm, draft-free place for 45 minutes. Bake in a preheated oven at 375 degrees F for 25 to 30 minutes. Remove the bread from the pan immediately and brush the crust with corn oil or glaze.

Glaze

2 tablespoons barley malt
    syrup
1 tablespoon mirin
1 tablespoon soy milk
1 tablespoon tahini

Stir together the ingredients to form a smooth glaze.

Boston Brown Bread

YIELD: *4 small loaves*
TIME: *40 minutes*
preparation; 60 to 90 minutes
cooking

1¼ *cups currants (or 1½ cups*
raisins, chopped)
¾ *cup mirin, brandy, or water*
(or ½ cup mirin or brandy
and ¼ cup water)
2 *cups dry whole wheat bread*
crumbs
1 *cup hot water*
1¼ *cups, plus 2 tablespoons,*
soy milk
2 *tablespoons cider vinegar*
¾ *cup molasses*
2 *tablespoons barley malt*
syrup (or honey)
3 *tablespoons corn oil*
¾ *cup unbleached flour*
1½ *cups rye flour*
¾ *cup cornmeal*
1 *tablespoon baking soda*
1½ *teaspoons sea salt*
¼ *to ½ teaspoon allspice*
¼ *to ½ teaspoon white*
pepper
¼ *teaspoon mace*

*B*oston brown bread is a yeast-free bread. Originally, this bread was formed into small loaves, steamed, boiled, or baked, and then served hot. It is a New England specialty and often is served with Boston baked beans. For this recipe, you will need four small empty fruit or vegetable cans (12- to 16-ounce cans).

Soak the currants in the mirin, brandy, or water for about 20 minutes. Then drain well.

Mix the bread crumbs in hot water and soak for about 2 minutes. Meanwhile, mix the soy milk and vinegar in a small bowl. When it has curdled, add the molasses, barley malt syrup, and corn oil. Immediately add the soaked bread crumbs.

In a large bowl, combine the flours, cornmeal, baking soda, salt, allspice, pepper, and mace. Add the bread crumb mixture and the soaked, drained currants. Blend all ingredients thoroughly.

Brush oil on the insides of the cans, and dust with flour. (As an alternative, you could line the cans with baking liner paper.) Fill each can about ¾ full with batter. Cover the can with aluminum foil and secure with a rubber band. Place the four cans in a pressure cooker with water. Begin cooking at a high temperature; when the pressure builds (after about 15 minutes), lower the heat to medium-low for 40 to 45 minutes; then remove from heat and leave the cans in the pressure cooker for a few more minutes. Remove the cans from the pressure cooker and cool on a wire rack.

As an alternative, you could steam the bread in the oven. Place the cans on a rack in a large pot with about a quart of water in it. Cover the pot and steam for about 90 minutes. Remove the cans from the pot and cool on a wire rack.

Desserts

*A*ppropriately, my family name, Pickarski, means "baker." It only stands to reason that baking would be one of my first loves in the kitchen. In fact, I consider pastry making a specialty of mine. This may seem ironic, since the word *dessert* is almost synonymous with empty calories and poor nutrition. So, over the past few years, I have been challenged to create desserts that will actually contribute nutritionally to the diet.

The nutritional density of desserts, like that of any part of a meal, is relative to the quality of the ingredients used. In general, traditional desserts contain a high percentage of sugar, fats, and highly refined flour. (It is natural, then, that we often associate desserts with diabetes, hypoglycemia, cardiovascular problems, and other health disorders.) But when desserts contain healthful ingredients, they can be good for you.

The secret to nutritious desserts is to use more healthful sweeteners, such as whole cane sugar (Sucanat) or brown rice syrup, and to reduce (or even eliminate) highly refined ingredients such as bleached white flour, saturated fats such as butter and shortening, and high-cholesterol ingredients such as eggs. Another key to increasing the nutritional density of desserts is to incorporate vegetables such as squash and carrots, which add nutrients and fiber as well as a delicate sweetness. In addition, you can replace dairy products with ingredients such as tofu and soy milk, which are high in protein and have no cholesterol. The use of such high-nutrition foods balances out the sweeteners that you do use and thereby helps prevent "sugar rushes" in the body.

All of the dessert recipes in this book are vegan, for the most part. (Some recipes include optional dairy products or eggs; but these truly are optional.) My desserts tend to be less sweet than traditional desserts. Partly, this is a result of my using more beneficial sweeteners instead of refined sugars. However, I also find that subtle sweeteners bring out the character of the primary food in the dessert and avoid overwhelming the taste buds. Later, I will discuss some important facts about sweeteners, which may help you make substitutions in recipes as appropriate.

Techniques for Vegan Cakes

With the cake recipes in this chapter, you can create delicious, versatile cakes that do not contain dairy products or eggs. You may find that the cakes are a little heavier than traditional layer cakes, though; you could, of course, add eggs to make the cakes lighter, but this is not essential. Using the following techniques will ensure greater success with making vegan cakes:

- When pouring batter into the cake pans, fill each pan no more than halfway. Otherwise, the cake either will not bake well in the center or will be burned on the outside.
- Handle the baked cake with care. (Vegan cakes are tender.) If the cake does not come out of the pan easily, place it in the freezer. When the cake is frozen, warm the pan on a stove burner for about 15 seconds. Then slide a knife around the sides of the pan, flip the pan over, and lightly tap on the bottom of the pan to remove the cake.
- A vegan cake may tend to be a little drier than non-vegan cakes. To compensate, spread a moist icing on the cake or serve it with fruit, nondairy ice cream, or a dessert sauce. Or you could just plan to serve the cake with a complementary beverage.
- Use a serrated knife to cut the cake. (Better yet, use a clean piece of strong fishing line. Holding the line tightly at both ends, gently descend upon the cake with a slight sawing motion. The advantage of the fishing line is that you don't end up with a sticky utensil.)

Sweeteners

Sugar is a natural refined product made mainly from sugar cane or sugar beets. Before it is refined, it contains calcium, phosphorus, iron, potassium, vitamin E, several B vitamins, copper, manganese, and zinc. Nearly all of these nutrients are gone after the product is refined. The result is sucrose.

Glucose, or dextrose, is derived from starches, such as corn. Fructose, also called levulose, occurs naturally in fruits. Because it is expensive to produce fructose from a fruit source, this sweetener is derived from sugar instead. (Sugar is about 50 percent fructose; honey is about 40 percent fructose.) Some medical researchers now believe that it is the fructose in sugar that is fattening.

Some researchers suggest that fructose may contribute to elevated cholesterol levels because the liver, which produces cholesterol, also stores excess sugars in the form of glucose.

Sorbitol, mannitol, maltitol, and xylitol are sugar alcohols. Like fructose, these sugars exist naturally in fruits but are usually produced from less expensive sources. Also like fructose, they can cause diarrhea if consumed daily in great enough quantities.

Lactose is a milk sugar. It is a natural product derived from milk. The ingredient lactose is made from whey and skim milk.

Raw sugar is much coarser than refined white sugar. Through the refining process, raw sugar retains some minerals but loses most of its vitamins. Turbinado sugar is more highly refined than raw sugar, although these terms sometimes are used interchangeably. Most brown sugar is simply white sugar with caramel coloring added. Some brown sugar, however, is less refined and contains molasses.

GRAIN SWEETENERS   Sweeteners are made from many grains, including corn, barley, and rice. All grain sweeteners are made by combining the grain starch with enzymes. The enzymes convert the starch to sugars, which provide the sweet taste desired. Most grain sweeteners do not need preservatives.

Corn syrup is classified as a modified corn sweetener. This product is made using sulfuric acid as a catalyst to cause the starch in the corn to become sugar. Because it is highly refined, and because the process is aided by an "unfriendly" chemical, I try not to use corn syrup very often.

Corn malt is classified as a natural sweetener. This product is a combination of unprocessed corn grits and barley malt extract. The barley extract, which is made from germinated barley seeds, contains enzymes that convert the starch in the corn grits to a sweet sugar.

Barley malt syrups are made basically in the same way as other grain sweeteners. There are many types of barley malt syrup, but the main difference between them is the percentage of barley malt syrup to other syrup (usually corn syrup). Some barley malt syrups are actually cut with corn syrup; in some, the barley and corn are fermented together. The latter type is preferable, because, as I mentioned, corn syrups generally are not friendly food.

Brown rice syrup is a cultured product made from brown rice, water, and a small amount of natural cereal enzyme. It has a light, delicate flavor, and it is about half as sweet as other sweeteners discussed here. Rice syrup can be used in place of honey or a fruit juice sweetener. Brown rice syrup is also available in powdered form.

SUCANAT   This sweetener arrived on the food scene a few years ago. Sucanat (short for "sugar cane natural") is probably the highest quality sweetener you can buy. It is made by processing the juice from sugar cane. The juice is spun at high temperatures through a vacuum funnel and then is milled into a powder. In this process, only the water and fiber are removed. Apparently, the mineral salts and vitamins naturally present in the sugar cane are retained. Sucanat is moist, like brown sugar, has a slight molasses taste, and can be used in place of white sugar. Because it is not a fully refined product, Sucanat cannot actually be labeled as a sugar.

HONEY   The nutritional value of refined honey is about the same as that of white sugar. Unrefined honey, on the other hand, contains bee pollen and bee propolis. Bee pollen is one of the most nutritious foods on earth, and bee propolis is a natural disinfectant. (The bees spread propolis on dead bees inside the hive.) Propolis may even have some healing properties. Honey is much higher in calories than refined sugar, but it also is much sweeter than sugar. When using honey to replace sugar in a recipe, you generally can use about half the indicated amount.

MAPLE SUGAR   To make a gallon of maple syrup, some 40 gallons of sap have to be collected and boiled down. During the boiling, the sap tends to foam up, impeding the syrup-making process. The best way to combat this foaming is to add a drop of fat or oil (lard, shortening, cream, butter, or vegetable oil). The package label will not indicate this "ingredient." However, some manufacturers produce kosher maple syrup using only vegetable-based oils (generally vegetable shortening). So vegans are safe consuming maple syrup labeled as kosher.

Maple syrup may also contain trace amounts of formaldehyde. This is because, after drilling a hole in the tree, formaldehyde is often used to keep the hole from closing up. The sap then runs over the formaldehyde, which contaminates the sap. The package label should indicate whether this chemical compound was used in collecting sap.

Assuming the product was made using vegetable-based defoamers, and assuming it is not contaminated with formaldehyde, maple syrup is a fine choice for a sweetener. Like honey, it is very sweet, so a little goes a long way. Also like honey, it imparts a special flavor that you may not want in all foods.

Chocolate

Chocolate is a common ingredient in traditional desserts. Some of my dessert recipes call for chocolate, although they may suggest carob as an alternative. I do not really endorse chocolate as a friendly food, but I acknowledge that most people consume this dessert food at least in small quantities. Two alternatives to regular chocolate—cocoa and tofu chocolate—are definitely worth exploring.

Chocolate is high in saturated fats and contains caffeine, which depletes the body of some vitamins. In addition, most chocolate contains milk, so it is not a vegan product. Cocoa, on the other hand, contains no fat and therefore has far fewer calories than regular chocolate. Cocoa is nondairy, but it still contains caffeine.

A wonderful vegan alternative to regular chocolate is tofu chocolate (Barat chocolate), which is widely available at natural foods stores. This product uses tofu powder in place of dairy ingredients and contains Sucanat as a sweetener. It has the creaminess of milk chocolate with the firmness of dark chocolate.

To determine if chocolate is of high quality, place a small piece on your finger to see if it melts. High-quality chocolate contains no wax and should melt at lower temperatures.

Carob Cake

YIELD: *Two 8-inch cakes*
TIME: *15 minutes preparation; 25 to 35 minutes baking*

1 cup unbleached flour
1¼ cups whole wheat pastry
   flour
1 teaspoon baking soda
¼ teaspoon salt
½ cup carob powder (or
   cocoa)
½ cup Sucanat
½ cup unrefined corn oil
¾ cup water
1¼ cups honey (or maple
   syrup)
1 tablespoon cider vinegar
2 teaspoons vanilla extract

1 carob cake, made according
   to the recipe above
7 cups nondairy ice cream
1 cup hazelnut butter
1½ cups Tofu Chocolate
   Ganache (page 234)

*T*his cake has many variables and is one of my old stand-
bys in dairyless, eggless cakes. You can use cocoa powder in
place of carob, if you want to make a chocolate cake.

Sift the two flours together, along with the baking soda, salt,
and carob powder. Stir in the Sucanat.

In a large mixing bowl, stir together the oil, water,
honey, cider vinegar, and vanilla until well blended. Then
add the dry ingredients, mixing at medium speed until well
blended (about 2 minutes).

Lightly oil and flour the cake pans. Divide the batter
equally between the two pans and bake the cakes in a preheated oven for about 20 minutes at 350 degrees F, or until
done (a toothpick comes out of the center clean).

Cool the cakes for about 10 minutes. Then remove them
from the pans and cool completely. Frost the cakes with an
icing of your choice. (See icing recipes, pages 234–237.)

VARIATION: *"Ice Cream" Cake*

Freeze the cake. Then slice it in half horizontally. Line a cake
pan with a large piece of plastic wrap. Place one layer of the
cake inside the pan. Beat the ice cream and nut butter just
until it is soft enough to spread. Spread it over the first layer
of the cake. Add the second layer of cake on top and gently
press to fill in the gaps between the layers. Freeze the cake
completely.

Heat the ganache icing to about 95 degrees F. Pour over
the frozen cake and spread the icing as necessary. Refreeze
the cake. Remove from the freezer about 5 minutes before
serving.

Kanten Cakes

T hese cakes are extremely versatile. A basic kanten cake consists of a regular thin single-layer cake, about one inch tall, spread with a thin layer of pastry cream; then you arrange fresh or stewed fruit on the cake, pour a semi-set kanten (agar) over the entire cake, and chill the cake until the kanten gels completely.

You can use any type of cake, pastry cream (or almond butter), fruit, and fruit juice with the kanten to make these cakes. You can also top the finished cake with any sauce, such as a sabayon or fruit sauce, if you wish. Here is one recipe for a kanten cake, along with a variation. As you can see, though, the variations are practically limitless.

Apple Kanten Cake

YIELD: *One 10-inch cake; 6 to 8 servings*
TIME: *40 minutes preparation (if the carob cake and pastry cream are made already); 2 hours for the cake to set*

1½ to 2 teaspoons agar powder (or 4 to 5 teaspoons agar flakes)
2 cups apple juice
2 tablespoons barley malt syrup
2 cups apples, peeled and thinly sliced

Dissolve the agar powder in the apple juice, along with the barley malt syrup, and simmer for 2 to 3 minutes. (If you are using agar flakes, you will need to cook the solution for 8 to 10 minutes for the flakes to dissolve.) Set aside at room temperature until the kanten sauce is semi-set (about 20 minutes).

Steam the apples until they are tender but still firm.

The carob cake should be about 1 inch tall. (If it is 2 or more inches tall, you should split it into two layers, reserving one layer for another use.)

Spread a thin layer of pastry cream on the carob cake and place it in a clean 10-inch springform pan. Arrange the cooked apples over the cake. When the sauce is semi-set, pour it over the cake. Refrigerate until the kanten is set completely (1½ to 2 hours).

one Carob Cake, made in a 10-inch springform pan (use half the recipe from page 217)

¾ cup Pastry Cream (page 260) or almond butter (optional)

To serve, release the pan spring. Slide a spatula around the sides of the cake. After removing the pan sides, loosen the cake from the pan bottom. Carefully transfer the cake onto a serving plate. (You may instead serve the cake directly from the springform pan.) Serve slices of the kanten cake with a sabayon sauce if you wish.

VARIATION: *Apricot Strawberry Kanten Cake*
Substitute 1½ cups of apricot nectar and ½ cup of papaya juice concentrate for the apple juice. Use slightly more agar than in the main recipe above. Place sliced fresh strawberries over the pastry cream (or very thin coating of almond butter) on the cake. Assemble the kanten cake according to the main recipe.

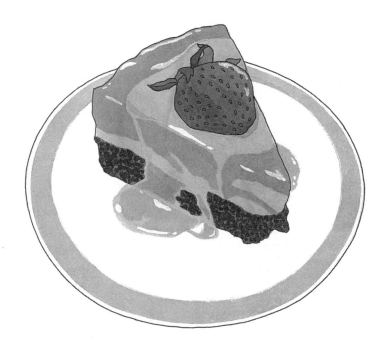

Chocolate Cream Couscous Cake

YIELD: *One 9-inch cake; 8 to 10 servings*
TIME: *40 minutes preparation; 2 hours to set*

¾ *cup pecans*
2½ *cups water*
1½ *cups Sucanat*
¼ *cup cocoa*
1 *cup couscous*
1 *tablespoon vanilla extract*
Chocolate Cream Filling
    (recipe follows)

Roast the pecans at 300 degrees F for about 30 minutes. Remove from oven and cool. Grind the roasted pecans in a food processor for 5 to 10 seconds. They should have the consistency of a coarse meal.

In a medium saucepan, stir together the water, Sucanat, cocoa, and couscous. Bring to a simmer and cook until thickened (5 to 10 minutes). Add the vanilla and stir well. Spread the mixture into a 9-inch springform pan. Sprinkle ¼ cup of the roasted pecan meal over the couscous cake. Pour the filling over the cake and top with the remaining pecan meal. Refrigerate the cake until it is set (about 2 hours). Serve cold.

Chocolate Cream Filling

1 *package (10 ounces) barley malt chocolate chips**
2 *packages (10½ ounces each) firm silken tofu, at room temperature*
3 *tablespoons maple syrup (or honey)*

*These chocolate chips, which are sweetened with barley malt syrup rather than sugar, are available at natural foods stores.

Melt the chocolate chips in a small saucepan over low heat, stirring constantly. Transfer to a blender, add the tofu and maple syrup, and blend until smooth.

It is best to use heavier sweeteners with cocoa or chocolate, because these ingredients are bitter. Sucanat, maple syrup, and honey are examples of heavy sweeteners. Use lighter sweeteners, such as rice syrup, barley malt, or fruit juice with carob, because carob is already somewhat sweet.

Silken Tofu Chocolate "Cheesecake"

YIELD: *8 to 10 servings*
TIME: *40 minutes*
preparation; 2 hours baking;
2 hours to chill

¾ cup finely ground pecans
2 tablespoons brown rice
 syrup
2 tablespoons barley malt
 syrup
2 tablespoons Sucanat
2 teaspoons arrowroot
½ teaspoon vanilla extract
Granola Crust for one 9-inch
 pie (page 226)
"Cheesecake" Filling (recipe
 follows)

Roast the ground pecans at 300 degrees F for 20 minutes or so. Transfer the pecans to a bowl and add the syrups, Sucanat, arrowroot, and vanilla. Set aside.

Prepare the granola crust and press the mixture onto the bottom and sides of an 8-inch cake pan, preferably a spring-form pan. Gently spread the pecan mixture evenly over the inside bottom of the pan, on top of the granola crust. Pour the "cheesecake" filling over the pecan mixture and spread evenly in the pan. Bake in a preheated oven at 300 degrees F, with a pan of water on the bottom shelf of the oven, for about 2 hours.

Remove the cake from the oven and let cool to room temperature. Then refrigerate the cake and serve cold.

"Cheesecake" Filling

2 packages extra-firm silken
 tofu, 10½ ounces each
¼ cup Egg Replacer
⅓ cup brown rice syrup
¼ cup tofu chocolate (Barat
 chocolate), melted
¾ teaspoon vanilla extract
⅓ cup Sucanat
3 tablespoons cocoa powder
3 tablespoons water
1 teaspoon agar powder

Put all ingredients in a blender and blend until smooth.

Key Lime Shamrock Torte

YIELD: *One 9-inch cake; 6 to 8 servings*
TIME: *20 to 25 minutes preparation (if carob cake is made already); 2 hours to set*

2 packages firm silken tofu, 10½ ounces each
¾ cup brown rice syrup
½ cup honey
¾ cup lime juice (preferably key lime juice)
1 tablespoon agar powder
4 tablespoons arrowroot
2 tablespoons corn oil
4 teaspoons barley green powder (optional)
one Carob Cake, made in an 8-inch cake pan (use half the recipe from page 217)
2 to 3 kiwi fruits (optional)
glaze (optional; recipe follows)

*T*his dessert is in honor of Father James Murphy, pastor of St. Patrick's Catholic Church in Miami Beach. Jim is one of those people who likes light desserts that aren't overly sweet.

Blend the tofu, brown rice syrup, honey, lime juice, agar, arrowroot, corn oil, and barley green powder (if you wish) until smooth. Transfer to a double boiler and heat until the mixture thickens. It should reach the consistency of heavy cream. Set aside to cool.

Split the cake into two layers. (For this recipe, you will need only one layer.) Line a 9-inch cake pan with a sheet of plastic wrap. Place one layer of cake in the bottom of the pan and refrigerate while the tofu filling is cooling.

When the filling is cool, pour it onto the cake and refrigerate until the filling sets completely (about 2 hours).

For added color and flavor, add the kiwi fruit: peel the fruit, cut it into thin slices, and fan out the slices over the entire torte. Glaze the cake, if you wish, by lightly pouring a thin layer of the glaze (still slightly warm) over the cool cake. (Use one-half to three-fourths of the recipe for a light glaze.) Refrigerate the cake again for 10 minutes or so before cutting it. To serve, remove the cake from the pan by lifting on the plastic wrap.

Glaze

1 teaspoon agar powder
½ cup water
½ cup brown rice syrup
1 to 2 drops mint extract

In a small saucepan, dissolve the agar in the water. Add the brown rice syrup and mint extract. Bring to a simmer and remove from heat. Allow to cool slightly. (The glaze provides an attractive presentation.)

Dream Bars

YIELD: *One 9- by 12-inch pan*
of bars; 8 to 10 servings
TIME: *20 minutes prepara-*
tion; 25 to 30 minutes baking

¾ *cup oil*
1¾ *cups honey*
2½ *cups whole wheat flour*
5 *teaspoons Egg Replacer*
½ *cup water*
1 *teaspoon baking soda*
½ *teaspoon salt*
2 *teaspoons vanilla*
1½ *cups chopped walnuts*
1 *cup unsweetened coconut*
1 *tablespoon lemon juice*
zested rind of half a lemon

In a bowl, mix the oil with ¼ cup plus 2 tablespoons of honey and 2 cups of flour. Spread the batter evenly in the bottom of a lightly oiled pan.

Mix the remaining honey and flour with the other ingredients. Stir to combine thoroughly. Spread this mixture evenly over the batter in the pan. Be careful that you don't cut through the batter; that would cause the topping to run beneath the batter and possibly stick to the pan. Bake in a preheated oven at 350 degrees F for 25 to 30 minutes.

Cake-like cookies use less oil, so they may be lower in calories than crisp cookies, which tend to contain more oil.

Teff Cookies

YIELD: *16 large cookies*
TIME: *40 minutes*
preparation; 20 minutes
baking

¾ *cup whole almonds*
½ *cup oat flour**
½ *cup teff flour*
1 *cup whole wheat pastry*
  flour
½ *cup unrefined corn oil (or*
  margarine)

*T*his cookie is a spin-off from the raspberry cookie recipe in Mary Estella's *Natural Foods Cookbook*. Both recipes, I think, result in superb cookies.

Roast the almonds in a preheated oven at 325 degrees F until lightly browned (about 15 minutes). Transfer them to a food processor and blend until they are the consistency of coarse flour. (Be careful not to overprocess them, or you will end up with almond butter.)

Mix the dry ingredients together. In a separate bowl, stir together the corn oil, syrup, and vanilla. Then add the dry

½ *cup maple syrup*
2 *teaspoons vanilla extract*
no-sugar fruit spread
   (optional)

*If you do not have oat flour, you can make it from oatmeal. Put ¾ cup oatmeal in a blender and blend for a minute or so. This should yield about ½ cup oat flour.

ingredients to the wet ingredients and mix until well blended.

To shape each cookie, roll about 2 tablespoons of dough into a ball. Place the cookie on a lightly oiled baking sheet. Press out the cookie slightly and make an indentation in the center of the cookie with your thumb. Fill the indentation with a small amount of fruit spread, if you wish. (Raspberry fruit spread is especially delicious.)

Bake the cookies in a preheated oven at 350 degrees F for about 20 minutes. The cookies should be lightly brown and firm to the touch. Remove from the cookie sheet immediately.

Polynesian Crisp

YIELD: *6 to 8 servings*
TIME: *15 minutes preparation; 45 minutes baking*

1/4 *cup unsweetened coconut*
5 *cups fresh pineapple, diced*
¼ *cup Sucanat*
⅓ *cup whole wheat pastry*
   flour
2 *teaspoons vanilla*
topping (see recipe below)

Combine the coconut, pineapple, Sucanat, flour, and vanilla. Press the mixture into a lightly oiled 10- by 12- by 2-inch pan. Spread the topping evenly over the pineapple mixture. Bake in a preheated oven at 375 degrees F for about 45 minutes, or until the top is crispy and the fruit mixture is bubbly. Cool for about 10 minutes. Serve warm or cold. You may wish to serve this dessert with a nondairy ice cream of your choice.

Topping

⅓ *cup whole wheat pastry*
   flour
¾ *cup rolled oats*
¼ *cup Sucanat*
⅓ *cup chopped walnuts*
¼ *teaspoon ginger powder*
¼ *cup soy margarine (or corn oil)*

Combine the dry ingredients in a small bowl. Cut in the margarine and mix until it reaches the consistency of a coarse meal.

Pie Dough

YIELD: *Two 9-inch pie crusts or one 12-inch crust*
TIME: *10 to 15 minutes preparation; allow 1 hour to freeze the ingredients beforehand*

¾ *cup whole wheat pastry flour*
¾ *cup unbleached flour*
¼ *cup unrefined corn oil (or 5 tablespoons soy margarine, softened)*
pinch of salt
½ *cup ice water*

*U*nlike most pie doughs, this one is extremely low in saturated fats. The way in which the dough is handled and the texture of the dough are similar to traditional pie crusts. Freezing helps the oil bind to form a crumbly mixture. If the oil is not frozen, the crust will still work but may not be as flaky.

Stir the flours together in a small bowl and freeze. Freeze the corn oil in a separate container. Both containers should remain in the freezer for 1 hour. (The oil need not be firm.)

Mix the oil into the flour until it forms a crumbly meal. Stir the salt into the ice water and add the water to the flour mixture. Mix only to bind the dough. The dough may seem a little wet at first, but it should become drier as it absorbs moisture. If it is still too wet, you can add a little whole wheat flour to the dough.

Roll out each half of the dough on a floured surface, rolling to a thickness of about ¹⁄₁₆ inch. Transfer the dough to the pie pan, and trim and crimp the edges.

If you are prebaking the pie crust, bake in a preheated oven at 400 degrees F for 10 to 15 minutes, or until it is lightly brown and firm. This crust will seem hard when it comes out of the oven but will become tender after a while. (In contrast, crusts made with saturated fats are flaky immediately after removing from the oven.)

Granola Crust

YIELD: *Two 9-inch pie crusts*
TIME: *15 minutes preparation*

3 cups commercial granola
    (crunchy-style)
½ cup Sucanat
½ cup corn oil
¼ cup Egg Replacer
½ cup water
¾ cup unbleached flour

Using a food processor, blend the granola until it is the consistency of coarse meal. Transfer to a large bowl and add the other ingredients. Press the mixture equally into two lightly oiled pie pans. Fill the crusts and bake as directed. If you are prebaking the pie crusts, bake at 350 degrees F for 15 minutes.

The oil will separate if the mixture isn't used and baked right away. If necessary, mix the granola crust and press into the pans again.

Fresh Mango Pie

YIELD: *One 9-inch pie*
TIME: *20 minutes
preparation; 30 to 40 minutes
baking*

Pie Dough for double crust
    (page 225)
3 tablespoons unbleached
    flour
¼ teaspoon cinnamon
2 large, very ripe mangoes,
    peeled and sliced (4 cups)
juice from half a lemon

When mangoes are in season in Miami, I walk the "mango tree beat," picking fresh fruit off the ground. Then I let the fruit ripen fully on my window ledge. When I have enough for a luscious dessert, such as this pie, I head for the kitchen and, well, you can guess the rest.

The mangoes should be very ripe and sweet for this pie. If they are not, you may wish to drizzle a tablespoon of rice syrup over the fruit before adding the top crust.

Roll out the pie dough for the bottom crust and line the pie pan. Set aside.

Mix the flour and cinnamon together in a small bowl. Set aside.

Arrange one third of the mangoes in the pie pan. Sprinkle a third of the flour mixture over the mangoes. Continue layering the mangoes and sprinkling the flour mixture on top. Then sprinkle the lemon juice on top.

Roll out the remaining pie crust and place it on top of the pie. Trim the crusts, seal them, and crimp the edges. Cut several holes in the top crust to allow steam to escape. Bake in a preheated oven at 400 degrees F for about 30 to 40 minutes, or until the crust is lightly browned.

VARIATION: *Blueberry Mango Pie*
Use 3 cups of mangoes and 1 cup of fresh blueberries. Add 2 tablespoons of Sucanat to the flour and cinnamon mixture. Otherwise, make the pie according to the directions for Fresh Mango Pie. Serve warm.

Squash Pie

YIELD: *One 9-inch pie; 8 servings*
TIME: *20 to 30 minutes preparation; 1 hour baking*

Pie Dough for single crust (or Granola Crust; pages 225–226)
4 cups peeled and cubed butternut squash, and 2 thin slices of squash for garnish
½ cup Sucanat
3 tablespoons arrowroot
2 tablespoons agar flakes
½ teaspoon cinnamon
½ teaspoon nutmeg
¾ cup soy milk
½ teaspoon ginger powder
1 teaspoon vanilla extract
1 tablespoon soy oil
½ cup pecan halves, for garnish
glaze (see recipe next page)

*T*his is one of the most delicious squash pies I have ever tasted. It is also one of the simplest; you just steam the squash, blend the filling, bake, and serve!

Roll out the pie dough and line a 9-inch pie pan. Trim and crimp the edges. Set aside.

Steam the squash in a covered saucepan, with about an inch of water, until the squash is soft. Drain immediately. Set aside the two slices for garnish. Put the steamed cubed squash in a blender, along with all the other ingredients, except the pecans and the glaze. Blend until smooth. Pour the filling into the pie shell. Arrange the pecans around the outer edge of the pie. Place the squash slices in the center of the pie, along with one pecan half. Bake in a preheated oven at 350 degrees F for 40 minutes. Then reduce the heat to 250 degrees F, cover the pie with aluminum foil, and bake for 20 minutes, or until the pie is done. (Insert a knife into the pie; if it comes out clean, the pie is done.) Cool the pie completely. Then brush the glaze on the pie.

Glaze

2 tablespoons barley malt
   syrup
¼ cup water
1½ teaspoons agar flakes

Place ingredients in a small saucepan and bring to a simmer. Cook until the agar flakes are dissolved (5 to 10 minutes).

Mocha Custard Cream

YIELD: *5 servings*
TIME: *20 minutes
preparation; 2 hours to set*

3 cups almond milk (or
   coconut milk)
1 cup cashew nuts
2 tablespoons carob powder
¼ cup grain coffee substitute
2 to 3 tablespoons agar flakes
½ to ¾ cup brown rice syrup
2 tablespoons arrowroot,
   dissolved in 2 tablespoons
   water
1 tablespoon vanilla extract
½ teaspoon salt
½ cup Sucanat
strawberries and halved
   almonds, for garnish

*T*his custard is a culinary ecstasy for the inquiring palate. The unique aspect is the genuine mocha taste, which is achieved without chocolate or coffee. I created this recipe on my second day at the Natural Foods Express, a natural foods delivery service in Miami Beach.

Blend 1 cup of almond milk with the cashews until smooth and creamy. (You should be able to feel very little grit when you rub the mixture between your fingers.)

Pour the mixture into a medium saucepan. Use a little of the remaining almond milk to rinse out the blender; then pour this liquid into the saucepan and add the rest of the almond milk, the carob powder, coffee substitute, agar flakes, and brown rice syrup. Whisk the mixture to dissolve the carob powder and coffee substitute. Simmer over a medium-low heat, stirring occasionally, for 7 to 10 minutes, or until the agar flakes dissolve. Remove from heat and vigorously stir in the dissolved arrowroot. Bring to a simmer again and cook for 30 seconds to 1 minute. Remove from heat and stir in the vanilla, salt, and Sucanat.

Lightly oil five 1-cup molds or one large mold. Pour the mixture into the molds and refrigerate until set (about 2 hours). To serve, unmold the custards onto serving plates and garnish with strawberries and halved almonds.

VARIATION: *Mocha Cream Pie*

Make the Mocha Custard Cream according to the recipe, using the greater amounts of agar and rice syrup. Allow the custard to cool at room temperature while you prepare a single pie crust (page 225) and prebake it. When the custard cream begins to set, spoon it into the cooled pie crust and spread evenly. Refrigerate until set completely (about 1½ hours). Garnish the pie with strawberries and halved almonds.

Dutch Apple Custard

YIELD: *4 to 6 servings*
TIME: *20 minutes preparation (if the Dutch Honey is made already); 2 hours to set*

24 ounces (1 large jar) unsweetened applesauce
2 tablespoons agar flakes
½ cup Dutch Honey (see recipe below)
¼ teaspoon cinnamon
1 cup soy milk
1 teaspoon vanilla extract

Dutch Honey

1 cup brown rice syrup
1 cup soy milk
1 cup Sucanat
½ teaspoon vanilla extract

Combine the applesauce with the agar flakes, Dutch Honey, and cinnamon in a medium saucepan. Bring the mixture to a simmer over a medium heat and cook until the agar is dissolved (10 to 12 minutes). Add the soy milk and vanilla, stir until well blended, and cook for a few more minutes. Pour the mixture into a lightly oiled 4-cup mold. Refrigerate until set (2 hours). Unmold and serve.

Dutch Honey

P ioneers of the American West used Dutch Honey when genuine honey was scarce. The recipe presented here is a natural foods version of the original recipe.

This recipe yields about 1½ cups of syrup. Refrigerated, it will keep for about two months. It is an excellent glaze for breads, pies, and other baked goods. It is also a wonderful dessert sauce for fruit, custards, and "ice cream."

Combine all ingredients, except the vanilla, in a medium saucepan. Bring to a simmer and cook until it is reduced by one half (about 90 minutes). Stir in the vanilla. Cool.

Pecan Baked Apples

YIELD: *6 servings*
TIME: *30 minutes preparation; 30 minutes baking*

6 baking apples, preferably Granny Smith
¾ cup finely ground pecans
2 tablespoons barley malt syrup
2 tablespoons brown rice syrup
½ tablespoon vanilla extract
½ tablespoon lime juice (or lemon juice)

Serve these baked apples warm with a sabayon sauce, if you wish.

Core the apples from the top, cutting a fairly wide opening but leaving the bottom intact.

Combine the ground pecans, syrups, vanilla, and lime juice. Fill the apples, dividing the pecan filling equally among the six apples. Place the apples in a baking dish and add about ¼ inch of water to the pan. Cover with aluminum foil and bake at 350 degrees F for 20 to 30 minutes.

VARIATION: *Pecan-Filled Apple Dumplings*
Prepare the dough from the Tofu Seitan Wellington recipe (page 250). Prepare the pecan filling according to the recipe above. Peel the apples and fill them with the pecan filling. Roll out the dough and cut it into six large squares. Wrap the apples individually in the dough, pinching the edges together. Place the dumplings on an oiled baking sheet. Bake at 350 degrees F for 30 minutes.

Piña Colada Pasta

YIELD: *4 servings*
TIME: *30 minutes preparation; marinate the pasta overnight; 1 hour to cool the sauce*

4 cups coconut milk
2 ounces (½ package) udon pasta
⅓ cup coconut liqueur

Bring the coconut milk to a simmer over a medium heat. Add the pasta and cook it, stirring occasionally, until tender but still firm (*al dente*). Immediately drain the liquid into a bowl and reserve it. Rinse the pasta in cold water. When the milk and pasta are cool, put them together and add the coconut liqueur. Cover and refrigerate overnight.

Blend the cashews with the pineapple-coconut juice until the nuts are well ground (about 10 minutes). Add the 1 cup of marinade liquid and the cornstarch, and blend until

¼ *cup cashew nuts*
1 *cup natural pineapple-
coconut juice*
1 *cup of liquid drained from
the pasta (the marinade)*
4 *teaspoons cornstarch*
½ *teaspoon vanilla extract*
¼ *cup unsweetened coconut*
half of a fresh, ripe pineapple
8 *strawberries*

smooth. Transfer to a small saucepan and cook over medium heat, stirring constantly, until the sauce thickens. Remove from heat and add the vanilla. Set aside and allow to cool completely (about 1 hour). Meanwhile, toast the coconut and prepare the fruit.

Spread the coconut on a baking sheet and toast it at 350 degrees F for 5 minutes, or until lightly toasted. (Watch it carefully, because it can burn quickly.) Remove from the oven and transfer to a bowl immediately to stop the cooking process.

Cut the half pineapple into quarters. Trim away the core and the skin. Slice the pineapple into bite-sized pieces. Stem the strawberries and cut them in half. Chill the fruit until ready to serve.

To serve, place the pasta on four serving plates and pour the sauce on top. Arrange the pineapple and strawberries around the pasta. Top with toasted coconut.

As an alternative, you may wish to serve the pasta in a hollowed-out pineapple shell. Combine the pasta with the pineapple and sauce before placing in the pineapple shell. Arrange the strawberries and toasted coconut on top.

Hazelnut Glennie

YIELD: *One 10- by 12-inch pan of bars; 8 to 10 servings*
TIME: *20 minutes preparation; 3 to 4 hours to set*

1¾ *cups brown rice syrup*
¼ *cup barley malt syrup*
½ *cup hazelnut butter*
1 *tablespoon vanilla extract*
8 *cups puffed wheat*
2 *cups crushed wheat flakes
(breakfast cereal)*

In a large saucepan, bring the two syrups to a boil and cook for 5 minutes. Add the hazelnut butter and mix well. Then stir in the vanilla.

In a large bowl, combine the two cereals. Add this to the syrup mixture and stir to coat the cereals thoroughly.

Press the cereal mixture into the lightly oiled pan, cover, and cool for 3 or 4 hours. (You may wish to line the pan with plastic wrap, since the mixture is quite sticky.)

Cut the glennies into squares using a lightly oiled knife; wipe the knife with a little oil before each cut.

Poached Pears with Raspberry Sabayon Sauce

YIELD: *4 servings*
TIME: *30 minutes*

*4 small ripe pears (Bartlett or
   Anjou)*
4½ cups raspberry lemonade
4 cloves
zest from one orange
*1 tablespoon apricot fruit
   spread*
*Raspberry Sabayon Sauce
   (see recipe below)*
*fresh raspberries, fresh
   orange zest, and mint
   leaves (for garnish)*

Peel the pears and core them from the bottom, leaving the stem in place.

Place 4 cups of raspberry lemonade in a medium saucepan with the cloves and orange zest. Bring to a simmer and add the pears. (Make sure the pears are covered completely by the poaching liquid. If they are not, add more lemonade.) Simmer, partially covered, for about 30 minutes, or until the pears are tender. Test the pears by inserting a toothpick; the toothpick should slide all the way into the pear quite easily. Remove the pears and cool them quickly in the freezer, but don't let them freeze. While the pears are simmering in the poaching liquid, you can begin making the glaze and the Raspberry Sabayon Sauce.

To make the glaze, combine the remaining ½ cup of lemonade with the apricot spread in a small saucepan. Bring to a simmer and cook until the liquid is reduced by one half. Let cool and then refrigerate.

To prepare each serving, set a pear in the center of a small bowl and drizzle glaze over the pear until a small pool of glaze forms around the pear. Pour the Raspberry Sabayon Sauce on top and garnish with fresh raspberries, mint leaves, and fresh orange zests.

Raspberry Sabayon Sauce

½ cup firm silken tofu
½ cup fresh raspberries
2 tablespoons honey
*1 tablespoon barley malt
   syrup*
¼ teaspoon lemon juice
3 tablespoons rum

Blend the tofu with the raspberries until smooth. Transfer to a small saucepan and place over a low heat. Whip the remaining ingredients into the tofu mixture and keep them warm until ready to use.

VARIATION: *Poached Pears in Crêpes*

Poach the pears according to the recipe above. To prepare the glaze, use half of the leftover poaching liquid with 1 cup of dry red wine and 2 tablespoons of apricot spread. Simmer this liquid until it is reduced by one half. Cool the glaze. Meanwhile, prepare the crêpes. (The recipe that follows yields 2 cups of batter, or about 16 crêpes.)

To serve, glaze each poached pear, wrap a crêpe around it, securing with a long piece of orange zest. Make a pool of glaze on a dessert plate, and rest the crêpe-wrapped pear on the glaze.

Dessert Crêpes

½ cup whole wheat pastry
   flour
½ cup unbleached flour
2 tablespoons Egg Replacer
¼ cup teff flour
¾ cup Sucanat
2 tablespoons unrefined corn
   oil
1½ cups water
zest from one orange

Stir together the dry ingredients. In a separate bowl, mix the corn oil, water, and orange zest; then add the dry ingredients, stirring until well blended.

To make the crêpes, lightly oil a crêpe pan or omelet pan and heat the pan. Pour the batter into the pan and cook until the crêpe is crisp on the edges and done in the center. (This recipe yields about 16 crêpes.)

Tofu Chocolate "Buttercream" Icing

YIELD: *3 cups of icing*
TIME: *15 minutes*
preparation; 1 hour to set

*½ pound tofu chocolate
(Barat chocolate)*
*½ pound firm tofu (or extra
firm silken tofu)*
½ cup brown rice syrup
*½ pound soy margarine (or
unsalted butter, if you
wish)*
½ teaspoon vanilla extract

*T*his is an elegant icing that is quick and easy to make. It uses a commercial nondairy chocolate that is sweetened with Sucanat. This icing will remain firm if it is kept cool; a cooler temperature will facilitate smooth spreading.

Three cups of this icing is sufficient to cover a large 2- or 3-layer cake.

Chop the chocolate into small pieces and melt slowly in a double boiler. (You can melt the chocolate over direct heat, if it is very low. However, you should stir constantly and watch carefully that the chocolate does not burn.)

Rinse the tofu and put it in a blender with the brown rice syrup. Blend until smooth. Transfer to a mixing bowl and add the margarine and vanilla. Beat until smooth, periodically scraping the sides of the bowl to ensure that the ingredients are well blended.

Slowly pour the chocolate into the bowl and gradually mix until the ingredients are well blended. Refrigerate the icing for 1 hour before using.

Tofu Chocolate Ganache

YIELD: *2¼ cups of icing*
TIME: *10 minutes*

¾ cup soy milk
2 ounces soy margarine
*¾ pound tofu chocolate
(Barat chocolate; or use
carob)*

*G*anache is a pourable icing. The traditional recipe calls for heavy cream and butter. This ganache uses more healthful ingredients but still has a rich, sweet, chocolate flavor. It is easy to make, easy to work with, versatile, and delicious.

When icing a cake, place the cake on a wire rack and slip a clean baking sheet beneath the rack. The baking sheet will catch the icing that drips from the cake; you can then collect this runoff and reuse it.

You can also dip fresh fruit, dried fruit, or confections in this ganache. Begin by heating a small amount of the ganache. When this runs low, add a little more. To avoid waste, try not to warm up more than you will use.

Bring the soy milk and margarine to a simmer. Chop the chocolate into small pieces and add it to the soy milk mixture. Continue to heat, stirring constantly until the chocolate has melted. Cool slightly.

Note: This icing may separate if it is not used immediately. If separation occurs, heat the icing in a saucepan, stirring vigorously.

VARIATION: *Bitter Chocolate Ganache*

1½ cups soy milk
1 cup maple syrup (or honey)
8 ounces bitter chocolate
4 ounces tofu chocolate
   (Barat chocolate)
1 tablespoon vanilla extract

This variation, which calls for genuine chocolate, has a robust, bittersweet flavor. This recipe yields 3½ cups of icing.

Bring the soy milk and syrup to a simmer. Chop both kinds of chocolate into small pieces and add to the soy milk mixture. Stir until the chocolate has melted. Remove from heat. If the icing tends to separate, add a little more chocolate. When the mixture is smooth and of the desired consistency, stir in the vanilla.

VARIATION: *Carob Ganache*

½ cup brown rice syrup
¼ cup soy milk
¼ cup Sucanat
1 cup unsweetened nondairy
   carob chips
2 tablespoons soy margarine
1 tablespoon cocoa (optional)
½ teaspoon vanilla extract

This is another quick and easy version of the original ganache recipe. It has a delicate but full-bodied carob taste.

Heat the brown rice syrup, soy milk, and Sucanat just to a brief simmer. Add the carob chips, margarine, and cocoa (if you wish), and continue to cook for 1 minute or so. Remove from heat and stir in the vanilla.

Peanut Butter Icing

YIELD: *2½ cups of icing*
TIME: *20 minutes preparation; 1 hour to chill*

¼ *pound firm tofu, crushed by hand*
½ *cup brown rice syrup*
½ *cup Sucanat*
½ *cup creamy peanut butter*
½ *pound soy margarine*

*T*his is a superb icing that does not impart a cloying after-taste so common with icings. The peanut butter flavor is present but is not overbearing. Rather, the peanut butter creates a delicate balance with the sweeteners. Try this icing on the Carob Cake (page 217). For a completely different flavor, substitute an equal amount of cashew butter or almond butter for the peanut butter. This recipe will be sufficient to cover a large two-layer cake.

Combine the tofu, brown rice syrup, and Sucanat in a small saucepan. Heat for about 5 minutes over medium heat, stirring constantly. Then pour the mixture into a blender and blend until smooth. Transfer to a mixing bowl. Add the peanut butter and margarine and beat until smooth. Refrigerate the icing for 1 hour, or until firm.

Red Pepper Sabayon Sauce

YIELD: *3¾ cups of sauce*
TIME: *40 minutes preparation*

4 *medium red bell peppers*
1 *cup sweet sherry or brandy*
¼ *cup Sucanat*
1 *package (10½ ounces) firm silken tofu*
½ *cup cashew nuts*
¼ *cup brown rice syrup*
½ *cup honey*
1 *teaspoon vanilla extract*

*Y*ou can serve this sauce with a layer cake, kanten cake, or baked fruit dessert (such as apple crisp), or poured over poached or stewed fruit. The color and flavor of this sauce is beautiful, and the ingredients will enhance the nutritional density of your dessert. This sauce will keep in the refrigerator for a few weeks.

Halve and seed the bell peppers. Roast them over an open flame (on the stove or in the broiler) until blisters form on the skin of the peppers. Peel the skin from the peppers and chop them. (You should have about 2 cups of chopped peppers at this point.) Place the peppers in a small saucepan. Add the remaining ingredients, bring to a simmer, and cook for about 5 minutes. Transfer the mixture to a blender. Blend at low speed, with the lid placed loosely over the opening so that steam can escape. Gradually increase the blender speed to purée the peppers. Secure the lid tightly and blend at high speed briefly to make a smooth sauce. Serve warm or cold.

DRINKS

Irish Coffee

YIELD: *2 servings*
TIME: *5 to 10 minutes*

2 teaspoons unsalted mirin
½ cup soy milk
½ teaspoon lime juice
¼ cup grain-based coffee substitute
½ cup boiling water
1 cup unsalted mirin

T his is a superb alternative to the original Irish Coffee, which has strong coffee, Irish whiskey, sugar, and heavy whipped cream. The key to making this coffee successfully is to make the soy milk float. To do so, you must pour it very slowly onto the prepared beverage. As an alternative, you can mix about a teaspoon of cooking oil into the soy milk before pouring it onto the coffee; this should enable the soy milk to float.

In a small bowl, mix the 2 teaspoons mirin into the soy milk and lime juice. Set aside for a few minutes.

When you are ready to serve the drink, combine the coffee substitute, boiling water, and 1 cup of mirin. Pour into two large cups. Set a spoon across the surface of each drink, with the back of the spoon facing upward. Pour the soy milk mixture very slowly onto the back of the spoon, letting it run onto the coffee drink. (Use half of the soy milk mixture for each cup.) Serve immediately.

Mocha Grain Coffee

YIELD: *4 servings*
TIME: *5 minutes*

2 cups boiling water
2 tablespoons grain coffee
  substitute
1 tablespoon cocoa
¼ cup brown rice syrup
½ cup soy milk

Measure the boiling water in a large measuring cup. Add the coffee substitute and cocoa and stir until the powders are dissolved. Gently stir in the brown rice syrup until dissolved. Then pour the drink into four large coffee cups. Add the soy milk to each cup, distributing equally. Serve hot.

Christmas Soy Nog

YIELD: *4 servings*
TIME: *30 minutes preparation; 30 minutes to chill*

1 cup peeled and cubed
  butternut squash
2 cups vanilla soy milk
3 tablespoons brown rice
  syrup
2½ tablespoons fruit-
  flavored lecithin granules
¼ teaspoon nutmeg
¼ teaspoon vanilla extract
4 tablespoons unsalted mirin
  (optional)

Steam the squash for about 20 minutes, or until soft. Drain and let cool for about 5 minutes. Transfer to a blender, add the remaining ingredients, and blend until smooth. Refrigerate for 30 minutes.

The Culinary Olympics

*E*very four years the International Cooks Society holds a cooking competition in Frankfurt, Germany. The event, known as the International Culinary Olympics, occurs in conjunction with the athletic Olympics. Member nations of this society assemble national teams, which converge on Frankfurt to compete for medals in various categories of artistic food preparation. One of the purposes of the competition is to stimulate chefs to new levels of culinary excellence.

The American Culinary Federation is the national organization in the United States that promotes the competition. Any member of this organization can compete for a position on the national team. In 1978, I won a gold medal in the national competition, which qualified me to compete in the 1980 Culinary Olympics. In 1980, I founded the American natural foods team and, with this team, entered the international competition to gain widespread recognition for vegetarian cuisine. In that year, I became the first professional vegetarian chef to compete in the Olympics and win a medal for totally vegetarian foods. I also competed in 1984 and 1988, and I look forward to competing again in 1992. This competition allows me to promote whole foods cuisine on the highest level possible.

Typically during the international event, thousands of chefs converge on the city a few weeks before the competition, which lasts for six days. Kitchens throughout Frankfurt and as far as 30 miles outside the city are humming day and night. Thousands of exhibits with some of the most beautiful food in the world are displayed during the competition. It is truly an exciting event.

My team won bronze and silver medals in all three years that we entered the competition. In 1988, we won silver medals in the categories of hot foods and desserts. (Actually, we missed winning the gold medal for hot foods by one point.) The theme for our desserts entry was bridging the nutritional gap; most of our pastries and confections included nutritious but sweet and tasty vegetables. Some of these recipes are included in this chapter.

In general, the recipes in this chapter are a little more challenging than those in earlier chapters. The international competition requires a certain level of professional ability. However, not all of the recipes are difficult or tricky; besides, you may enjoy the challenge of tackling those recipes that are more difficult.

Baked Tofu Pâtés

*T*hese pâtés were developed for the 1984 Culinary Olympics and won a bronze medal. Simple and elegant, these pâtés are also versatile. They may be served as appetizers; as a salad, on a bed of Boston or other loose-leaf lettuce and garnished with julienned carrots, tomato wedges, and pickled peppers; or as a dinner entrée, for which you might make a combination pâté, using one and one-quarter cups of the mixture for each of the different pâtés (spinach, tarragon, and carrot), layering them in a pan in that order, baking them according to the directions for carrot pâté, and serving two slices arranged on a pool of sauce, accompanied by a complementary vegetable and starch.

The vegetable purées used in these pâtés are delicate. At an internal temperature of 220 degrees F, the steam in the mixture begins to rise, the starch is cooked, and the agar is activated and gels. Therefore, it is important to use only enough heat to make the formula set and not so much that it becomes rubbery. The pâté is cooked when it has risen up in the pan; it should rise, like custard, and then drop when it cools.

Basic Pâté Mixture

YIELD: *4 cups*
TIME: *15 to 20 minutes
preparation; 2 hours baking*

2 pounds firm tofu
¼ cup olive oil (or canola oil)
1 teaspoon minced garlic
*2 tablespoons nutritional
    yeast*
2 teaspoons arrowroot
½ teaspoon salt
*scant ½ teaspoon agar
    powder*
pinch of white pepper
*2 tablespoons white wine
    (optional)*

Place all ingredients in a food processor and blend until smooth. The base mix is now ready.

Spinach Tofu Pâté

*basic pâté mixture (see recipe
    above)*
*one 10-ounce package of
    frozen spinach, thawed
    and squeezed dry*
½ teaspoon ground nutmeg
*2 teaspoons chopped basil (or
    1 teaspoon dried basil)*
1 teaspoon salt
*1 tablespoon cornstarch
    (or arrowroot)*
2 teaspoons minced garlic

Place all ingredients in a food processor and blend well. Prepare the loaf pan and bake the pâté as directed for Tarragon Tofu Pâté (above).

Tarragon Tofu Pâté

basic pâté mixture (see recipe
previous page)
1 teaspoon chopped tarragon
½ teaspoon salt
¼ teaspoon white pepper
1 teaspoon savory

Mix all of the ingredients together until evenly dispersed (3 to 5 minutes). Oil a loaf pan, line it with plastic wrap, and spread the pâté mixture evenly in the pan. Cover the top of the pâté with plastic wrap. Then place the loaf pan in a larger pan, with about an inch of water, and cover the water pan with aluminum foil. Bake in a preheated oven at 325 degrees F for 1½ to 2 hours. The pâté will be done when a toothpick, inserted into the middle of the pâté, comes out clean. You can also tell that it has baked sufficiently when it rises.

Carrot Tofu Pâté

basic pâté mixture (see recipe
previous page)
3 cups peeled and chopped
carrots
½ teaspoon salt
1 tablespoon arrowroot
(or cornstarch)
1 tablespoon dill weed

Steam the carrots until they are soft. Then drain them, pat them dry, and place them in a food processor with the remaining ingredients. Blend until smooth. Prepare the loaf pan and bake the pâté as directed for Tarragon Tofu Pâté (above).

Tofu and Sea Vegetable Quenelles

T hese recipes, which won a silver medal in the 1988 Culinary Olympics, are a spin-off from traditional quenelles, which call for egg yolks, butter, milk, and fish. You may add eggs to these recipes, if you want additional protein. If you do, you should also add another teaspoon of Egg Replacer (or arrowroot) to compensate for the moister batter.

Normally, quenelles are poached in a rich fish stock. Because these special quenelles are delicate and do not include eggs, I prefer to steam them on a rack in a covered pan. They can be poached, however. Serve these quenelles with any creamy vegetable-based sauce.

Beet Sea Vegetable Quenelles

YIELD: *4 to 6 servings as an appetizer*
TIME: *15 minutes*

½ cup cooked, chopped beets
½ pound firm tofu
5 tablespoons arrowroot
1 teaspoon corn oil
⅛ teaspoon white pepper
⅛ teaspoon nutmeg
¼ teaspoon agar powder
2 teaspoons nutritional yeast
1 teaspoon dill weed
½ teaspoon minced garlic (or
    ¼ teaspoon garlic powder)
½ teaspoon salt
1 tablespoon finely chopped
    arame (optional)

Drain the beets and the tofu. Put all ingredients (except the arame) in a food processor and blend to make a smooth paste. If you are adding arame, mix it in by hand. Form the quenelle shapes and steam or poach as directed for the Spinach Sea Vegetable Quenelles.

Spinach Sea Vegetable Quenelles

YIELD: *4 to 6 servings as an appetizer*
TIME: *15 minutes; allow several hours to thaw the frozen spinach*

½ pound firm tofu
5 ounces frozen spinach,
    thawed
small amount of dried arame
    (about ¼ handful)
5 tablespoons Egg Replacer

Rinse the tofu and steam it for 4 to 5 minutes, if you wish. Drain for several minutes and then pat dry with a cloth. Squeeze the spinach dry. (If you have thawed a 10-ounce package of spinach, form the spinach in a ball, cut the ball in half, and reserve half of it for another use.) Blend the spinach and tofu in a food processor.

Soak the arame in warm water for a few minutes. Drain, chop up, and measure out 1 tablespoon. Add this arame, along with all other ingredients, to the spinach mixture. Form quenelles, or dumpling shapes, using about 2 tablespoons of the mixture for each quenelle. Place these shapes

½ teaspoon salt
2 tablespoons white miso
1 tablespoon corn oil
½ teaspoon agar powder
⅛ teaspoon nutmeg

on a lightly oiled steamer rack. Lower the rack into a large saucepan with 1 to 2 inches of water. (The water should almost reach the level of the rack.) Cover the saucepan and steam the quenelles for 5 minutes.

As an alternative, place the shaped quenelles on a lightly oiled pan and gently pour a simmering vegetable stock into the pan, half covering the quenelles. Place a lid on the pan. Poach the quenelles over low heat for about 5 minutes. Gently remove and serve immediately.

Carrot Sea Vegetable Quenelles

YIELD: *4 to 6 servings as an appetizer*
TIME: *25 minutes*

½ pound firm tofu
1 cup peeled and chopped
    carrots
small amount of dried arame
    (about ¼ handful)
3 tablespoons Egg Replacer
1 teaspoon corn oil
¼ teaspoon agar powder
¾ teaspoon dill weed
⅛ teaspoon nutmeg
¾ teaspoon salt
⅛ teaspoon white pepper
pinch of powdered thyme
2 teaspoons nutritional yeast
    (optional)

Drain the tofu and pat dry. Steam the carrots until they are soft. Run them under cold water for about a minute to cool. Pat dry with a towel. Blend the carrots and tofu until smooth.

Soak the arame in a little warm water for a few minutes. Drain, pat dry, chop up, and measure out 1 tablespoon of arame. Add this, along with all other ingredients, to the carrot mixture. Form the quenelle shapes and steam or poach as directed for the Spinach Sea Vegetable Quenelles.

Leek Aspic

YIELD: *1 large loaf; 8 servings*
TIME: *1 hour preparation; 2 hours to chill*

5 medium leeks
3 cups water
6 tablespoons (or more) agar flakes
2 tablespoons Vogue Vegy Base
1½ teaspoons salt
1 teaspoon minced garlic
several pitted black olives

*T*his cold appetizer dish won a bronze medal in the 1984 Culinary Olympics.

Cut the roots from the leeks, trim away any wilted parts, and split each leek in half lengthwise. Wash the leeks under running water, carefully separating the layers. Blanch the leeks, one at a time, in boiling salted water for 30 seconds, or until the green part changes to a deeper, slightly darker color. Place the leeks in a large bowl of cold water to stop the cooking process. Drain the leeks thoroughly and pat the leaves dry. Set aside.

Mix the 3 cups of water with the agar flakes, soup base, salt, and garlic. (If you want a firmer aspic, you may wish to add a little more agar.) Simmer, stirring occasionally, until the agar flakes dissolve (about 5 minutes). Strain the liquid and pour it into a shallow dish that can be kept warm during the next step in the preparation.

Lightly oil a large loaf pan, preferably the type that has rounded corners. Dip the leek leaves, one at a time, in the warm agar solution, and line the bottom and sides of the pan with the leaves, letting them hang over the edges of the pan. The inner surface of the mold should be completely covered with a layer of leek leaves, layered to create an attractive pattern on the inside bottom of the pan. Continue layering the leeks, but now cut the leaves individually so they fit into the pan lengthwise without curling up at the end. After placing four layers in the bottom of the pan, pour 1 to 2 tablespoons of warm agar liquid evenly over the leaves. Continue this pattern of layering the leeks and adding agar liquid after every fourth layer of leaves. (For an optimal visual effect, use the deepest green part of the leaves for the first layers and the white part of the leaves for the center of the loaf.) When you have filled the loaf about halfway, line up several olives down the center of the loaf, along the length of the pan. Continue layering the leeks as before until the pan is full. Fold the overhanging leaves back over the aspic, and refrigerate for at least 2 hours.

To serve, dip the mold in a bowl of hot water for a few seconds and turn out the aspic onto a serving dish. Slice the aspic and serve with Tahini Lemon Sauce (page 165), if you wish.

Tempura Vegetable Nori Roll

YIELD: *2 servings*
TIME: *45 minutes; allow a few hours to soak the cabbage*

1½ cups shredded red cabbage
cider vinegar (or red wine vinegar)
1½ cups peeled and julienned carrots
1½ cups watercress
¼ cup tamari
2 cups hot water
about ½ cup dried arame
3 sheets nori
tempura batter (see page 48)
cooking oil

Dip the shredded cabbage in a small amount of vinegar and rub the cabbage by hand. Let it soak for a few hours. Drain and press dry. Meanwhile, prepare the other vegetables.

Mix the tamari in hot water and soak the arame in this mixture for 30 minutes. Drain and press dry.

Lightly toast the nori sheets by holding them about 6 inches over medium heat for 5 to 10 seconds on each side. Place a nori sheet on a flat surface. Lay all the vegetables in a row along the nori sheet. Roll up the vegetables tightly in the nori sheet, squeezing hard to eliminate as much juice as possible. Roll up this nori roll in the second sheet. Wet the ends of the second sheet with water and seal the edges. Repeat with the third nori sheet.

Heat the cooking oil to 375 degrees F in a deep skillet. Dip the whole roll into the tempura batter. Then fry it in the hot oil until lightly brown. Remove and drain.

Serve slices of the nori roll along with a sauce of your choice. Sweet and Sour Sauce (page 166) is delicious with this appetizer.

New York Cima Roll

YIELD: *8 servings*
TIME: *1 hour*

1½ pounds firm tofu
1 tablespoon oil
3 tablespoons arrowroot
1 teaspoon salt
¼ teaspoon white pepper
1 teaspoon agar powder
1 teaspoon dried marjoram
1 teaspoon dried thyme
1 tablespoon minced garlic (or
  1 teaspoon garlic powder)
½ teaspoon black pepper
2½ cups Cima Mixture (see
  recipe below)

*T*his entrée meal won a silver medal at the 1988 Culinary Olympics. The Cima Mixture recipe is quite versatile. It can be used as a filling, as in the main recipe presented here. You can also form the mixture into patties or small balls and sauté them as one might make hamburgers or meatballs.

Wash the tofu and pat it dry. Cut it into small pieces. Place the tofu in a blender, along with all other ingredients except the Cima Mixture, and blend until smooth.

Shape the Cima Mixture into a 12- by 3-inch roll. Spread the tofu mixture evenly on a piece of plastic wrap about 28 inches long by 12 inches wide. Gently place the cima roll on the tofu mixture and wrap the coated plastic around the roll. Smooth out the tofu mixture seam around the cima roll. Steam the roll for about 30 minutes. Remove from heat, cool for 10 minutes, and remove the plastic wrap. Then slice and serve with Tomato Sauce or Béchamel Sauce (pages 159–163).

Cima Mixture*

½ cup finely chopped onions
2 tablespoons soy margarine
  (or olive oil)
1 cup whole wheat bread
  crumbs
¼ pound ground seitan
¼ pound finely textured soy
  grits
¼ pound firm tofu, crushed
  by hand
⅓ cup nutritional yeast
  (optional)
2 teaspoons dried marjoram

In a large, deep skillet, sauté the onions in the margarine until they are translucent. Remove from heat. Add the bread crumbs, seitan, soy grits, tofu, yeast (if you wish), seasonings, and water to the onions. Mix together until the ingredients are evenly dispersed. Add the spinach, roasted pepper, pistachios, and green peas, if you wish, to the onion mixture.

In a small bowl, mix the agar powder with the gluten flour. Warm the liquid lecithin and add it to the onion mixture and mix in. Then add the gluten mixture to the onion mixture and mix well. This recipe yields 4½ cups of Cima Mixture.

2 teaspoons dried thyme

2 teaspoons sea salt

1½ cups water

1 cup chopped spinach,
    packed tightly (or ½ cup
    packaged spinach,
    measured after it is
    thawed, squeezed dry, and
    chopped)

¼ cup roasted red bell pepper,
    peeled and finely diced

½ cup pistachio nuts

1 cup green peas (optional)

1 tablespoon agar powder

½ cup gluten flour

2 tablespoons liquid lecithin

*This recipe yields 4½ cups of mixture. Because this mixture is so versatile, you may wish to make an entire recipe of it and use any leftover amount to make cima burgers or other dishes.

VARIATION: *Cima and Pasta with Broccoli Fennel Sauce*

½ cup chopped fresh fennel

¼ cup chopped shallots

1 clove garlic, minced

2 tablespoons corn oil (or soy
    margarine)

2½ cups Broccoli Sauce (page
    167)

2 cups Cima Mixture

4 cups cooked udon pasta (or
    other pasta)

Sauté the fennel, shallots, and garlic in 1 tablespoon of oil for 5 minutes. Add these sautéed vegetables to the broccoli sauce and simmer for 10 to 15 minutes.

Form the Cima Mixture into about 12 small balls. Sauté the cima balls in the remaining tablespoon of oil until lightly browned. For each serving, place the cima balls on top of the pasta and pour the sauce over it.

Tofu Seitan Wellington

YIELD: *4 servings*
TIME: *1 hour preparation (if the Mushroom Duxelles is made already); 20 to 30 minutes baking*

Wellington Dough (see recipe below)*
1⅓ cups Mushroom Duxelles (page 51)
8 slices firm tofu, each 3″ × ¼″ thick
fresh herb paste (see recipe below)
8 slices seitan, each 3″ × ¼″ thick
¼ cup barley malt syrup dissolved in ¼ cup water

*You may use a puff pastry dough instead of the Wellington Dough, if you wish.

*T*his elegant entrée won a bronze medal in the 1984 Culinary Olympics. This dish blends the robust flavor of seitan with the simple flavor of tofu. You may wish to serve the entrée with a Bordelaise Sauce and an attractive vegetable side dish, such as Bouquetière of Vegetables.

Wellington Dough

¾ teaspoon sea salt
½ cup water
1¾ cups finely ground whole wheat flour
1½ teaspoons honey (or maple syrup)
2 tablespoons oil

Roll out the dough to a thickness of about ⅜ of an inch. Cut into four strips, each about 4 inches wide. Use the following procedure for each strip of dough:

Spread ⅓ cup of Mushroom *Duxelles* mixture at one end of the strip of dough. Place a slice of tofu on the mushroom mixture. Then spread 1½ teaspoons of fresh herb paste on the tofu. Stack a slice of seitan on top of the tofu, and spread more herb paste on the seitan. Repeat this layering procedure using another slice each of tofu and seitan and more herb paste. Wrap the dough around the block of layered ingredients, totally encasing it. Flip the piece over so the *dux-*

Fresh Herb Paste

1 cup loosely packed fresh
  basil
¾ cup fresh cilantro
¼ cup fresh thyme
½ cup fresh dill weed
3 cloves garlic
¾ cup cooking oil
½ cup cashew nuts
1 teaspoon salt
¼ teaspoon black pepper

elles mixture is on top. Seal the open edges and place on a baking sheet. Punch a few small holes in the top crust and brush with the dissolved barley malt syrup. Bake in a preheated oven at 400 degrees F for 20 to 30 minutes, or until the dough is lightly browned.

Wellington Dough

Dissolve the salt in the water. Add it to the flour, along with the honey and oil, and mix to form a medium-stiff dough.

Fresh Herb Paste

Put all of the ingredients into a blender and blend to form a smooth paste. Refrigerate until ready to use.

Vegan London Broil

YIELD: *Eight 6-ounce steaks*
TIME: *30 minutes
preparation; 1½ to 1¾ hours
cooking*

2½ pounds of freshly made
  but uncooked seitan
½ gallon water
1½ cups tamari
one 7-inch strip kombu
6 thin slices fresh ginger
sauce, such as Bordelaise or
  Miso Sauces (see pages
  161–164)

*F*or the 1984 Culinary Olympics, I presented this dish with miso sauce, and I scored the steaks using the hot tip on a portable propane torch. The presentation was simple but lovely, and it earned the dish a bronze medal. Vegan London Broil is a wonderful dish for dinner guests.

Place the seitan in an 8-inch square cake pan. Allow it to rest until it takes the shape of the pan. Then place this pan inside a second, larger pan that is half-filled with water. Cover the larger pan. Bake in a preheated oven at 375 degrees F for 1 hour.

When the seitan is done, remove it from the pan. Divide it into eight equal pieces.

To the ½ gallon of water, add the tamari, kombu, ginger, and the seitan steaks. Cover the pot, bring to a simmer, and cook for about 45 minutes. (If you are using a pressure cooker, reduce the liquid by one half and cook for 20 to 25 minutes.) You may leave the steaks in the stock for several hours, if you wish.

Remove the steaks from the stock and drain them. Brush the steaks with a little sauce, and broil them so they will be lightly browned. Serve the steaks hot with additional sauce.

Garbanzo Parsnip Gnocchi

YIELD: *4 servings*
TIME: *35 minutes*

1½ tablespoons olive oil
2 cups coarsely diced parsnips
¾ cup finely diced onions
1 tablespoon minced garlic (or
    2 teaspoons garlic powder)
½ cup garbanzo flour
¼ cup gluten flour
2 teaspoons nutritional yeast
1 teaspoon salt (optional)
¼ teaspoon white pepper
cooking oil for frying the
    gnocchi

*T*his recipe was created for the 1988 Culinary Olympics and was awarded a silver medal. It was presented as an accompaniment to the New York Cima Roll. You can serve small portions of these gnocchi as a side dish or make larger portions for an entrée.

Heat the oil in a skillet. Sauté the parsnips, onions, and garlic until the onions are translucent and the parsnips are soft. Place in a food processor and process until a smooth paste is formed. Add the flours, yeast, salt, and pepper, and blend until the ingredients are well integrated.

Begin heating the cooking oil in a deep frying pan. (The oil should be about 2 inches deep in the pan.) Meanwhile, you can make the gnocchi.

Oil a tablespoon. Spoon out the gnocchi batter, making oval-shaped pieces, and use a second spoon to remove the pieces from the first spoon.

Drop the gnocchi into the oil, heated to 375 degrees F. Because the gnocchi may burn easily, don't put too many in the pan at one time. Remove from the oil and drain on paper towels.

Serve the gnocchi warm with a colorful, flavorful sauce. I like to serve the gnocchi around a nest of spaghetti squash or pasta, topped with a tomato sauce. Together with a side dish of zucchini, this is a beautiful and excellent meal.

Buckwheat Potato Caraway Pasta

YIELD: *4 to 6 servings*
TIME: *30 to 40 minutes preparation; allow 1 day for pasta to dry*

2 large baking potatoes
1 cup buckwheat flour
¾ cup gluten flour
½ cup unbleached flour
1 tablespoon ground caraway seeds
1½ teaspoons sea salt
¼ cup liquid lecithin
½ cup cold water
2 tablespoons olive oil

*T*he flavor and texture of this pasta are superb. This recipe won a silver medal in the 1988 Culinary Olympics.

Peel the potatoes, cut them into small pieces, and steam them until soft (about 15 minutes). Purée the cooked potatoes using a food processor. Measure out 1 cup of puréed potatoes. Reserve any leftover potatoes for another recipe.

In a medium bowl, mix the 1 cup of puréed potatoes with the flours, caraway seeds, 1 teaspoon salt, lecithin, and water. Mix to form a medium-stiff dough. Roll out the dough to ¹⁄₁₆ of an inch thick, either by hand or using a pasta machine, and cut into ¼-inch-wide strips. Hang the pasta on a rack to dry for about 24 hours.

Bring a large pot of water to a simmer. Add the olive oil and ½ teaspoon of salt. Then add the pasta, stirring with a wooden spoon to separate the noodles. Cook for about 2 minutes, drain, and serve with Tomato Sauce, Carrot Sauce (pages 159–168), or other complementary sauce.

Southern Blackened Tempeh with Tomato-Apricot-Ginger Coulis

YIELD: *4 servings*
TIME: *25 minutes preparation; 10 to 15 minutes cooking; allow 40 minutes to make the coulis*

1 cup Soysage (page 105), or instant black bean mix
two 8-ounce pieces tempeh

*T*his dish won a silver medal at the 1988 Culinary Olympics. To make a quick version of this recipe, you can use Fantastic Foods instant black bean mix instead of the 1 cup Soysage. Instant bean mixes are available at natural foods stores. For this recipe, add three-fourths cup of hot water to one-half cup of bean mix.

Serve the blackened tempeh with any complementary sauce. I like the coulis because it seems to have a cooling effect on this spicy dish.

2 tablespoons prepared cajun
  spice mixture (commercial)
2 tablespoons water
2 tablespoons tamari
1 tablespoon Sucanat
2 tablespoons cooking oil
Tomato-Apricot-Ginger
  Coulis (see recipe below)

If you are using the instant black bean mix, place the contents of the mix in a bowl. Add the hot water and stir until well blended. Set aside for about 5 minutes.

Slice each piece of tempeh in half. Then prepare to stuff the tempeh by making a cut along the length of each piece of tempeh, keeping the edges intact. Gently open and fill the tempeh, using ¼ cup of the bean mixture for each piece. Press the tempeh closed and set aside.

In a small bowl, mix the cajun spices with 2 tablespoons of water, the tamari, and the Sucanat. Brush the mixture on both sides of each piece of tempeh.

Heat the oil in a skillet and sauté the tempeh on both sides until brown (about 1 minute on each side). Place the browned tempeh in a baking dish. Bake, covered, in a preheated oven at 350 degrees F for about 10 to 15 minutes. Serve immediately with the coulis or other sauce.

Tomato-Apricot-Ginger Coulis

3 medium tomatoes
5 medium fresh apricots*
2 tablespoons minced onions
  or shallots
2 tablespoons Sucanat
2 tablespoons white wine
2 tablespoons olive oil
1 tablespoon lemon juice
⅓ teaspoon ginger powder

*If you are using canned apricots instead of fresh apricots, you will need about 10 small apricot halves. Choose fruit that is canned in a fruit-juice concentrate rather than a sugar syrup, and use only 1 tablespoon of Sucanat. Drain the fruit well.

Blanch, peel, seed, and chop the tomatoes. (You should end up with 1 cup of tomatoes.)

Cut the apricots into small pieces. Place them in a saucepan with the tomatoes and other ingredients and simmer until the liquid is reduced by one half (about 20 minutes). Serve this sauce hot or cold.

Jamaican Cakes

YIELD: *Forty 1-inch confections (or twenty 2-inch cakes)*
TIME: *30 minutes preparation; 2 hours cooking*

4 cups grated fresh coconut
1½ cups water
3½ teaspoons peeled and chopped ginger
1 cup Sucanat
1 stick of cinnamon
1 cup brown rice syrup

*T*his recipe is quite versatile, since you can use it as a confection, for cookie filling, or in an ice cream cake. Jamaican Cakes won a silver medal in the 1988 Culinary Olympics.

Blend together 2 cups of coconut, the water, and ginger in a bowl. Set aside.

In a small saucepan, combine 1 cup of coconut, the Sucanat, cinnamon, brown rice syrup, and coconut-ginger mixture. Cook over a low heat until the mixture thickens (about 2 hours). Stir occasionally to prevent burning. Set aside to cool.

When the mixture has cooled enough to handle it, form small spherical cakes (each 2 inches in diameter), or smaller confections (each 1 inch in diameter), rolling the mixture by hand. Then roll each ball in the remaining 1 cup of coconut.

Carrot Cream in Squash Shell

YIELD: *4 servings*
TIME: *35 to 45 minutes preparation; 2 hours to chill and set*

1 small butternut squash
1½ cups peeled and chopped carrots
1½ teaspoons corn oil
1½ cups vanilla soy milk
3 to 4 tablespoons agar flakes
2 tablespoons shredded unsweetened coconut, toasted

*T*his dessert dish was presented as part of a special vegetable dessert tray, created especially for the 1988 Culinary Olympics. It was awarded a silver medal in that event.

Peel the squash and cut off the top. Remove the seeds. Steam the squash in a large saucepan with about 1 inch of simmering water. Cook it until tender but still firm. Set aside.

Sauté the carrots in oil over medium heat, stirring occasionally to prevent burning. Cook the carrots until soft. (You may wish to steam the carrots instead of sautéing them.) Set aside.

Pour the soy milk into a small saucepan along with the agar flakes and cook over medium heat until the agar is dis-

⅓ cup firm tofu, crushed by
   hand
1½ to 3 tablespoons honey
½ teaspoon vanilla extract
2 tablespoons carob powder

solved and the liquid is reduced by one half. (Use the larger quantity of agar for a firmer filling.)

Place the cooked carrots, toasted coconut, and the soy milk mixture in a blender. Add the tofu, honey, and vanilla to the carrot mixture and blend until smooth. Set aside.

Sift the carob powder and coat the inside of the squash shell. Shake out the excess powder and discard. Pour the carrot mixture into the squash shell and gently shake it to release bubbles from the carrot mixture. (Pour any remaining filling into individual molds.) Chill until the filling is set (about 2 hours). Cut the squash into 1½-inch slices and serve with yellow pepper pastry cream.

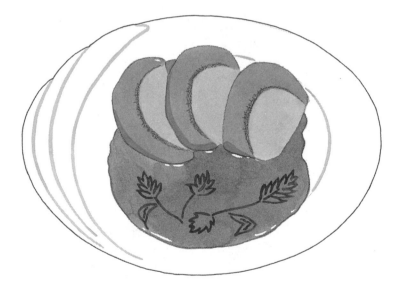

VARIATION: *Carrot Cream in Poached Pears*
Add ¾ teaspoon ginger powder to the carrot filling and omit the coconut. Pour the carrot filling into halved, hollowed-out, poached pears (see page 232).

Swiss Burnt-Pecan Torte

YIELD: *One 11-inch torte*
TIME: *70 minutes
preparation; 1 hour baking*

4 cups pecans
1 cup barley malt syrup (or ½
  cup barley malt syrup and
  ½ cup honey)
¼ cup brown rice syrup
1 heaping tablespoon
  arrowroot
1 teaspoon vanilla extract
Pie Dough (page 225)
2 teaspoons barley malt
  syrup, dissolved in 2
  teaspoons water

*T*his torte is one of my signature "friendly foods" pastries and has always been a four-star dessert. The original recipe on which this recipe is based calls for caramelized sugar, whipping cream, and butter. Not only is my version more healthful, since it eliminates these ingredients, but the flavor and texture of this dessert are more delicate than the original dessert. The barley malt syrup in this recipe gives the torte a subtle caramel flavor. After tasting it, you will know why it won a bronze medal in the 1984 Culinary Olympics.

Roast the pecans at 275 degrees F for about 40 minutes. (Slow roasting is essential to this dessert, because it allows for a delicate pecan flavor.)

Using a food processor, grind the pecans to the consistency of coarse flour. Mix the finely ground pecans with the syrups, arrowroot, and vanilla. Set aside while you make the pie dough, if you haven't made it already.

Roll out half of the pie dough and place it in an 11-inch fluted torte pan, trimming the edges. Add the pecan mixture on top of this bottom crust. Then roll out the remainder of the pie dough, place it over the filling, and trim the edges. Seal the edges of the top and bottom crust together. Cut a few holes in the top crust to let the steam escape.

Bake in a preheated oven at 350 degrees F for 35 minutes. Then brush the top crust with the dissolved barley malt syrup, and bake until lightly browned (5 to 10 minutes). Cool and serve.

VARIATION
Instead of the brown rice syrup, substitute ¼ cup of honey.

4 cups almonds

½ cup unsweetened coconut,
   toasted

3 tablespoons cornstarch (or
   arrowroot)

¼ cup honey

1¾ cups brown rice syrup

1 teaspoon vanilla extract

VARIATION: *Almond Coconut Torte*

Use these ingredients to make the torte filling.

Roast the almonds at 325 degrees F until lightly browned (15 to 20 minutes). Remove from the oven and spread the almonds on another pan to cool. Grind the almonds to a fine meal but be careful not to overprocess them (or you will end up with almond butter). Add the coconut, cornstarch, honey, brown rice syrup, and vanilla to the ground almonds. Roll out the pie crusts, fill the torte, and bake it as directed in the recipe above.

Florida Bonbons

YIELD: *about 6 dozen bonbons*
TIME: *20 minutes
preparation; 1 hour to cool*

1 cup water

1 cup orange juice
   concentrate

½ cup brown rice syrup

½ cup honey

4 cups finely ground
   unsweetened coconut,
   toasted

1½ cups cooked couscous

½ cup soy margarine

1 cup cocoa butter

½ cup oat bran

1 tablespoon vanilla extract

1 tablespoon minced orange
   zests

Orange Coconut (see recipe
   next page)

*T*his dessert confection won a silver medal in the 1988 Culinary Olympics.

In a small saucepan, stir together the water, orange juice concentrate, brown rice syrup, honey, and coconut. Heat to a simmer, and remove from heat. Add the couscous, margarine, cocoa butter, oat bran, vanilla, and orange zests. Let stand until cool. Form the mixture into 1-inch balls and roll in the Orange Coconut. Store the bonbons in an airtight container between layers of waxed paper. They will keep, refrigerated, for at least a week.

Orange Coconut

2 cups finely ground
    unsweetened coconut
2 tablespoons grated orange
    peel

In a bowl or on a nonporous surface, rub the coconut and orange peel between your fingers until the coconut takes on the color and flavor of the orange.

Chocolate-Squash Confection

YIELD: *3 dozen pieces*
TIME: *45 minutes prepara-*
tion; 2 hours to chill and set

1 large butternut squash
2 medium sweet potatoes
1 cup almond milk
3 tablespoons agar flakes
¼ cup honey
½ cup cocoa butter*
2 tablespoons soy margarine
¼ teaspoon sea salt
Tofu Chocolate Ganache
    (page 234)

*Cocoa butter is available at gourmet food shops.

*T*his dessert won a silver medal in the 1988 Culinary Olympics.

Peel the squash and sweet potatoes, cut them into small pieces, and steam them until soft. Drain thoroughly and separate the squash pieces from the potato pieces. Purée the squash and measure out 2 cups of purée. Purée the sweet potatoes and measure out 1 cup of purée. (Use any remaining purée for a soup, sauce, or other dish.) Set aside.

Cook the almond milk and agar in a medium saucepan until the agar is dissolved and the milk is reduced by about one half. Stir in the squash and sweet potato purées, honey, cocoa butter, margarine, and salt. Continue cooking over medium heat, stirring constantly, just long enough to blend the ingredients. Pour the mixture into clean, plastic tubes, ¾ inch in diameter and 8 inches long. (As an alternative, pour the mixture into a lightly oiled 9- by 9-inch pan.) Refrigerate until the mixture has set and is very cold (60 to 90 minutes).

Warm the Tofu Chocolate Ganache to about 80 degrees F using a double boiler or small saucepan. Push the squash filling out of the tubes and dip each squash roll in the ganache. Place the coated roll on a sheet of waxed paper and let the ganache set. Then slice the roll into small pieces. (If you used a 9- by 9-inch pan instead of the plastic tubes, cut the cold squash mixture into ¾-inch pieces and dip each piece in ganache.)

Store the confections in an airtight container, layered between waxed paper, and refrigerate.

Yellow Pepper Pastry Cream

YIELD: *5 cups of pastry cream*
TIME: *1 hour preparation; 45 minutes to cool*

4 *medium yellow peppers*
2 *cups soy milk*
1 *tablespoon agar powder*
½ *cup apple juice*
¾ *cup brown rice syrup*
2 *tablespoons unsweetened coconut, toasted*
6 *tablespoons kuzu (or arrowroot powder)*
2 *teaspoons vanilla extract*

*T*his pastry cream recipe won a silver medal in the 1988 Culinary Olympics.

Roast the peppers over a flame, or under the broiler, until the peppers begin to soften and the skin blisters. (As an alternative, lightly oil the peppers and bake them at 350 degrees F until they blister, begin to brown, and collapse.) Then peel the peppers and blend them until smooth. Measure out 2 cups of purée. (Use any remaining purée for another recipe.)

Add the soy milk, agar, apple juice, brown rice syrup, and coconut to the puréed peppers and blend until smooth. Pour 1 cup of this mixture in a saucepan. Heat slowly, stirring occasionally to prevent burning.

Meanwhile, blend the kuzu with the remaining 1 cup of soy milk mixture. Add to the heated soy milk mixture, stirring vigorously, and cook until it makes a smooth, creamy sauce. Remove from heat and stir in the vanilla. Cool.

Spoon the cooled pepper cream into a pastry bag and use it to pipe filling in fruit tarts or decorative designs on cakes. You may also use this pastry cream as a light filling between cake layers, or as a sauce to complement desserts such as the Carrot Cream in Squash Shell (page 255).

GLOSSARY

ADUKI BEANS   These small maroon-red beans are considered by the Japanese to be the king of beans. They cook more easily than other dried beans, have a rich-bodied flavor, and are a good source of carbohydrates, amino acids, potassium, iron, calcium, and some of the B-complex vitamins. Aduki beans are a common macrobiotics food and in the macrobiotic philosophy of nutrition are used as nutritional therapy for the kidneys.

AGAR   Agar (or kanten) comes from the algae *agar-agar*. It is rich in calcium, iron, phosphorus, vitamins A, B-complex, C, D, and K. Used mainly as a thickener, agar is an excellent vegan substitute for gelatin, which is an animal product. Agar is cleansing to the colon and may retard radiation poisoning. Far superior to traditional gelatin, which offers few health benefits, it can be used in much the same way that gelatin is used. However, agar will set at room temperature.

Agar comes in three forms—powder, flakes, and bars. Agar flakes and agar bars are basically the same. Both need to be cooked about ten minutes to completely dissolve. Never cook agars in any liquid that contains oil; the oil seems to bind the agar, which then never has a chance to absorb the liquid. When foods require limited cooking, it is best to use agar powder because it absorbs the liquid immediately. About one teaspoon of agar powder is equivalent to one tablespoon of agar flakes.

APPLE-PEEL ROSE   A garnishing technique in which you peel an apple in one continuous piece from top to bottom and roll up the peel to make the shape of a rose.

ARAME   This mild-flavored sea vegetable does not need to be cooked before eating (although it can be). You can soak it in room-temperature water and use it on salads or add it to cooked vegetables or grain loaves for additional flavor and nutritional value. It's so delicate that, when soaked, falls apart easily. Alone, arame cooks in a few minutes. I recommend cooking it separately, because the black color of the arame can permeate other foods while cooking.

BARLEY GREEN POWDER   This Japanese product is a natural food coloring. It is available at many health food stores and Asian markets.

BARLEY MALT SYRUP   A sweetener made from sprouted whole barley that has a caramel flavor and generally is about half as sweet as sugar or honey. Barley malt syrups that are cut with corn syrup are not as desirable as pure barley malt syrup. However, in barley-corn malt syrup, the two grains have been fermented together, producing a high-quality food.

Barley malt syrup is high in carbohydrates and contains some vitamins and minerals. It tends to be the least expensive of natural sweeteners. This syrup must be stored in a sanitary jar and kept in a cool, dry place. If it begins to ferment, heat the syrup to kill the active enzymes.

BOK CHOY   Also known as Chinese chard or Chinese cabbage, bok choy, a crisp cabbage that has a delicate flavor, is often used in stir-fry dishes or with other vegetables in a sauté. Bok choy is widely available in Asian markets and has a great shelf life if stored in ventilated plastic bags.

BRAGG'S LIQUID AMINOS   A vegetarian liquid flavoring similar to tamari but with a low-sodium content, Braggs Liquid Aminos is a good source of amino acids and can be used to give stocks a strong, beef-like flavor.

BROWN RICE SYRUP   This cultured product is made from brown rice, water, and a small amount of natural cereal enzyme. The light and delicate syrup is about half as sweet as sugar. In combination with other sweeteners such as Sucanat or honey, it helps neutralize the dominant flavor of those sweeteners.

BULGUR   Steamed, dried, and cracked whole wheat, bulgur has its origins in the Middle East and is commonly used in the traditional dish *tabbouleh*. To cook this light grain, pour boiling water over it, cover, and let stand for a few hours until tender.

COUSCOUS   Traditionally, couscous is made from the endosperm remnants of refined durum wheat. It is therefore a refined food and has less nutritional value than whole wheat. However, a new product, called whole wheat couscous, is now available through natural foods stores and in some supermarkets. Darker in color than traditional couscous, it is a whole, more nutritious food.

CORN GRITS   Because grits are coarser in texture than meal, they must be cooked longer than cornmeal or corn flour.

DAIKON   Daikon, a white radish that has the shape of a carrot but is much larger, is commonly used in macrobiotic cooking. This root vegetable counters or breaks up fats in the body and therefore complements fried foods. Shred-ded daikon is often served as a relish condiment or cooked with other vegetables.

DULSE   A sea vegetable, which sometimes goes by the poetic name "Neptune's girdle," once eaten as a snack like potato chips in Western Europe and New England. Found in the waters of the North Atlantic and the Pacific Northwest, it is purplish-red and fast cooking. Dulse is good in salads, with broccoli and carrots, and can also be used in grain dishes. You can use dulse in any recipe that calls for wakame. Keep in mind that dulse is softer than wakame and will need to be handled with a little more care if you want to keep it intact.

EGG REPLACER   This powdered egg substitute is available at natural foods stores—usually near the flours, sugars, and other baking needs. Egg Replacer is made primarily from potato starch and tapioca flour, and contains no animal products, lactose, sodium, preservatives, sugar, or artificial flavorings. Although Egg Replacer is a dry ingredient, you can use it as you would use eggs—in breads, cakes, muffins, crepes, and so on.

FU   Fu are sheets of dried wheat gluten. Like tofu, fu has virtually no flavor and takes on the flavor of surrounding ingredients. Reconstituted fu can be sliced and added to soups or other dishes. You can use whole fu sheets in place of crepes, but they are a little tough—although they tear easily. I have used fu sheets to wrap around a tofu loaf, but the sheets are not easy to work with whole.

GARBANZO FLOUR   Made from garbanzo beans, or chickpeas, this flour is a good source of protein and carbohydrates. It is available at most natural foods stores.

GLUTEN FLOUR   Gluten flour is not the same as high-gluten flour, which is bread flour or stone-ground whole wheat flour that has a high gluten content. Gluten flour is pure gluten; it contains no carbohydrates but rather is all protein.

HIJIKI This sea vegetable has a strong flavor. For that reason, I generally cook it with tamari and ginger to lighten up the taste. A longer cooking time helps mellow out the flavor. If you are new to sea vegetables, I would recommend you begin with the milder ones, such as arame or wakame, rather than with hijiki. Because it grows close to the bottom of the ocean, hijiki has a dark color. The dried hijiki usually is quite dirty and must be washed carefully.

Hijiki is delicious cooked with onions and tofu. It also complements green beans especially well. Hijiki is a good diet food because it is very filling and adds a crunchy texture and nutty flavor to soups and salads.

JERUSALEM ARTICHOKES Also known as sunchokes, these are actually the roots of sunflower plants. The vegetable does not originate from Jerusalem, nor is it related to artichokes. This tuber is small, white, and sweet. Unlike most root vegetables, Jerusalem artichokes do not contain starch. It is a popular food among many Native American tribes. Jerusalem artichokes can be deep-fried, used in stir-fry dishes, and used for sauces. They do not freeze or can well, so they are mainly available fresh. However, commercial pastas made from Jerusalem artichokes are sold through natural foods stores and gourmet food stores.

JICAMA The tuber of a legume plant from South America, jicama has the texture of water chestnuts and a delicate flavor. Jicama can be used in fruit or vegetable salads, and can be eaten raw or cooked. Jicama will keep for several weeks; once cut, though, should be used within several days.

KASHA Kasha is roasted buckwheat that origi-nates from the Volga region of the Soviet Union. Originally, it was called beechwheat, because the triangular seed resembles the beech seed. The chestnut-colored kasha has a much heartier flavor than the greenish-white unroasted groats.

KELP This sea vegetable usually is available in a powdered form, mainly as a salt substitute. In this form, it is delicious sprinkled over popcorn or salads. You may also find packages of dried kelp sold whole. Sliced kelp can be used in soups and stews as well as in vegetable side dishes. Kelp is tasty when fried or when toasted until crisp.

KOMBU Sold dried, in flat sheets or in strips that measure seven to eight inches, the sea vegetable kombu is used most commonly as a flavoring. For example, you can cut off small pieces of the kombu strip to use in soup stock. (I like to add cooked kombu to sandwiches.) Kombu often is used in cooking beans and seitan, since it improves the flavor and digestibility of those products. Kombu also is used in miso soup; it is cooked with the soup and then taken out, sliced thinly, and added back into the soup.

KUZU This powder is a concentrated starch from the kuzu (or kudzu) plant and can be used as a thickener, similar to cornstarch or arrowroot. In macrobiotic terms, kuzu is a yang starch. Kuzu is sold in Asian markets and health food stores. In Japan, it is used for its medicinal properties; in the southern United States, Kuzu is considered a noxious weed.

MIRIN Mirin, or Chinese cooking wine, is a flavoring agent made from sweet rice, rice koji (a natural rice culture used to convert the starches into sugars), water, and alcohol. The 13- or 14-percent alcohol solution evaporates quickly when mirin is heated.

There are two types of mirin—one with salt and one without. The one with salt is appropriate in savory foods; the one without salt can be used in savory or sweet foods. Mirin can be used in sauces, salad dressings, pastries, fruit liqueurs, and so on.

MISO   A fermented paste made from beans and/or grains and salt, miso is 10 to 12 percent protein. Because it is actually a predigested food, miso is a remarkable digestive aid. It is used mainly as a flavoring agent or a soup or sauce base and comes in a wide range of flavors, depending on the bean or grain from which it is made.

Shiro miso and chickpea miso are two types of light (or white) miso. These are delicately flavored and can be used in creamy sauces, salad dressings, delicate soups, sweet vegetables, and so on. Barley miso, brown rice miso, red miso, and hatcho miso (made from soybeans) are a few types of dark miso. These varieties of miso are stronger in flavor and have a dark, rich color. The darkest ones are great substitutes for beef-based stock.

NORI   Nori is a high-protein red seaweed originally called laver in English. Japanese nori is tricky to buy because it is sometimes dyed. Avoid buying nori sheets that are a uniform green; instead, choose those that are multihued. Asakusa nori, the most popular nori in Japan, is known in the United States as the paper-thin wrapper in which sushi is rolled. The Koreans call it kim, and they season it with sesame oil, soy sauce, and hot peppers. Nori that grows in North American coastal waters is dried in its natural shape. Toasted, nori has a sweet, nutty, and salty taste. Sliced thin, it is a good garnish for soups.

To toast nori, hold it about six inches over a medium flame, moving it at a moderate pace to prevent burning a hole through the sheet. When the nori turns light green, it is ready to use.

OKARA   This is a fiber by-product of tofu. Couscous can be used in place of okara.

RICE VINEGAR   Rice vinegar has about half the level of acid as cider vinegar and therefore has a more delicate flavor. It is widely available at natural foods stores, Asian markets, and many supermarkets. Some rice vinegars may be made from white rice and contain additives. Those labeled *brown rice vinegar* have greater nutritional integrity.

RIZCOUS   Widely available at health food stores and even many supermarkets, this packaged product resembles couscous, but it is made from rice rather than wheat. There are some flavored RizCous products as well as the plain.

SEA LETTUCE   Swaying in the ocean, this vegetable actually looks like lettuce. Fresh sea lettuce, which has the texture of romaine lettuce and a spicy taste, makes a good salad ingredient. Dried sea lettuce can be used as a condiment or crumbled into salads or soups.

SEA VEGETABLES   (see Agar, Arame, Dulse, Hijiki, Kelp, Kombu, Kuzu, Nori, Sea Lettuce, and Wakame)

SEITAN   This meat substitute, also known as kofu, wheat meat, or Buddha food, is a wheat gluten protein. Seitan is essentially a bread dough made from water and stone-ground whole wheat flour and cooked in a broth. (For more on seitan, see pages 140–143.)

SHOYU   Shoyu, also called soy sauce, is made from soy salt and wheat. The fermentation process that creates shoyu is similar to the process used in making miso, though shoyu is not a whole food like miso. As such, it has neither the nutritional value nor the robust flavor of miso.

SOBA   Buckwheat (soba) noodles are available at Asian markets and most natural foods stores.

The noodles have a brownish-gray color. Cook soba noodles in the same way as regular pasta.

SOY GRITS   Soy grits are a natural whole food made from raw or partially cooked soybeans. The texture depends on the degree they have been cracked; soy grits come in two different sizes—small and large. I usually use the larger grits. Soy grits cook much faster than whole soybeans.

SOY MILK   To a vegan, soy milk is an important replacement for dairy milk. It has no cholesterol but about the same amount of protein, one third the fat, less calcium, and fifteen times as much iron as cow's milk. Because soy milk is lower on the food chain than dairy milk, it has fewer contaminants.

In my opinion, the best tasting soy milk comes in aseptic containers. A good soy milk should not have an offensive flavor.

SUCANAT   Short for "sugar cane natural," Sucanat is made by processing the juice from sugar cane. It is probably the highest quality sweetener available; 100 grams of Sucanat contains 386 calories, 389 mg of calcium, 53 mg of magnesium, 291 mg of potassium, 95.9 grams of carbohydrates, 3.41 mg of iron, and no fat. Sucanat is moist, like brown sugar, has a slight molasses taste, and can be used in place of white sugar. Because it is not a fully refined product, Sucanat cannot actually be called "sugar," according to FDA standards.

SURIBASHI   A bowl with a wooden rod used to crush sesame seeds when making gamasio. The bowl has a coarse surface with many ridges that facilitate the seed crushing.

TAHINI   An ingredient, which is also called sesame butter, made from ground sesame seeds. It is popular in Middle Eastern cooking and can be found in natural foods stores and large supermarkets. Tahini has an overpowering flavor and therefore has limited use in sauces and as a flavoring agent. It is not hydrogenated, which is an asset in terms of nutrition but means that the butter must be mixed before using since the oil separates from the ground seeds. Refrigerating tahini may prevent separation and will extend the life of the product.

TAMARI   Tamari is a by-product of miso; it is the liquid that rises to the surface in making hatcho (or soybean) miso. It is generally a higher quality product than shoyu (soy sauce). Tamari holds up well in intense heat. Therefore it is more appropriate to use tamari in cooked dishes, such as a stir-fry; shoyu can be used in recipes that do not require cooking.

TEFF   This grain, an Ethiopian staple, is one of the smallest grains in the world but is also a good source of protein, iron, and minerals. The calcium content of teff is seventeen times greater than that of wheat or barley. Teff flour is available at natural foods stores and can be used in making baked goods. Teff is also available as a breakfast cereal.

TEMPEH   Tempeh is a meat substitute made from soybeans that is rich in protein and vitamin B_{12}. In making tempeh, the cooked soybeans are incubated with a bacteria that acts as a binding agent. Tempeh has a strong, fermented flavor and tends to compete with other ingredients. Tempeh is available at many natural foods stores.

TOFU   To make tofu, the soybeans are cooked and the soy milk is extracted. Then a curdling agent such as nigari is added to the soy milk. The product is pressed to compact the curd and separate the soy whey. There are three types of regular tofu—firm, extra firm, and soft. Regular tofu must be refrigerated and used within a week or so, because it will spoil. If regular tofu is being used in a cold dish, it should first be boiled for at least three minutes to kill bacteria.

Silken tofu actually is produced within its package. It does not need to be refrigerated and will keep, unopened, for several months. Silken tofu also comes in three forms—soft, firm, and extra firm. The custard texture of silken tofu makes it excellent in desserts. (For more on tofu and how to use each type, see the discussion on pages 101–102.)

UDON   A thick, chewy, beige-colored wheat noodle from Japan, Udon noodles are available at Asian markets and some natural foods stores. They are prepared in the same way as other pastas.

UMEBOSHI   Umeboshi are sour, immature plums fermented in salt with the herb *beefsteak*. This Japanese product is considered a seasoning agent. Actually, the plum is used more often for its medicinal properties; umeboshi paste is used more often in cooking.

Umeboshi vinegar is made from the pickling juices used in making umeboshi. It has a fruity flavor, a cherry aroma, and a reddish color. Because umeboshi vinegar contains salt, it is not technically a vinegar, but it can be used in place of other vinegars and is especially appropriate in salad dressings. When using this vinegar, avoid adding salt.

VOGUE VEGY BASE   This is a powdered vegetarian soup base that simulates chicken stock. It has no chemicals or MSG, and it is very low in salt.

WAKAME   Wakame, available dried and fresh-packed with salt, is among the most popular seaweeds in Japan. It can be used to help soften the tough fibers of other vegetables. Rehydrated wakame looks like slippery spinach. Wakame is essential to miso soup and it combines well with onions, soba noodles, bamboo shoots, rice or barley, and many vegetables. You can also fry pieces of wakame to eat as "chips."

Wakame is harvested primarily in the northern seas of Japan, where it thrives in about 20 to 30 feet of water. About two thirds of Japan's 150,000-ton wakame crop is cultivated on about 19,000 sea farms. This vegetable grows quickly and needs only minimal weeding. It is ready to harvest by mid winter, when it is cut, rinsed, and sun-dried. Wakame is delicately textured. When soaking wakame, you should handle it with care or it tends to fall apart.

YEAST, NUTRITIONAL   This product is similar to brewer's yeast but has a less bitter taste; it has a gentle cheese-like flavor. Some brands of nutritional yeast use whey in the formula, so you have to read labels carefully if you want to avoid this dairy by-product.

YEAST, SMOKED   You can use this nutritious, dairy-free yeast that has been smoked to give a dish the same smoky flavor that cured meats have.

APPENDIX

This appendix is primarily a listing of companies that produce and/or distribute high-quality natural foods. I frequently use products from most of these companies in my own cooking. If you are unable to find certain products at your local store, you may want to ask the store manager about distributing products from these companies, or you can contact the company directly. Many of them will allow you to order direct and even have toll-free phone numbers.

Arrowhead Mills, Inc.
P.O. Box 2059
Hereford, Texas 79045
(806) 364-0730

Arrowhead Mills sells many high-quality products, including grains, flours, dried beans and legumes, peanut butter, tahini, corn oil and olive oil, instant seitan, and breakfast cereals. Arrowhead's tahini is my favorite because the company uses a process in which the sesame seeds are hulled mechanically, rather than chemically, and lightly roasted. The tahini does not have the bitter taste so common to tahini.

Eden Foods
701 Tecumseh
Clifton, Michigan 49236
(517) 456-7424

A wide range of high-quality products, including soy milk, barley malt syrup, sea vegetables, organic pastas, Oriental pastas, grain coffee substitute, tamari, shoyu, kuzu, black sesame seeds, gamasio, quinoa, rice vinegars, bottled organic beans is produced by Eden. Their soy milk rates best in consumer guides, and it is also my favorite soy milk.

Fantastic Foods
106 Galli Drive
Novato, California 94949
(415) 883-7718

I think this company has the best line of instant foods on the market, including instant bean mixes, couscous, hummus, and so on.

Fearn Natural Foods
Division of Modern Products, Inc.
P.O. Box 09398
Milwaukee, Wisconsin 53209
(414) 352-3333

This company sells soy grits, liquid soy lecithin, and lecithin granules.

Frontier Cooperative Herbs
P.O. Box 299
Norway, Iowa
(319) 227-7991

The retail division of this company is called Herb & Spice Collection. The company sells herbs, spices, and health care products. They are a good source of lecithin granules.

G's Herbs International
2344 N.W. 21st Place
Portland, Oregon 97210
(503) 241-1131

Specializing in herbs and spices, G's handles just about every herb that is used for cooking, as well as some superb blends. The company also offers different varieties of some herbs, such as thyme. None of the spices or herbs has been irradiated, and the herbs are fresh-dried, which means they will be quite potent. The company distributes about eighteen organic herbs.

Garden of Eatin'
5300 Santa Monica Boulevard
Los Angeles, California 90029
(213) 462-5406

They sell fruit juice sweetened sorbets, tempeh burgers, whole wheat pita breads, and various other wholesome products.

Lakewood Natural Products
P.O. Box 420708
Miami, Florida 33242
(305) 324-5932

This company sells juices and juice concentrates.

Lundberg Family Farms
P.O. Box 369
Richvale, California 95974
(916) 882-4551

Lundberg sells high-quality rice syrup, short-grain rice, sweet rice, wehani rice, and rice cakes. They also produce RizCous.

The Macrobiotic Mall Catalog
P.O. Box 2402
Gaithersburg, Maryland 20879
(301) 963-9235

This mail-order catalog carries many grains, sea vegetables, juices, pastas, misos, condiments, oils, nuts, seeds and beans, finger foods, cookies, mixes, grain coffee substitutes, and some kitchen equipment. The company also offers a macrobiotic foods starter kit.

Maine Coast Sea Vegetables
Shore Road
Franklin, Maine 04634
(207) 565-2907

Kelp, alaria, nori, and other sea vegetables harvested within the coastal U.S. can be obtained through Maine Coast Sea Vegetables. The company's dulse is one of the best on the market. The plants are wild, uncultivated, and dried by sun and wood heat. They also sell a line of sea vegetable seasonings, such as kelp with cayenne and nori with ginger.

Morinaga Nutritional Foods, Inc.
5800 Eastern Avenue Suite 270
Los Angeles, California 90040
(213) 728-4325

Morinaga produces aseptically packaged silken tofu.

Nasoya Foods Ind.
23 Jytek Drive
Leominster, Massachusetts 01453
(508) 537-0713

Nasoya makes Nayonaise, a 100 percent cholesterol-free mayonnaise. The company also offers a variety of high-quality tofu.

Northern Soy, Inc.
545 West Avenue
Rochester, New York 14611
(716) 235-8970

An incredible soy "hot dog" called Not Dog, as well as some good breakfast link sausages, are produced by Northern Soy. These products are totally vegetarian and contain no meat, eggs, or dairy products.

Ocean Harvest
P.O. Box 1719
Mendocino, California 95460
(707) 964-7869

Domestically harvested sea vegetables, including a very special one called sea palm, are sold through this California company.

Once Again Nut Butters, Inc.
12 State Street
Nunda, New York, 14517
(716) 468-2535

Once Again Nut Butters sells a range of high-quality nut butters and tahini. I use their pistachio, almond, and cashew butters in my cooking and baking.

Sovex Natural Foods, Inc.
P.O. Box 310
Collegedale, Tennessee 37315
(615) 396-3145

This company produces a hickory-smoked yeast that has a delicious bacon-like flavor and contains no sugar, animal products, or added salt.

Soyco Foods
Northgate Industrial Park
R.D. #3
P.O. Box 5204
New Castle, Pennsylvania 16105
(412) 656-1102

The soy cheeses produced by Soyco are high-quality. The Soymage line is 100 percent casein free.

Spice of Life
P.O. Box 1287
Fallbrook, California 92028
(619) 237-3677

An up-scale line of herb blends that are not irradiated and that do not contain regular salt can be purchased from Spice of Life.

Taylor's Herb Gardens
1535 Lone Oak Road
Vista, California 92083
(619) 727-3485

Taylor's distributes fresh herbs nationwide. The company has a growing garden in Phoenix, Arizona, but all herbs are shipped from the Vista location. You also can buy the herbs or the seeds and grow them yourself.

Vermont Country Maple, Inc.
Industrial Products Division
Jericho Center, Vermont 05465
(802) 864-7519

Granulated maple sugar and powdered maple sugar are produced by Vermont Country Maple. These sugars have potassium, calcium, magnesium, phosphorus, manganese, and sodium, and can be used in place of rice syrup sugar, barley malt sugars, and regular sugar.

Vogue Cuisine, Inc.
437 Golden Isles Drive
Suite 15 G
Hallandale, Florida 33009
(305) 458-2915

Vogue Vegy Base, produced by Vogue Cuisine, is a basic seasoning in my kitchen.

BIBLIOGRAPHY

Bailey, Covert. *Fit or Fat?* Boston: Houghton Mifflin, 1989.

Ballentine, Rudolph. *Diet and Nutrition*. Honesdale, PA: Himalayan Publishers, n.d.

Ballentine, Rudolph. Transition to Vegetarianism: *An Evolutionary Step*. Honesdale, PA: Himalayan Publishers, 1987.

Blackman, Jackson F. *Working Chef's Cookbook for Natural Whole Foods*. Vermont Publishers, 1989.

Eckhardt, Linda W. *Satisfaction Guaranteed: Simply Sumptuous Mail Order Foods with Recipes and Menus for Fast and Fabulous Meals*. New York: Jeremy P. Tarcher, 1986.

Elliot, Rose. *Complete Vegetarian Cuisine*. New York: Pantheon, 1988.

Erasmus, Udo. *Fats and Oils*. Burnaby, BC: Alive Books, 1986.

Estella, Mary. *Natural Foods Cookbook*. Briarcliff Manor, NY: Japan Publications, 1985.

Gates, June C. *Basic Foods*. 3rd ed. New York: Holt College Department, 1987.

Harrington, Geri. *Real Food, Fake Food, and Everything in Between: The Only Consumer's Guide to Modern Foods*. New York: Macmillan, 1987.

Hunter, Beatrice Trum. *Consumer Beware!* New York: Touchstone Books, 1972. (out of print)

Jacobs, Barbara, and Leonard Jacobs. *Cooking with Seitan: The Delicious Natural Foods from Whole Grain*. Briarcliff Manor, NY: Japan Publications, 1987.

Kadans, Joseph. *Encyclopedia of Fruits, Vegetables, Nuts, and Seeds for Healthful Living*. Englewood Cliffs, NJ: Reward Books, 1975.

King, Jonathan. *Troubled Water: The Poisoning of America's Drinking Water*. Emmaus, PA: Rodale Press, 1985. (out of print)

Lang, Jenifer H. *Tastings: The Best from Ketchup to Caviar*. New York: Crown Publishers, 1986.

Lappé, Frances M. *Diet for a Small Planet*. rev. ed. New York: Ballantine Books, 1975.

Lappé, Frances M., and Joseph Collins. *Food First: Beyond the Myth of Scarcity*. New York: Ballantine Books, 1981.

Moyer, Roger, ed. *Water Treatment Handbook: A Homeowners' Guide to Safer Drinking Water*. Emmaus, PA: Rodale Press, 1985. (out of print)

Robbins, John. *Diet for a New America: How Your Food Choices Affect Your Health, Happiness, and the Future of Life on Earth*. Walpole, NH: Stillpoint Publishing, 1987.

Sale, Kirkpatrick. *The Human Scale*. New York: Coward, McCann & Geoghegan, 1982. (out of print)

Schneider, Elizabeth. *Uncommon Fruits and Vegetables: A Common Sense Guide*. New York: Harper Trade Books, 1986.

Walker, N. W. *Fresh Vegetable and Fruit Juices*. Prescott, AZ: Norwalk Press, 1970.

Wood, Rebecca. *The Whole Foods Encyclopedia: A Shopper's Guide*. New York: Prentice Hall, 1988.

Additional Resources

California Certified Organic Farmers
P.O. Box 8136
Santa Cruz, California 95061

Campaign to End Hunger
Project Planet Earth Foundation
2701 First Avenue, Suite 400
Seattle, Washington 98121

Government Accountability Project
25 E Street NW, Suite 700
Washington, DC 20001

Project Cure
2020 K Street NW
Washington, DC 20069

The Vegetarian Resource Group
P.O. Box 1463
Baltimore, Maryland 21203
(301) 752-VEGV

INDEX